Sexual Violence and Armed Conflict

For Catharine Crockett, MD, and Julie Maschhoff, Ed.D
for your love, support, and friendship

Sexual Violence and Armed Conflict

Janie L. Leatherman

polity

First published in 2011 by Polity Press

Polity Press
65 Bridge Street
Cambridge CB2 1UR, UK

Polity Press
350 Main Street
Malden, MA 02148, USA

ISBN-13: 978-0-7456-4187-4
ISBN-13: 978-0-7456-4188-1(pb)

A catalogue record for this book is available from the British Library.

Typeset in 10.25 on 13 pt Scala
by Servis Filmsetting Ltd, Stockport, Cheshire
Printed and bound in Great Britain by MPG Books Group Limited, Bodmin, Cornwall

The publisher has used its best endeavours to ensure that the URLs for external websites referred to in this book are correct and active at the time of going to press. However, the publisher has no responsibility for the websites and can make no guarantee that a site will remain live or that the content is or will remain appropriate.

Every effort has been made to trace all copyright holders, but if any have been inadvertently overlooked the publisher will be pleased to include any necessary credits in any subsequent reprint or edition.

For further information on Polity, visit our website: www.politybooks.com

Contents

Preface and Acknowledgments

When I read Domitila Barrios de Chúngara's autobiography, *Si me permiten hablar: testimonio de una mujer en las minas de Bolivia* (*Let me Speak*) (1978) as an undergraduate, it set me thinking about gender for the first time. I never forgot her feeling of alienation and marginalization from the liberal struggles of women from the global North whose voices were prominent at the first World Conference on Women sponsored by the United Nations in Mexico City in 1975. This launched the UN Decade for Women and laid the groundwork for many initiatives that would eventually include a global campaign to overcome violence against women. Despite this early introduction, gender did not figure too much in my early academic work in peace and conflict resolution studies, nor did it much in the literature at that time.

However, as a visiting fellow at the Kroc Institute for International Peace Studies at the University of Notre Dame, I carried out fieldwork and collaborated on projects dealing with conflict in the Balkans through grants from the United States Institute of Peace, consulting for Catholic Relief Services, and participation in the South Balkans Working Group at the Council on Foreign Relations (New York). During one trip to the region, I found myself in a meeting with the former Yugoslav President Slobodan Milosevic. I saw for myself the steely, red anger in his eyes, and heard straight from his curled-back lips the kind of propaganda and dehumanization that stirred ethnic hatreds and sexual violence in the Balkan

Wars. Later, in meetings with women activists from various communities in the former Yugoslav Republic of Macedonia, I learned also about the fears and threats they experienced, even before armed conflict touched their country.

Nevertheless, when I read Ervin Staub's 2001 review[1] of a book I wrote with colleagues at the Kroc Institute, *Breaking Cycles of Violence: Early Warning and Conflict Prevention in Intra-State Crises* (co-authored with Raimo Vayrynen, Patrick Gaffney, and William DeMars), I was dumbfounded. As Staub rightly points out, we failed to include a gender analysis. When Louise Knight at Polity approached me with the opportunity to write this book on *Sexual Violence and Armed Conflict*, I was ready to take it on.

I owe a special debt of gratitude to Preety Sthapit and Shyan Bajracharya, my graduate assistants of the last two years (from Nepal), whose assistance on this project was as unflagging as their insights were instructive. I have also been fortunate to prepare the final manuscript thanks to summer research assistance from Kathryn Keane, one of our fine undergraduate majors in International Studies, who, like Preety, has brought good cheer and a quick mind to the tasks at hand. I also had the pleasure of teaching a seminar at Fairfield University during spring 2010 on the topic of "Gender, War, Peace" to a group of ten women with family ties and life experiences spanning Iran, Afghanistan, Turkey, Argentina, Morocco, Senegal, and different parts of Latin America. I am grateful for support from Fairfield University for research assistants, the chance to teach this seminar, and especially for encouragement on this project from Associate Academic Vice President, Dr Mary Frances Malone.

I have been fortunate to take students and meet on several occasions with staff at UNIFEM in New York. I owe a special thanks to Felicity Hill, Stephanie Ziebell, Sarah Douglas, and Carol Cohn for their time, resources, and contacts they provided over the years and also Pamela Delargy at the United Nations Population Fund for feedback on the early conceptualization of this book. All these experiences and the collective journey they represent have sharpened my own understanding of women in the world. Their voices are folded into the pages of this book.

I want also to thank colleagues and friends, in particular Drs Jyl Josephson and Jocelyn Boryczka, for fielding queries from me on feminist theory, and Ana Siscar, and Carmen Djuro Goiricelaya for their feedback on the draft manuscript and perspectives from their experiences in the areas of human rights and social justice in the Philippines and Venezuela, respectively.

I want to express very special thanks to Nadezdha Griffin, my collaborator on other projects relating to the topic of this book. She has shared with me reports and articles from regions where she is working in humanitarian affairs, while keeping me grounded in the realities of that work – the possibilities and the limitations. She has endured many questions, read drafts, and helped me think through ideas and arguments. The book carries her voice, too.

Finally, I owe special thanks to anonymous reviewers of the original book proposal and the draft manuscript. Their feedback has also helped in many ways to shape this volume, and I am grateful for the guidance their insights provided. I have a deep debt of gratitude to Louise Knight, my editor at Polity, for her support, good cheer and ready encouragement for my work on this emotionally challenging book.

As I finish writing this week, the connection between sexual violence and armed conflict is very much in the news, particularly with the 50th anniversary of the Democratic Republic of Congo's independence from Belgian colonial rule. This has cast the spotlight on the exploitation of conflict minerals in Eastern Congo, what has been called "the worst place in the world to be a woman." It is also one of the worst places in the world to be a man. Sexual violence affects both genders. Neither is spared in conflict zones. But thanks to the efforts of activists in many parts of the world, both in war zones and outside it, the link between sexual violence and profit making in the global marketplace is also coming to light. This book is my contribution to that global effort. Readers will bring their experiences to bear on the pages that follow, too. Between the covers of this book and beyond their embrace, I also hope to create a safe space for discussions on these difficult matters, and a context to shape action. It is my deepest hope that the voices of survivors contained within the pages that follow will reach new audiences and inspire them to support the multi-faceted cause of preventing sexual violence in armed conflict and bring urgently needed aid to those who have suffered so greatly.

Janie Leatherman
Fairfield University
July 22, 2010

Abbreviations

BBC	British Broadcasting Company
CNDP	Congrès nationale pour la defénse du peuple (National Congress for the Defense of the People)
DDR	disarmament, demobilization, and reintegration
DRC	The Democratic Republic of the Congo
ECOMOG	Economic Community of West African States Monitoring Group
FARDC	Forces Armées de la République Démocratique du Congo (Armed Forces of the Democratic Republic of the Congo)
FDLR	Forces démocratiques de libération du Rwanda (Democratic Forces for the Liberation of Rwanda)
GBV	gender-based violence
GHI	Global Hunger Index
GTZ	Deutsche Gesellschaft für Technische Zusammenarbeit (German Society for Technical Cooperation)
HIV/AIDS	Human immunodeficiency virus/Acquired immune deficiency syndrome
IASC	The Inter-Agency Standing Committee
ICC	International Criminal Court
IDP	internally displaced person
IPTF	International Police Task Force

IRC	International Rescue Committee
IRIN	Integrated Regional Information Networks
LRA	The Lord's Resistance Army
LTTE	Liberation Tigers of Tamil Eelam
MONUC	United Nations Mission in the Democratic Republic of the Congo
MSF	Médecins Sans Frontières (Doctors without Borders)
NGO	nongovernmental organization
NPFL	National Patriotic Front of Liberia
OCHA	United Nations Office for the Coordination of Humanitarian Affairs
OSS	Overseas Security Services
RCD	Rassemblement Congolais pour la Démocratie (Congolese Rally for Democracy)
RPF	Rwanda Patriotic Front (Rwandan army)
RUF	Revolutionary United Front
SFOR	The Stabilization Force in Bosnia and Herzegovina
SPLA/M	Sudanese People's Liberation Army/Movement
SS	Schutzstaffel (Protective Echelon)
UAE	United Arab Emirates
UPC	The Union of Congolese Patriots
UPDF	Ugandan People's Defense Force
UN	The United Nations
UNAMID	African Union/United Nations Hybrid operation in Darfur
UNAMSIL	United Nations Mission in Sierra Leone
UNESCO	United Nations Educational, Scientific and Cultural Organization
UNFPA	United Nations Population Fund
UNHCR	United Nations High Commissioner for Refugees
UNICEF	United Nations Children's Fund

UNIFEM	United Nations Development Fund for Women
UNMIBH	United Nations Mission in Bosnia and Herzegovina
US	United States
WHO	World Health Organization
WSB	West Side Boys

CHAPTER ONE

Ending the Silence

"One day when my husband went into the forest to gather rubber, the sentry Ikelonda came, finding me in my hut where I stayed, and asked me to give myself to him. I rejected his proposition. Furious, Ikelonda fired a gun shot at me, which gave me the wound whose trace you can still see. I fell on my back; Ikelonda thought I was dead, and to get hold of the brass bracelet that I wore at the base of my right leg, he cut off my right foot." (Boali of Ekolongo, 1905)[1]

Boali is one of 13 women who had the courage to testify before the King's Commission investigating atrocities in the Congo Free State in the early 1900s at a time when King Leopold II himself was organizing the conquest, slave labor system, and plunder of his personal colony for the collection of rubber that brought him enormous wealth. Her testimony stands as one of the great exceptions among survivors, not the rule. Mostly, the historical record is silent when it comes to the voices of victims, especially from sexual violence. Nonetheless, sexual violence in armed conflict has been part of the spoils of war from time immemorial. It has carved a path of humiliation and destruction, turning the lives of women and girls into the currency of chattel and slaves, and the feminization and emasculation of men and boys. References to rape are found in the earliest documents of recorded history and in early religious texts, such as in Homer's *Iliad* and the Old and New Testaments of the Bible. The founding of Rome, the Crusades, colonialism, slavery,

I

and the spread of settlers across Native American lands all encompass a history of rape.

Sexual violence in warfare is among the darkest legacies of the twentieth century, and it continues to ravage societies in the new millennium. Instances of widespread use of sexual violence include: the 1915 Armenian genocide by Ottoman Turkey; the Japanese assault on the Chinese in Nanking during World War II, and in the Chinese civil war; the partition of India and creation of Pakistan; and Bangladesh's 1971 war of liberation. Sexual violence has been prevalent in many other conflicts during the Cold War and after, including the Korean War, Vietnam War, and Cambodia; in the wars and conflicts in Central and Latin America, and in Haiti; and in many African conflicts, such as Angola, Djibouti, Liberia, Mozambique, Sierra Leone, Somalia, and Sudan. In Asia, war rapes are found in East Timor, Sri Lanka, Burma, Kashmir (India), Papua New Guinea; and in wars and conflicts in Central Europe and Eurasia, including Afghanistan, Turkey, Kuwait, Georgia, Bosnia, and Kosovo. No part of the world has been unaffected by wartime sexual violence.

The estimates of numbers of raped women in post-Cold War conflicts are staggering: as many as 500,000 women were raped in the Rwandan genocide; 60,000 in the wars in Bosnia and Herzegovina and Croatia; and 64,000 internally displaced women were victims of sexual violence in Sierra Leone during the decade of civil war from 1991–2001.[2] The wars in the Democratic Republic of Congo (hereafter DRC) since the mid-1990s encompassed widespread and horrific forms of sexual violence, particularly in Eastern Congo.[3] United Nations (UN) Emergency Relief Coordinator John Holmes tells of "sexual violence so brutal it staggers the imagination." More than 32,000 cases of rape and sexual violence have been registered in South Kivu Province alone since 2005 – a fraction of the total number of women subjected to such extreme suffering.[4]

Historically speaking, investigating sexual violence in armed conflict has been taboo. One of the reasons for silence on sexual violence in war is the seemingly impossible task of understanding it. Incomprehension is a typical response to egregious violence. Normal people (by definition) cannot understand cruel acts. Such assumptions have their own perils, however. Dismissing cruel perpetrators as mad, crazy or demonic alienates the observer from the perpetrator, rendering the perpetrator a "monster, inhuman, *unlike me*."[5] The impulse to dissociate serves many functions. Most significantly, dissociation from sexual violence in war is a means of silencing that suppresses awareness and accountability. Until recently, this produced a great gap in international law, among scholars in disciplines across the academy, and in national and international policy-making circles and practice. This silence has been an integral part of the institutions that make sexual violence in war possible, and permissible. To borrow from Hilary Charlesworth, the silence is a critical element of the stability of the institution in question, not a weakness in its structure.[6]

The silence on sexual violence has undergirded the economic, social, cultural and political power structures of patriarchy. Patriarchy is a hierarchical social order centered on dominant or hegemonic forms of masculinity. It requires an investment of time, social organization, and resources to sustain such disciplinary practices as honor killings; bride dowry that values men over women; cultural codes on adultery (that fail to differentiate it from rape); practices to ensure the purity of the girl child, whether through surveillance or cutting (such as female genital mutilation); forced marriage or child marriage.

Sexual violence in conflict does not develop in isolation from the society's preexisting socioeconomic and culturally shaped gender relationships. The extent of gender-based violence

(GBV) in society is a predisposing condition for sexual violence in war and is a principal reason why women and girls in
countries with high levels of gender-based discrimination and
inequality are at a much greater risk of victimization and revictimization of sexual violence from the onset to the aftermath
of violent conflict. GBV involves many forms of human rights
violations, such as rape, domestic violence, sexual assault and
harassment, sex trafficking, and harmful traditional practices
ranging from female genital mutilation, early marriage and
bride inheritance to honor killings. Men, women and children
can be targets of GBV, and this affects all the social institutions in society, including family and community structures
and relationships. GBV often intensifies and becomes more
extreme in a crisis, even escalating into a tool of war. In some
armed conflicts, the brutality and systematic use of sexual violence rises to the level of a crime against humanity, a war
crime and an aspect of genocide.[7] To understand what drives
men (and infrequently, women) to commit sexual violence
in armed conflict, this book draws especially on theories of
constructivism to explore systemic factors like hegemonic
masculinity and how it links up with situational factors in
conflict to produce other masculinities that are subordinate,
violence laden and catastrophic.

Contemporary war amplifies gender injustice in a context of
globalized militarism and weak states. Where gender injustice
is highest in the world, so too are indices of poverty, hunger,
state fragility, and war. The region where these factors coalesce most intensively is called an "arc of instability" that
runs from the west coast of Africa, including the important
oil-producing state of Nigeria across the African continent
through the Persian Gulf region and into Central Asia and
beyond, reaching Afghanistan, nuclear-armed Pakistan, and
Nepal. This arc of instability has a heavy concentration of
the 20 failed or weakest states in the world that represent a

population of 880 million people. Sub-Saharan Africa has an especially high concentration of states in crisis or war, or in a post-conflict period.[8]

Historically, claims to state sovereignty have protected governments from external scrutiny (regarding human rights, for example), which is the international analogy to the domestic divide between the public and private. This separation reverberates across many divisions in society and internationally, including between state and community, state and market, the market and the family, and so on, with different impacts depending on race, class, (dis)ability, sexual identity, nationality, or location (global North versus global South), for example. It also is intrinsic to globalizing capitalist processes that separate capitalist production and human reproduction in gendered terms. By the late twentieth century, globalization has defined these processes by the accelerating pace and the global reach and penetration of flows of capital, information, culture, production, and people across boundaries. While globalization itself is presented as gender neutral, the designation of the productive economy as the formal, monetarized economy, and reproduction as the domain of informal, noncompensated pay, reveals the hidden gendered nature of economic relations of domination and subjugation, as well as class, race/ethnicity, geography, and history (such as the legacies of colonialism and postcolonialism).[9] Women have been traditionally subordinated in both the productive and reproductive spheres of the global economy under the institutions of hegemonic masculinity.

Global capitalism takes a position of nonresponsibility regarding the economies of reproduction that involve the private sphere of family economies. This is where life is generated, children nursed and reared, family members' needs cared for, the roots of community life and socialization laid, and intergenerational relations sustained.[10] The position of nonresponsibility for the reproductive economy has been sustained globally through the dominance of European and American capital via colonization, empire, and more recently globalization. This capitalist ideological organization of labor contrasts starkly with the reality that women in most parts of the world have been involved in the productive, as well as the reproductive, economy and continue to contribute to the formal economy by growing crops, making goods to buy and sell at the market, and so on.[11]

The rules of the ordinary capitalist workplace are also embedded in assumptions about the division of the productive and reproductive economy, so that such activities as child rearing, breast-feeding, caring for elderly parents or feeding the family are excluded from its arena of responsibility. These claims to nonresponsibility normalize unpaid labor for women and extend into other realms, such as nonresponsibility for exploitation of laborers who are not directly under the employment of multinational corporations (as sweatshop workers, for example), or the negative impacts of capitalism on the environment and its sustainability. As this study will demonstrate, corporations also take a position of nonresponsibility for marginalized people in war zones whose exploitation is a function of global networks of profit making in diamonds, gold, tin, coltan (short for ColumboTantalite), and other valuable commodities. This system connects corporate headquarters with plundering militaries on the ground that use extreme forms of violence against the reproductive economy in general, and more specifically through sexual violence against women as a profit-making strategy to gain access to and control of natural resources. Through such developments, the global political economy has become militarized and violence-laden.

The divide between public and private is also marked by the development of male-oriented human rights protections in the public sphere as the domain for men (where they work and engage in politics) and the absence of legal protections in the private sphere as the domain for women (where they are responsible for family and home).[12] Liberal human rights serve to protect masculine modes of thinking and rights, as seen in the United States (US) Bill of Rights, for example. Forms of oppression that women face in "marriage, procreation, labor, property ownership, sexual repression, and other manifestations of unequal citizenship that are routinely viewed as private, nongovernmental, and reflective of cultural differences" have not historically been part of liberal activism on rights.[13] This has left women vulnerable to inequalities, despite their involvement both in and outside the home, and to domestic violence and other forms of discrimination and marginalization in public.[14] It has also left them vulnerable to sexual violence in war.

Nothing about sustaining a patriarchal system is inherently "easy." Patriarchy is not natural; it requires great effort to reproduce and sustain it every day.[15] Patriarchal institutions depend on hegemonic leadership, enforcement and reenactment, in which many women and men in society actively participate.[16] For example, women who circumcise girls are participants in patriarchal institutions, though they may do so to earn a living or as a source of power and leadership in secret societies. Patriarchy is also facilitated by its incorporation into or "colonization" of other forms of social organization, such as ethnic cleavages, race and class relations, economic development, militarization, and militarized masculinity. In war zones, access to and control of local resources like diamonds, coltan, gold, tin, timber, illicit drugs and underground trade in weapons and other commodities enrich local commanders and political backers, while guaranteeing profits to multinational corporations who negotiate lucrative contracts and concessionary rights with failed states and rebel groups that skirt accountability or transparency. Social disintegration and chaos facilitate economic exploitation, while sexual violence is one of the key tools in the arsenal of the global political economy of war. War strategies are always political strategies about who remains in control and what assets are theirs. In that sense, sexual violence is part of the political economy of war – one of its most efficient tools.

Few other strategies can so fundamentally unravel the fabric of society. This is because sexual violence encapsulates the violation of multiple taboos, including but not limited to those involving rape. Other forms of sexual violence encompass exploitation and abuse through sexual slavery, forced pregnancy, forced marriage, mutilation, cannibalism, violation of breast-feeding or pregnant and elderly women, the forcing of children to commit rape of others, or family members to commit incest. In armed conflict, rape is often part of a systematic campaign of terror, resulting in mass or collective rape. Gang rape is especially horrific. It involves multiple perpetrators sexually assaulting a particular victim and results in devastating physical and psychological consequences. Sexual assaults also leave victims at risk of HIV/AIDS (Human immunodeficiency virus/Acquired immune deficiency syndrome) and sexually transmitted diseases. Dealing with the health and psychosocial consequences of sexual violence is an urgent need, but most countries lack the specialized surgical resources.

Literature on sexual violence and war generally refers to those who have lived through the experience as *survivors*, and reserves the term *victims* for those who died or as a legal term of reference.[17] This book follows these conventions. Nevertheless, like men, women have many identities in war, not only that of victim. They navigate its treacherous waters as mothers, daughters, wives, farmers, traders, smugglers, caretakers, internally displaced persons (IDPs), and refugees, among many other roles and identities, including as combatants. This underscores the complexity of gendered power relations in war where rape is much more prevalent than in peacetime.[18]

Conceptualizing sexual violence

Sexual violence in armed conflict happens in a *place*, and involves *violent acts, perpetrators, victims, survivors* and *impacts* ranging from health to a broad array of social consequences. Sexual violence is also a *tool* or *strategy* of war that encompasses the *pre-conflict, conflict escalation* and *post-conflict phases*. It *breaks taboos*, thereby violating rules and crossing thresholds that society sets on acceptable conduct. Sexual violence in war is a runaway norm for these reasons, and also because it causes the subversion of traditional sexual hierarchies and social order through its political economy of violence. Rape is only one of many types of sexual violence in warfare, though probably the most widely mentioned. Rape is a sexual assault through penetration using a body part or other object, including vaginal copulation, or oral and anal penetration. The perpetrators of rape may be women or men; boys or girls (e.g. coerced as child soldiers). However, most often men are the perpetrators. Those at greatest risk are married women, adolescent girls, female-headed households, orphans and unaccompanied minors, young girls and boys, and women in general. In some conflicts, men also are the direct targets of sexual violence; this may be on their own bodies, or they may be forced to commit sexual violence against family members or witness it being done to emasculate them. Sexual violence is thus a crime faced by both genders, even if women and young girls are most often the direct object of assault and exploitation.

The *place* where sexual violence is perpetrated is almost

always of significance in its own way. Sexual violence in armed conflicts occurs in all manner of locations, including in homes, gardens or fields, at work and in many places considered safe havens, such as hospitals, clinics, schools, and religious sites (e.g. churches, mosques, synagogues). As a survivor of an attack in Sierra Leone explains:

> "We were hiding in the mosque when two rebels dressed in civilian [clothing] entered. It was dark but they shone their flashlights looking for girls and said, "We are coming for young girls, for virgins; even if they tie their heads like old grandmothers, we will find them." They also said that if the people did not hand over the young girls, they would open fire on all of us."[19]

This account confirms the challenges victims face even when they try to find protection through various strategies, such as shelter in a sacred space that under international humanitarian law should provide safe refuge, staying together in large groups, and wearing disguises. This account of a gang rape also illustrates how the place (a mosque) becomes a stage or theater of horror complete with "cast and audience."

While sexual violence in armed conflict is used against men, women, and children, there are some important differences in terms of its *impact* or *effects*. The social construction of gender varies across cultures, and thus perceptions of victims and perpetrators of sexual violence in armed conflict may differ, as well as the consequences they face.[20] Some of these differences are marked biologically. For example, one way that women greatly differ from men in the experience of rape is forced pregnancy. In addition, in many cultures, a woman internalizes rape as though she were herself guilty or responsible for it occurring. What kind of help she may receive or not, as well as the mechanisms for marginalization or re-inclusion in society also vary according to prevailing cultural norms and practices. The effects of rape of men may also be different from women, and vary culturally. Sexual violence against a male is often used to denigrate and feminize him, a maneuver that is ultimately aimed at further denigrating women. Thus, a gendered analysis is essential for understanding the suffering and social implications that sexual violence causes.

Explaining sexual violence in armed conflict

Is sexual violence in contemporary conflicts a new kind of politics of violence, with new tactics and techniques of domination, or does sexual violence today reproduce old forms of subjugation? Has it increased since the end of the Cold War, as the Vice-President of the International Criminal Court (ICC) and some scholars argue?[21] Finding answers to these questions is challenging. The heightened awareness of sexual violence in armed conflict stems from many factors. First, reconceptualizing conflicts after the Cold War as "new wars" as though they were something fundamentally different from previous wars may lead to premature conclusions that sexual violence is more prevalent as a weapon of war than ever before. Second, the growing coverage by the global news media, human rights and other nongovernmental organizations (NGOs) and international organizations reporting on sexual violence in armed conflict also heightens awareness – often with advocacy and fund-raising campaigns that draw on and exploit images of the victimization of women and girls.[22] Third, all this attention may be partly a function of the attenuation of taboos against speaking out on sexual violence, given the creation of international laws and tribunals to prosecute violators, and the empowerment and willingness of survivors and witnesses to come forward. Normatively speaking, this signals progress in the development of feminist law and global governance; however, it may also risk inviting a backlash against women. At the same time, putting the media and public focus on the prevalence of sexual violence in post-Cold War conflicts might also serve as a diversionary tactic. While essentializing women and girls as victims, it directs attention away from the effects of economic exploitation under neoliberal globalization and how sexual violence in armed conflict serves economic interests.

Complicating the search for explanations for sexual violence in armed conflict is the fact that some societies appear to be at higher risk than others. For example, there is some evidence that high levels of state terrorism – government-sponsored murder, torture, imprisonment, and state-sponsored campaigns of terror and assaults on villages – is the most consistent predictor of collective rape.[23] Alternatively, analysis of conflicts in South Asia and Bosnia suggests that mass rape tends to occur in conflicts that involve the partition of the territory and the population when the state is fragile with limited control of the territory and people. In contrast, conflicts that do not pose imminent threat of partition may avoid rape, even when murder is acceptable.[24]

But even in the same conflict, some parties may resort to sexual violence and others not, or the incidence will vary significantly from one armed group to the next, or among factions of one side in a conflict.[25] For example, the notorious West Side Boys, a gang spun off from other rebel forces in the civil war in Sierra Leone, committed horrific atrocities, including sexual violence against civilians, abduction and rape of children, forcing victims to become "wives" of the gang members, or drugging and forcing them to perpetrate atrocities themselves. In contrast, the government forces of Sierra Leone were found to have committed far less sexual violence. The conflict in Sierra Leone involved neither partition nor preexisting high levels of state terror, but the government was fragile, and preexisting levels of gender-based violence were high.

There are other contradictions. The presence of a significant number of female combatants may actually serve to decrease violence against women in armed conflict. Alternatively, sexual violence was carried out in Rwanda with the complicity of some women,[26] and sexual violence against prisoners held by the United States in Afghanistan, Iraq and Guantanamo have occurred in instances where women played central roles.[27] Other explanations focus on revenge and hyper-masculinity, although military training and discipline within the ranks of armed groups can also work to prevent or minimize sexual violence in war.[28]

Three different schools or theoretical approaches to the study of sexual violence in armed conflict provide alternative ways of understanding the many contradictions and variations the topic presents: *essentialism, structuralism*, and *social constructivism*. Each approach makes some key assumptions about gender relations in society, especially in terms of power, freedom, autonomy, agency, and choice. These assumptions lead to different insights and analytical frameworks for studying sexual violence in armed conflict and inform strategies for remediation and prevention.

Essentialism

Essentialism is a theoretical approach that carries a number of basic assumptions about human nature. It tends to offer universalizing perspectives on questions relating to gender and global solutions to the problems. For example, it assumes that women share the same basic experiences or interests, regardless of culture, class, race or other identities and socio-cultural contexts and experiences.[29] Essentialist accounts treat sexual violence as an inevitable aspect of fighting, especially as a reward or tool for revenge for the winning side. Sexual violence simply is considered a natural part of war, a given, a normal thing to do. It does not warrant questioning. It is what men do to women when they can or must. One of the patterns of violence against women that emerges from archeological records, literature, and anthropology is the competition for women as a function of warfare: men have fought each other throughout the ages for a fundamentally biological reason: the shortage of female reproductive capacity (a function of menopause in *Homo sapiens*) relative to male demand. This essentialist argument about scarcity offers one answer to the question "why men fight."[30]

A radical feminist critique of rape offers a different essentializing account. Women have subjugated themselves to men because of their fear of "an open season of rape" and because women alone and together lacked sufficient physical strength to protect themselves. The consequences were sweeping. "The historic price of woman's protection by man against man was the imposition of chastity and monogamy. *A crime committed against her body became a crime against the male estate.*"[31] Brownmiller links the practice of bride capture – forcible seizure – to both the institutionalization of marriage and to "the full-blown male solidification of power, the patriarchy."[32] Thus, woman becomes man's property, who, together with his children, defines the minimal boundaries of his estate. This initial subjugation of women lays the foundation for their exploitation, which continues today under such hierarchical institutions as hegemonic masculinity, slavery (through trafficking, for example) and private property (the great majority of which still remains in the hands of men in most countries). In this account, women lack freedom, autonomy, agency, and choices in life. In contrast, for men war is an opportunity to release their suppressed sexual drive. According to the essentialist school, men are perpetrators and women are victims.

The war zone accentuates differences between men and women under the institution of patriarchy by polarizing gender roles. Women are at greater risk of sexual violence in conflict because men are called to fight in war and women to keep the home fires burning. Men are not just to be men in war, but militaristic men.[33] Sexual violence in war is a tool to reaffirm patriarchal hierarchies. The breakdown of social institutions and authority in wartime thus opens the gate to increased violence against women as a means to reassert gender roles. At the same time, marginalized males can take advantage of the social chaos of war to subvert traditional sexual hierarchies and acquire women and wealth ordinarily denied them by their low status. In a similar vein, Mackinnon argues that war grants license for further subversion of sexual relations by becoming an arena to realize men's sexual fantasies: rape camps turn into the wartime version of pornography. Indeed, documented films from rape camps in Bosnia-Herzegovina were shown on television in Banja Luka and Belgrade, and later distributed through the international pornographic market.[34] This perspective emphasizes understandings of sexual violence in war from the perspective of the perpetrator, focusing on the category of undifferentiated aggressive males.

Structuralism
Structural theories of sexual violence take a more nuanced perspective. Unlike essentialism, which posits that all women are at greater risk of sexual violence in war than in peace, structuralism points to structural factors as predisposing certain women to a greater likelihood of sexual violence in war. These factors include economic and other gendered forms of oppression and marginalization, injustice and structural violence. It also includes identities like ethnicity, race, religion, or political affiliation. When these structural factors intersect with gender, it makes some members in society more vulnerable than others, including women and girls, and

marginalized men or boys. As Skjelsbaek explains, the understanding of patriarchy in this school is more complex. Here it is no longer a matter of men having power over women but of "belonging to the most powerful ethnic, religious or political groups having power over 'their' women (in order to protect them) and over the women of the 'other' (by potentially attacking them)."[35] In other words, identity matters where the risk of rape in war is concerned. Important examples include the ethnic cleansing in Bosnia-Herzegovina; the genocide against the Armenians by the Ottoman Turks; and the 1994 Hutu-led Interahamwe genocide in Rwanda that targeted Tutsi and Hutu moderates (viewed as traitors) for extermination.

This approach emphasizes understanding sexual violence in war and solutions to it mostly from the perspective of the victim. As important as such attention is for raising awareness about the plight and extreme suffering of women and girls in armed conflict, it is also imperative not to let the framing of women as victims exclude all other considerations. Such reductionism tends to simplify blame and place it narrowly and reflexively on factors internal to the nation and culture where sexual violence in war is occurring, so that the "brutal, savage men" of "uncivilized" societies are especially at fault. This essentializes men by casting perpetrators in contemporary conflicts as male. However, men like women, have many different identities in war, and not only as perpetrators. Men do not always fight, while sometimes women do. Indeed, women have gained reputations as fierce and able fighters in many parts of the world, including in the Maoist insurgency in Nepal, the civil war in Liberia, or the National Liberation Army and the Revolutionary Armed Forces of Colombia in Colombia.[36]

Social constructivism

Constructivism asks questions about how the actions of actors in world politics are shaped and constrained by the system of power relations, and how their behavior either reproduces and reinforces that system, or transforms it – the so-called agent/structure debate.[37] Constructivists focus on hegemonic masculinity instead of patriarchy to underscore the role of many different kinds of masculinities – dominant, allied and subordinate – as there are also different femininities. Constructivists emphasize the role of norms, rules, beliefs, ideas, and principles influencing expectations for social behavior. Their diffusion in global politics determines how social institutions are formed and transformed. Social constructivism provides theoretical approaches that avoid reifying women's and men's roles in war that tend to emerge from essentialist and structural accounts. Instead of emphasizing victimization, this approach helps us to understand how structural violence limits a person's agency.[38]

While both genders pursue a wide range of coping strategies in war, the social construction of hegemonic masculinity is particularly crucial. Hegemonic masculinity refers to a male-centered order that gives men, instead of women, primary access to power and privilege. Hegemonic masculinity is a Gramscian concept, drawing from the Italian Marxist scholar's understanding of hegemony as cultural/moral leadership that secures popular consent and support to a particular form of rule. Hegemonic masculinity organizes the power relations between women and men and the political agenda that sustains this hierarchy.[39] Hegemonic masculinity is defined more by its successful claim to authority than its use of direct violence.[40] However, by linking hegemonic masculinity to masculinist power, hierarchies are created among masculinities that depend variously on complicity, control, or disempowerment of males. Allied masculinities are empowered, while subordinate and marginalized masculinities are ostracized or exploited along with womanhood and femininity. Access to the inner sanctum of hegemonic masculinity is open not just to men but even to women – as long as they do not threaten the link between hegemony and masculinist power.[41] If they do, they are expelled from its inner circle.

Because masculinity is a social institution, it is an open-ended process, in constant flux, renegotiation, reconstitution, and contestation.[42] No society has only one true, fixed masculine identity. Masculinity, like femininity, is not a monolithic, universal phenomenon, and neither is its expression in local circumstances. Rather, the social construction of gender produces various masculinities that are always in competition and constantly being restructured as historical contexts change.[43] Even during armed conflict, men assume different masculine identities. This signals that different masculinities are at stake, struggling for the determination of socially acceptable practices. For example, some husbands support their wives and care for them regardless of their injuries in war, including rape, without respect to customary (and gendered) expectations that might lead them to do otherwise. Thus, gendered relationships revolve around both power and resistance to hegemonic models or identities.[44]

Scholars place the emergence of hegemonic masculinity as a function of the development of a Western bourgeois ideology in the nineteenth century[45] that formed a global, racialized hierarchy of masculinities. These were "created as part of the institutionalization of a complex set of race and gender identities sustaining European imperialism – identities that still have a cultural legacy today."[46] Societies confront competing models of masculinity that come from within their cultural traditions and from models imposed or promoted from the outside. There are colonial models of hegemonic masculinity and also local, traditional models of masculinity that may compete or reinforce each other to define the ideal masculine type.

Women have also played a role in the imperial expansion of Western societies in their capacity as wives of military men, or colonial administrators, for example. Thus, international affairs have depended on the ways both genders relate to hegemonic control.[47] The construct of hegemonic masculinity enables us to see the ruling pattern of masculinity that functions "at the level of the whole society and shore[s] up male power and advantage."[48] Many mechanisms of dominance, such as military service, or the management of the national security state, help sustain and reinvigorate it.

Although the concept of masculinity is linked to the male body, masculinity does not exist in and of itself. It is relational. Hegemonic masculinity sets up oppositional masculinities through a system of power relations that affect both women and men. Hegemonic masculinity is reinforced in part by the opposition it sets up along the lines of race and class (for example, in terms of toughness or physicality). Working-class men and Black, Latino, Native American, Asian and other men of color in the United States have a marginalized position in relation to hegemonic males. They are alienated by the gap between the expectations of hegemonic masculinity and the obstacles they face in their own lives to achieve it through the accumulation of wealth or access to power. Consequently, marginalized masculinity "creates a feeling of emasculation and powerlessness in the arenas of class and race, even though dominance is maintained in the arena of gender."[49] Marginalized masculinity is especially threatened in natural or man-made crises. For example, disasters and wars destroy social, political and economic institutions that people depend on for employment, status, and prestige in society, and leave women and men with devastating personal, professional, and economic losses. Hyper-masculinity provides men with an alternative role model to regain their lost status and aspiration to the power of hegemonic males.

Hyper-masculinity exaggerates noncatastrophic masculinities, draws on excessive forms of toughness, and deploys violence in order to maintain or reassert dominance and control in the limited arenas available under extreme circumstances. Women become a target for sexual violence because violence over them is socially constructed as a principal means for men to reestablish lost hegemony. The weaker the position of women under noncatastrophic masculinities, the more vulnerable in catastrophes they are. Hyper-masculinity takes advantage of gendered sources of injustice and resulting vulnerabilities to assert power. As societies edge toward war's abyss, images of hyper-masculinity are deployed to mobilize marginalized men in particular and drive gender polarization. Men who resist are targeted, too, for emasculation (for example, by forcing them to witness the rape of their wives or daughters, or by being raped and violated themselves), while women and girls are at particular risk. Poststructuralist theories focus on the symbols, language, and discursive practices to understand how power operates in these kinds of situations and knowledge is produced.[50]

The problem of consent and proving rape

Despite the widespread and heinous purposes for which sexual violence has been committed in armed conflicts, proving rape was committed without consent has remained a high bar for women. One overarching reason historically is women's lack of standing. Reviewing Babylonian and Mosaic Law, the Code of Hammurabi, passages from the Old and New Testament of the Bible, Talmudic law, and early English law, Brownmiller documents the precarious position and limited recourse of raped girls or women. The affront was to her father, husband or family, not to the raped girl or woman herself. She could be married to the rapist, or rejected by her family, tainted and devoid or significantly reduced of value for any future marriage. Restitution lay in restoring the father's, family's, or husband's honor. It was their loss, not hers, that mattered.

Only at the end of the thirteenth century under Edward I and the Statutes of Westminster was a more fully developed, legal concept of rape evident, covering not only virgins, but also married women, nuns, matrons, widows, concubines, and even prostitutes. These provisions are the origins of modern law on statutory rape, instances where the victim is below the legal age required to give consent. Despite these efforts, protection for the victim of rape remained limited until well into the twentieth century, especially because of the burden on the victim to prove that she had not consented in any way, nor brought the rape on herself. Brownmiller quotes the famous British jurist William Blackstone, who died in 1780, for his views on rape (that still echo in the silencing of victims in the twenty-first century). Blackstone commented:

> "If she be of evil fame and stand unsupported by others, if she concealed the injury for any considerable time after she had the opportunity to complain, if the place where the act was alleged to be committed was where it was possible she might have been heard and she made no outcry, these and the like circumstances carry a strong but not conclusive presumption that her testimony is false or feigned."[51]

The effect of the silencing mechanisms has been to prevent women from speaking out. One of the resulting gaps is a lack of *detailed* historical narratives of rape, or analysis. Speaking out violates taboos, and often places the victim at further risk. Rape survivors evoke memories of the defeat and humiliation of a family and community, as do children born of rape.[52]

Survivors are often ostracized or banished from their own families and communities because they evoke such memories and may be thought to carry bad spirits in them. The entire community comes to internalize the assault against it, while the women carry the markers of this memory and evidence of the ruination of family and community structures.[53]

For such multifaceted and complex reasons, documenting the incidence of rape is difficult in peacetime, and even more so in war. Establishing reliable numbers of incidence of rape and other forms of sexual violence historically and in contemporary armed conflicts is enormously challenging. Barriers to reporting include fears among survivors of cultural taboos and reprisals against them. These concerns emanate from within their own families and even patient relationships with doctors and nurses or international humanitarian staff. Ironically, there may be risks of overreporting rape, too. Utas raises this difficult question from the interviews he conducted with child soldiers and women survivors of the civil war in Liberia and Sierra Leone who were motivated to represent themselves as victims partly because this was the imposed frame of aid agencies, and it promised access to humanitarian programming.[54]

The changing nature of warfare also poses its own challenges for reporting on sexual violence in armed conflict. The fate of civilians has varied with the transformations in the nature of warfare, especially in relation to technology, changing political-economic systems, authorities and ideologies, and consequently, the issues at stake. Recent studies have found that the greater reliance on small arms and light weapons in intrastate wars through the 1990s and first decade of the new millennium has resulted in fewer direct civilian war-related deaths since the start of the Cold War (though counting war deaths is always fraught with difficulties). Indeed, the year of the highest number of casualties from war since the end of World War II was 1950. Because of the high death toll in the

Korean War especially, the average conflict during that year killed 33,000 people, whereas in 2007 the average death rate from armed conflicts involving a government force was 1,000 over the course of a year. That is a dramatic decline. In the new millennium, the average loss of life from armed conflicts kills 90 percent fewer people each year than lost their lives from war in the average conflict in the 1950s.[55] Three interrelated causes may explain this decline: first, the smaller size of armies and more geographically limited war zones within the country; second, dramatic long-term improvements in public health since especially the 1970s; and third, significant increases since the end of the Cold War in the level, scope, and effectiveness of humanitarian aid to people affected by conflict.[56]

Nonetheless, civilians have not been spared in the post-Cold War conflicts. The pervasive denial of neutrality and safe space is one of the alarming features. As political authority fragments, and there is no effective monopoly of violence by the state authorities, getting aid to civilian victims (who are typically the main targets of the new wars) becomes increasingly complex and challenging. Second, for the most part, fighting in state-based conflicts is highly localized. For example, a survey of eleven conflicts in sub-Saharan Africa found that serious violence affected on average only about 12 percent of the territory of the country in question.[57] People outside the areas of fighting still have a chance to carry on with their daily lives without threats to their physical security, but there are undoubtedly opportunity costs of war in the country that limit their nutrition, access to education, functioning police, and other aspects of civilian and economic development that go lacking. They still have to deal with the reality of national resources directed in the first instance to the war effort, the scarcity of international investment in unstable regions, and the criminalization that spreads through much of the economy from the proliferation of illicit war markets.

While the lack of rebel capacity to project their strength over larger geographical areas spares much of society from the direct horrors of war, one of the consequences of the localization of violence is its greater intimacy. Violence is neighbor on neighbor or may even divide families (especially in ethnically or tribally mixed families, as happened in the ethnic cleansing in Bosnia or the genocide in Rwanda). The localization of conflict also facilitates sexual violence as a tool of war, and is probably the most dramatic manifestation of the intimacy of modern warfare. It leads directly to the collapse of safe space in society. Fighting in Bosnia, Rwanda, or the DRC manifests many of these characteristics of the post-Cold War conflicts.

The impact on civilians is directly evident in the large numbers of internally displaced persons and refugee populations totaling in 2009 an estimated 43.3 million, with 27.1 million internally displaced. This is the highest number of forcibly displaced persons recorded since the 1990s. The amount of IDPs assisted or protected by the United Nations High Commissioner for Refugees (UNHCR) was the highest on record at 15.6 million.[58] The number of stateless persons also signifies the loss of safe space for civilian populations. At the end of 2009, the UNHCR identified 6.6 million stateless persons in 60 countries but estimates the number could be as high as 12 million.

The enduring civilian impacts of state-based wars are evident not only in the persistently high numbers of refugees but also in the low rates of resettlement: only approximately 251,500 in 2009 were voluntarily repatriated – the lowest number since 1990 (although IDPs fared better, with 2.2 million IDPs returning home). The low rate of repatriation is also linked to protracted conflicts. In 2009, 5.5 million persons remained in a protracted refugee situation in 21 different countries, coming from 25 different protracted situations. The main hosts of the world's refugees are developing countries, who bear four-fifths of the burden, with Pakistan hosting the largest number, 1.7 million Afghans. Best estimates indicate that more than half of the global population of refugees lives in urban areas, and only one third in camps, although in sub-Saharan Africa the number of refugees in camps rises to 60 percent. Contrary to the image that most refugees are women and children, UNHCR reports they only represent 49 percent of persons of concern under their care.[59] That means the balance consists of men or boys. This also signals that the new wars are not total wars – they do not mobilize the general population for war and men for conscription, as during and before World War II.

Ending impunity

Against this backdrop, the wheels of justice have started turning in the direction of the victim, if slowly. The development of international humanitarian law in the late 1800s led to war laws prohibiting crimes of a sexual nature, but the means and will for punishment have been lacking. This enabled cover-ups by states of widespread instances of sexual violence in war. For example, a review of the transcript of the Nuremberg Trials that followed World War II found no mention of the words "woman" and "rape," despite widespread documentation of it. In the east, the Chinese of Nanking suffered two atrocities during World War II – first, the actual mass rape and violence the Japanese perpetrated against the civilians of the city, and then subsequently their efforts to erase evidence of the atrocities from public consciousness. The 22 volumes of the Tokyo trial's transcription include rape in the list of atrocities, but only four references were made during the trial and no one was condemned for this crime.[60] The Japanese were further bolstered by the silence of the Chinese victims and by the emerging Cold War. For its part, the United States sought to rehabilitate Japan as a postwar friend and ally rather than hold it accountable for the crimes against humanity committed in Nanking, or for the Japanese use of Korean and other Asian and Dutch women and girls as "comfort women," for example.[61]

By the 1990s, groundwork had been laid in the development of women's human rights, while the launching of the global campaign to prevent violence against women also galvanized international law and policy making on sexual violence in armed conflict. The first major breakthrough came in the mid-1990s when the United Nations created ad hoc tribunals on the wars in the former Yugoslavia and Rwanda to prosecute violations of international humanitarian law. The widespread evidence of rape in both conflicts notwithstanding, the original Statutes drawn up for these ad hoc tribunals did not include rape among the serious breaches of the Geneva Conventions, of law or the practices of law, or among the elements of genocide. Odio Benito, Vice-President of the ICC, notes that in the Statutes developed for the ad hoc tribunal convened to address war crimes during the Balkan Wars, "only in the list of crimes against humanity article [article 5] can we find 'rape' mentioned. In the Statute for the Rwanda Tribunal, rape was also and only included as a crime against humanity."[62] This was an important, though narrowly delimited, point of departure.

Nevertheless, a number of precedents were forthcoming. The first one came in the Rwanda Tribunal with the prosecution of General Jean-Paul Akayesu. Accused of killing Tutsi men and women, he was found guilty on nine of fifteen counts, becoming the first person convicted of genocide. The final verdict also found him guilty of rape in one of the counts covering crimes against humanity.[63] The judges did not limit rape to physical invasion of the body. This yielded a broader definition. Second, in response to pressures from radical feminists lobbying the court, the judges did not allow defendants any recourse to a defense based on consent in any context. The victim had no burden to disprove this, unlike the allowance of implicit consent in many domestic legal systems. Instead, the judges found that recourse to implicit consent is "inapplicable in any circumstances of genocide, crimes against humanity or war crimes."[64]

The Tribunal for the Former Yugoslavia also laid new groundwork in international law. For example, it established for the first time in history a definition of sexual slavery as a crime against humanity. The judges emphasized that under conditions of slavery, there could be no voluntary consent, and therefore neither could international law require proof of enforcement, or enforced threat or coercion. The court recognized the absurdity of such a requirement when the perpetrators had unconditional access; they were in complete control of the victim, physically, emotionally, sexually, and psychologically. This verdict was also important for ruling out commercial transaction (such as prostitution). In the Appeal Court, this decision was affirmed, noting that there were no provisions in international customary law that would require the victim to show resistance in order to qualify the crime as rape.[65] The Yugoslav Tribunal also established other breakthroughs in international jurisdiction on crimes of sexual violence. For example, in the 1998 Celebici case, the tribunal considered sexual violence an element of torture, and allowed for sexual violence against a sole victim to be classified as a war crime.[66]

With the establishment of the ICC,[67] the 1998 Rome Statute created a standing court with its own organic law, including the necessary mandates and mechanisms for the Court to carry out investigations, bring cases before the Court, and impose compulsory cooperation and legal assistance to participant states. The jurisdiction of the ICC only concerns "persons for the most serious crimes of international concern." Its jurisdiction is complementary to state criminal jurisdictions. The ICC becomes involved when national authorities cannot or have not exercised appropriate judicial review. The ICC's mandate is focused on four concerns: the crime of genocide, crimes against humanity, war crimes, and the crime of aggression. Furthermore, the jurisdiction of the Court encompasses war crimes defined both as international armed conflicts and armed conflicts not of an international character. The Rome Statute embraces a clear gender perspective, evident in Articles 6, 7, 8, 21, 36, 43, 53, 54, and 68, and articulates prohibitions on crimes involving sexual violence in the context of genocide, crimes against humanity, and war crimes.

The legal precedents and normative groundwork laid by the ad hoc tribunals on Rwanda and the former Yugoslavia, together with the 1998 Rome Statute, added to the political momentum for another key initiative of the international campaign to end violence against women: the adoption of the landmark United Nations Security Council Resolution 1325 on October 31, 2000.[68] Resolution 1325 embraces a number of initiatives that address violence against women in the context of armed conflict. The resolution sets out a broad agenda, although it remains largely rooted in conceptions of the victimization of women, while men are not considered possible noncombatants also needing protection.[69] United Nations Security Council (UNSC) Resolution 1820 takes 1325 a step further to stress overcoming impunity for crimes of a sexual nature in armed conflict.[70]

Overview of the book

The remainder of this study seeks to understand why sexual violence is a devastating weapon of war in many armed conflicts, how it impacts victims and their communities, why perpetrators do it, and how it is linked into a global political economy of war that uses such violence as a means of plunder and profit. Chapter 2 develops these arguments by introducing sexual violence as a runaway norm that justifies and normalizes extreme forms of violence through many different tactics, techniques, and venues of domination, humiliation, and extermination. This conceptual approach leads to a four-part typology of sexual violence as a runaway norm that overtakes cultural, religious, or legal thresholds on: (1) the *type of violence* (e.g. gang rape, mutilation, cannibalism); (2) the *targets of the violence* (e.g. children, disabled, elderly); (3) the *agency of the violence* (e.g. forcing children to commit atrocities; fathers to rape daughters); and (4) the erosion of *neutrality* in conflict regarding *who* can signal it (e.g. medical or health professionals, clergy, or peacekeepers) and the *spaces* in which it can be claimed for *safety* and *refuge* (e.g. hospitals, churches, mosques, schools, refugee camps).

Chapters 3 and 4 trace the perpetration of sexual violence in armed conflict from the onset or pre-conflict phase to the escalation of conflict and its impact on families and communities fleeing violence through forced displacement as IDPs or refugees (displaced persons who have crossed international borders). Chapter 4 also examines how oftentimes, in ways that might seem counterintuitive, sexual violence is transformed into new threats and risks of victimization in the post-conflict phase, especially for women and girls and boys, including through their vulnerability to human trafficking and sex work when few alternatives exist, and when the women and girls have been thrown out of their homes by relatives or disowned by their husbands.[71]

Chapter 5 develops a framework of analysis for explaining sexual violence in armed conflict by examining the link between the social construction of gender, especially hegemonic masculinity, and the global political economy of war and sexual violence in local conflict settings. It begins with a detailed account of these relationships in the wars in Eastern Congo since the spillover of the Rwanda genocide in 1994. The balance of the chapter develops the framework of analysis that explores these relations of domination through the lens of hyper-masculinity, taboo violations, and victims' loss of bodily integrity.

Chapter 6 concludes this study with a critique of neoliberal globalization, especially its political economy of violence, and how this relates to the disciplinary functions of sexual violence and its paradoxes. One question that emerges is whether the subversion of sexual hierarchies that happens in war (in spite of pressures to polarize gender roles) leads to a backlash against women or the undermining of hegemonic masculinity. The summary remarks conclude by examining how the problem of sexual violence is being tackled through such strategies as protection and accountability versus an ethic of care that includes community strategies for responsibility and reconciliation. The objective is to discern the strengths and limitations and possible unintended consequences of these efforts, while underscoring the importance of mobilizing international action to stand in solidarity with communities that have struggled to overcome sexual violence in armed conflict.

Conclusions

Sexual violence in conflict is both a challenging and difficult topic in many ways, but lifting the veil of silence and ending impunity are the first steps to social change and the more complete realization of human rights. Sexual violence in war is a socioeconomic and political strategy for terrorizing, controlling, displacing, and even eliminating targeted groups. It has the effect of eliminating safe space in society, and making women and girls in particular vulnerable to multiple instances of victimization throughout a conflict's trajectory. These traumas are intensified by the fact that civilians are taken captive in war and forced to commit atrocities. Victimhood is extremely complex. The gross violation of human rights and crimes against humanity that sexual violence in armed conflicts entails underscores the urgency of concerted and effective international action to prevent it; commitments to enforce international law banning it; and the development of security measures in the context of humanitarian operations to ensure the greater safety of war survivors during conflict and its aftermath. This also requires an ethic of care committed to scaling up the delivery of health and trauma-related service to survivors, and vocational and educational programs that are culturally sensitive and appropriate to support reintegration into their families and communities.

CHAPTER TWO

Dimensions of Sexual Violence in Conflict

Sexual violence takes many forms in armed conflicts across time and cultures. These range from the rape of a particular person to gang rape and mass campaigns of rape as a strategy of ethnic cleansing or genocide. Sexual violence in war is often accompanied by torture, mutilation, and cannibalism. Sexual violence in war can even involve forcing family members to commit incest; or child soldiers to commit sexual violence or be killed. There is little doubt that sexual violence in war is abhorrent in and of itself. But it is more than that. The multiple violations that sexual violence encompasses signal that it is a runaway norm. It is repulsive because it is human depravity without limit; it is the crossing of all thresholds on acceptable conduct even when measured against the inhumanity of war. It is a weapon and strategy of war aimed at domination, humiliation, expulsion, and extermination of the targeted group. In the history of sexual violence, there are no taboos left untouched.

This chapter develops a typology of sexual violence in armed conflict by conceptualizing it as a runaway norm that crosses four kinds of thresholds on violence. The first two categories of thresholds concern the *type of violence* and its *target*. The third concerns *agency*: especially how perpetrators coerce or compel others to commit sexual violence. The fourth is the *loss of neutrality and safe space*. As sexual violence overtakes one threshold after another, it "normalizes" extreme forms of violence.

What's normal? The good and bad about norms

Norms function as rules, principles, and expectations for behavior in society. They provide the basis for behavior according to social, cultural, and legally acceptable standards. There are different classes of norms: regulating norms discipline action in a given area, constitutive norms create new categories of actors or action, and prescriptive norms stipulate what should be done according to the respective principles at stake. In practice, these categories of norms overlap. By having a prescriptive character, they implicitly tell what should be done, and what is prohibited.[1]

Much of the discussion of norms in international relations comes from the social constructivist camp of theorists whose focus has been on the prescriptive force of norms to produce or uphold public goods and progressive ideals to promote and support peace, democracy, social justice, breathable air, clean water, and so on. Thus, the violation of norms provokes disapproval, stigma or sanctions, while conforming leads to praise or, if the norm is entrenched, then possibly no reaction at all. Things are as they should be. Good people uphold norms because of the shared moral assessment associated with that rule of conduct. A logical corollary to emphasizing the prescriptive force of norms is that, from the vantage point of those who promote the norm, it cannot be bad.[2] Nonetheless, the universality of norms has to be tested against the validity of the moral claims on which they rest. To understand whether the prescriptive force of a norm produces public goods or social harms requires independent moral discernment on the part of the observer.

Slavery provides an example of an oppressive social institution that once carried strong prescriptive force in society: its social acceptance was finally ended by an international movement to ban it. Similarly, the missionary zeal that

European imperial powers and citizens brought to the notion of "civilization" was part of a larger moral, albeit colonizing and economic, enterprise. However, the assumption that imperialism then or in its contemporary form provides public goods also has come into question.[3] To take another example, international security norms can drive states to acquire more and more dangerous weapons, undermining common security, as the nuclear arms race did during the Cold War. Thus, some norms, despite moral claims to their prescriptive force, may not stand the test of time as providing public goods.

Runaway norms are a special class of norms that produce social harms or public bads. They open the floodgates to abuse and exploitation without limit. Runaway norms colonize or operate through fear and other conflict dynamics that undermine the sense of personal and group safety or security. For example, the promotion of propaganda and groupthink and other strategies that polarize different communities reinforce solidarity within the group, while justifying dominance over the out-group(s). Runaway norms legitimize these conflict processes, and "come to be seen as the 'right thinking' by most members of a group. They are taught to new members and imposed on old members who appear to question them."[4] Central to the emergence and internalization of norms is the way the dominant group shares them and can bring others to internalize them. Negative attitudes such as stereotyping, dehumanization, and zero-sum thinking – the psychological dynamics of conflict escalation – are tools for pushing the internalization of runaway norms, so that the norms gain strength and stability throughout the group. Runaway norms are fueled by the proliferation of hate propaganda and with it the mobilization of communities on the basis of hatred for the "Other." This creates an insidious climate that incentivizes and rationalizes the mass violation of human dignity and life.

As a runaway norm becomes part of the group's self-identity, perceptions, goals, or part of behavior patterns as a means of projecting authority and eliciting obedience, it gains force and is more likely to contribute to conflict escalation and other social harms. Norms also tend to be self-perpetuating, and this is true of runaway norms. A couple of the mechanisms that propel and sustain runaway norms are social pressure and claims to their "moral" force. As Rubin, Pruitt and Kim explain, "people who challenge a norm tend to be punished by the group. Others who doubt the validity of a norm remain silent for fear of being labeled deviates or, in the case of intergroup conflict, traitors."[5]

Norms are at the center of the acceptability of discipline and punishment in society.[6] The rhetorical power of norms establishes the boundaries of normality and deviance from it. They are the foundational elements of discourse and shape its power to discipline and punish. Repetition in discourse is one tool for reinforcing the acceptability of the norm, such as when US President George H. W. Bush justified the US-led international coalition efforts to turn back Saddam Hussein's 1990 invasion of Kuwait by saying, "We are united in the belief that Iraq's aggression must not be tolerated. No peaceful international order is possible if larger states can devour their smaller neighbors . . . In the face of tyranny, let no one doubt American credibility and reliability. Let no one doubt our staying power. We will stand by our friends," and so on.[7] Norms set boundaries on what is acceptable in society by framing and defining (naming) what the problem is (for example, Saddam controlling 20 percent of the world's oil reserves; or after 9/11, Muslim fundamentalism requiring a "war on terror"). Norms direct where attention should be focused; what the policy response and tools for carrying it out should be; whether and when the problem becomes a crisis needing more urgent response, and who has a say in all this or is excluded from the debate.[8] When runaway norms gain ground and set the terms for society to torture, ethnic cleanse or commit genocide, moral collapse is certain. In these circumstances, runaway norms lead to a "kind of false, explosive liberation."[9]

Runaway norms have several effects on conflict escalation. They justify actions by a group that cross cultural, legal, or other prohibitions and limits that set thresholds on violence. Runaway norms overtake thresholds in terms of the *type of violence* (e.g. rape, torture, mutilation, cannibalism) and the *intended targets* of the violence (sexual violence against pregnant women, or elders). They also coerce, threaten, force, and compel others to carry out violent acts, resulting in *oppressive agency* (child soldiers, sexual slavery) in situations where the victims' autonomy, choice or control over their situation is greatly circumscribed. They violate traditional methods of signaling *neutrality* (for noncombatants, women, children, elderly, infirm, disabled, refugee, etc.), and deny *safe space* or safe haven where refuge is sought (such as churches, schools, refugee camps, hospitals, UN compounds).[10]

Norms are rhetorical devices that conflict parties use to justify their strategies and targets of warfare. Runaway norms push societies into the abyss, while the norms of international humanitarian law attempt to rein in warring parties. Relationships are never fixed and evolve historically as actors use different kinds of power and moral justifications among their own people and against opposing side(s) to dominate, rule, and resist. Runaway norms colonize social institutions, and war is one such vehicle. In fact, the just war theory and international humanitarian law attempt to limit the runaway effects of war by proscribing certain behaviors of combatants and developing protections for civilians.

However, these protections have their own deep roots in gendered conceptions of war and chivalry,[11] while the category of civilian itself is deeply ambiguous. International humanitarian law defines civilians by what they are not ("noncombatants") rather than in a positive sense of who should be counted as civilian. Hugo Slim suggests that when faced with "superordinate enemy identities," the civilian ethic calls for rising above them to affirm a different identity – the deeper attachment to humanity as a whole.[12] In practice, civilians carry on with their lives in war with the same or more complexity of identities than they had before. To the extent that the new wars sweep many civilians under their shadows (smuggling goods to raise money and feed their family, selling supplies to armed groups, working as porters or forced laborers for them, and so on), maintaining the distinction between combatant and noncombatant is compromised, a reality reflected in the extent to which so many members of society bear the brunt of wars, even child soldiers.

Impact of armed conflicts on civilians: More of the same?

Strategies and targets of warfare have evolved over the centuries, especially in relation to technology, changing political systems and authorities, the issues at stake, and the civilian impact. For example, major changes transpired with the shift from the feudal system based largely on mercenaries to modern standing armies in service of the nation-state that prevailed through World Wars I and II. The fate of civilians has varied with the changes in the nature of warfare. Although the prevailing model of fighting during the first half of the twentieth century centered more on battlefield conflict with opposing armies than the targeting of civilians per se, noncombatants were not spared.[13] The "total" nature of warfare in World Wars I and II has to be counted among the factors that placed people in the direct line of conflict.[14]

War strategies following World War II developed in new ways that, despite the further development of humanitarian law, continued to place civilians at risk. These conflicts included wars of liberation accompanied by guerrilla and counterinsurgency strategies. They were mostly subsumed by the Cold War and fueled by the military-security interests and the largesse of superpower competition. At the same time, the earlier predominance of interstate war was replaced by state-based conflict (violent conflict involving the government and opposition forces). The type of weapons and their impact has also changed with the shift away from the use of tanks and other heavy artillery, as was customary with large conventional forces, to the use of small arms and light weapons in state-based conflicts (though there are some signs even these wars are moving toward heavier weaponry in the new millennium).

Many government military face well-armed and equipped rebel forces, as Sri Lanka has with the Liberation Tigers of Tamil Eelam (LTTE). At the height of their power, the Liberation Tigers of Tamil Eelam counted among their resources a field army equivalent to three brigades, armed with artillery, armor, radios with encryption devices, and even light aircraft they used for bombing. The protracted nature of many state-based conflicts, such as Sri Lanka's long-running civil war that dates to 1983, or Sudan (which experienced a low intensity civil war from 1955 to 1972, and then renewed fighting from 1983 to the present, involving both North–South conflict and later Darfur), suggest that opposition groups are able to acquire training, equipment, and capability sufficient to thwart government-led military efforts to suppress them. The number of active conflicts around the world has also changed over time. Since the aftermath of World War II, the number of state-based armed conflicts peaked in 1992 with 52 active conflicts – a high watermark coinciding with the instability of the end of the Cold War and widespread changes within and across international systems and regions. That trend then began a dramatic post-Cold War decline, reaching a low of 29 state-based conflicts in 2003, although the number rose to 34 by 2007.[15]

The post-World War II period has tended to draw scholars separately into either the study of intrastate or interstate wars. However, the spillover of conflict from one state into a neighboring country is one area where this division clearly breaks down. Another instance is in the case of conflict over territory of co-nationals on the other side of the border which may result in irredentist wars (annexation of territory of another state), revanchist wars (to reverse territorial loss), or secessionist wars (e.g. to secede from one state and form an independent state). There are other ways that interstate and intrastate wars are linked and may be outcomes of the same processes. For example, the German school has emphasized the study of war within the context of globalization, suggesting that globalization has accelerated state decay and provided rebels with new opportunities. Together with the growing availability of small arms and light weapons, the number of wars has increased.[16]

The literature on the "new wars," pioneered by Mary Kaldor, focuses on state-based conflicts in the post-Cold War context, which encompassed the dismantling of the Soviet "empire" and multiethnic states like the former Yugoslavia, as well as the shift from one-party states to democratic elections that brought conflict in the Balkans and elsewhere, especially Africa. These conflicts are no longer dragged into the ideological contestations of the superpower-driven bipolar system, where the parties came under some disciplinary influence of their patron[17] – not least because of the funding and military weapons they provided. This has put new pressures on conflict parties to fund their own war efforts. With the collapse of the superpower rivalry and the rapid withdrawal from regional conflicts and proxy wars, the Cold War means of international leverage over combatants have also been lost. On the other hand, the selling off of Cold War weapons stockpiles greatly increased the supply of arms (especially small arms and light weapons) on the world markets, helping to fuel the new wars.[18] The use of small arms and light weapons on the beds of pickup trucks or backs of rebels (even child soldiers) moving by foot often through rural areas in fairly delimited zones of conflict has also facilitated more intimate and localized violence, and with it, sexual violence. Thus, the new wars literature stresses changes in warfare from the Cold War days and earlier, such as the shift away from ideological conflicts to identity- or resource-based conflicts; the fractionation of warring parties; and the illicit sources of funding.

These changes in conflict patterns have to also be situated in the context of globalization. A closer analysis suggests that wars in the so-called failed states in Africa and elsewhere are, in fact, linked directly into the complex ties of the global political economy. The insertion of postcolonial states in the global economy was conditioned by 1980s World Bank and International Monetary Fund (IMF) structural adjustment programs aimed at greater transparency (less corruption), balanced national budgets, and debt restructuring. To achieve these goals, political leaders had to downsize the state apparatus by cutting subsidies for food, health care, education, and other social welfare policies and sources of civil servant jobs. At the same time, they were forced to open up to foreign investment. These policies, known collectively as the "Washington Consensus," removed political control of the national economy from the state, a move that was exacerbated by the 1990s push for democratization that unleashed political contestation along ethnic, tribal, racial or clan lines, exacerbating internal conflicts, often a legacy of colonialism.

The collapse of the state in Sierra Leone in the early 1990s provides a useful example of the impact of the Washington Consensus. Sierra Leone's "shadow state foundations," already in place from the early colonial period when the British administrators made accommodations with local rulers, came to the fore as neopatrimonial rule and clientelism when the state failed in the early 1990s. Then President Momoh used foreign investment to enrich himself and his cronies while marginalizing domestic foes. Instead of improving Sierra Leone's dismal economic performance, the strategy further fragmented internal conflicts and the state – opening the door to a brutal civil war funded through the illicit trade in diamonds.[19] Even the agricultural sector in Sierra Leone collapsed as labor shifted to the mines and smuggling operations that were central to the war economy. Sierra Leone was left importing basic foodstuffs, including rice when it was previously a rice-exporting country.[20]

The new wars have a couple of other novel features. Unlike wars of liberation, in which civilians (both men and women) supported rebels and fought alongside them (for example, Mozambique or Nicaragua), in the "new wars" rebels like the Lord's Resistance Army (LRA – formerly based in Northern Uganda) or the al-Shabab in Somalia have no ideology and no reason to mobilize civilian support. Since the main goal is wealth accumulation through criminal means, it is irrelevant whether warlords and rebel factions have the sympathy of civilians. To get new recruits, they kidnap children for child soldiering and women for camp duties and sexual slavery. In the case of the LRA, some of the patterns of violence, such as raiding, pillaging, and abduction of women to become "wives," follow precolonial practices in the region. In that sense, the LRA could be said to draw on enduring traditions,[21] but generally it has simply turned sadomasochistic, cutting off lips or ears of victims, amputating limbs, and engaging in forced cannibalism and the widespread use of sexual violence. *New York Times* East Africa bureau chief Jeffrey Gettleman calls this kind of violence against civilians for its own sake the "unwars."[22]

The patterns in post-Cold War conflicts reveal why civilian populations still bear a great deal of the burden of war, the evidence of lower mortality rates across them notwithstanding. Among the countries with conflicts that generate the most refugees, Afghanistan leads the pack for the last three decades with over 6.4 million seeking refuge during the peak years of the conflict. In 2009, there were still 2.9 million Afghan refugees (96 percent of them in Pakistan and the Islamic Republic of Iran). Iraq is the second largest source country of refugees, with 1,785,200 refugees. Somalia and the DRC are the third and fourth largest sources of refugees respectively. There were some 678,000 Somalis under UNHCR responsibility in 2009 (up from 2008), and 456,000 Congolese refugees from the DRC, of whom 144,000 fled in 2009 alone.[23] Despite the lessening lethality of war in the late twentieth and early twenty-first centuries, the civilian toll remains high, pervasive, and protracted.

Crossing thresholds: Impact of sexual violence as a runaway norm

Threshold 1: Type of sexual violence
Sexual violence takes many forms in war. As the 1998 Rome Statute articulates, sexual violence can be a component of genocide, crimes against humanity, and war crimes. Rape is perhaps the type of outrage most commonly associated with sexual violence in warfare. From an essentializing perspective, the long history and frequency of rape in armed conflict suggests that it is a standard form of conduct in difficult times, a normal way of being human. For their part,

structural theorists emphasize the role that identities play in why rape becomes a tool of ethnic extermination, such as Catharine MacKinnon's analysis of rape in the former Yugoslavia. She argues that in situations of armed conflict even a specific violation has to be understood as part of a larger strategy of violence against women and their ethno-religious community.[24]

Like Bosnia, the Rwandan genocide also stands out for the organized nature of the sexual violence. It was very public, with rapes committed in view of others at schools, churches, roadblocks, or government buildings. Even women who hid in the bush were found and violated. Rape victims' corpses "were left spread-eagled in public view, as a reminder of the brutality and power of the genocide's perpetrators."[25] Rape was also used as a weapon of genocide to kill and to spread HIV/AIDs by perpetrators who often knew they carried the disease. The United Nations Special Rapporteur on Rwanda, Rene Degni-Segui, estimated in a 1996 report that between 250,000 and 500,000 Rwandese women and girls were raped.[26] In Rwanda, 15 years after the genocide, an estimated 70 percent of rape survivors are HIV-positive.[27]

In contrast to essentialist and structuralist accounts, social constructivism helps to understand other gendered complexities of war rapes, including the fact that women are sometimes involved as perpetrators, too. This realization disrupts commonly held assumptions about the relationship between women, power, and agency, along with their purity and innocence. Much of the literature dealing with women perpetrators has struggled to come to terms with the role of women in sexual violence. More frequently the identities of women perpetrators are collapsed into such essentializing categories as mothers, monsters, or whores. Relying on stereotypical images marginalizes violent women and denies their agency, while failing to uncover the complex identities and power relations (and changes in them during war) that affect women, not unlike men.[28]

In the Rwandan genocide, both men and women were among the perpetrators. Hutu women from all segments of society (even nuns) carried out rapes, either using objects or ordering men to commit rape of Tutsi women.[29] Among the prominent women Genocidaires is Agnes Ntamabyariro, daughter of a Tutsi mother and Hutu father, and former Minister of Justice in Rwanda serving in the interim government at the time of the genocide. She was convicted for conspiracy and incitement related to the genocide and received a life sentence. In her memoir *The Blue Sweater*, philanthropist Jacqueline Novogratz tells of her incomprehension when she learned of Agnes's involvement in the planning and incitement to genocide. Agnes had been one of the original founders of Duterimbere, a women's empowerment organization Novogratz helped establish, that worked to bring microfinance credit to rural Rwandan women. Agnes was one of the first women in Africa to serve in her country's parliament. Novogratz had considered her a pioneer in the women's movement and role model for other women committed to social justice.[30] Novogratz could not reconcile her friend's social justice activism before the genocide with her role in the Hutu-led government's perpetration of it. Her incredulity was exacerbated on learning of Agnes's role in inciting genocide in Butare, a prefecture near the southern border of Rwanda with Burundi, where another one of their friends and original founder of the organization had fled with her family for protection.[31]

Eventually, Agnes was convicted of the murder of Jean Baptiste Habyarimana, who, until his death, had succeeded in preventing the spread of the genocide to the prefecture where he served as governor. She was also convicted of planning and holding meetings to organize the genocide in her own hometown region and of participating in campaigns to distribute weapons. Still, a third member of Novogratz's team ended up in jail for two years under suspicion of genocide for her work with the interim government, but she was later released, never charged with any crimes. For Novogratz, the paths taken by her former colleagues recalled Hannah Arendt's exposition of the "banality of evil:" "Agnes had helped me internalize what I hadn't wanted to see before – monsters do exist, but not in the way I had imagined them. I grew up believing in Frank Capra's world, where everyone was good except the bad guys who wore black hats and either died or found redemption."[32] She had never imagined that her friend, head shaven and wearing a pink prison uniform, long eyelashes and soft eyes, with whom she had created an institution of social justice, could be such a war criminal. Nevertheless, Agnes's continued anger and hatred that boiled over in her attempt to justify the genocide to her friend belied how far she had strayed from her former principled self.[33]

Women also played some leading roles in the ethnic cleansing that unfolded in the war zones of the former Yugoslavia. The most prominent woman official convicted is Dr Biljana Plasvic, a former member of the Presidency of the Republika Srpska, who served as its Acting President in 1992 and from 1996–8. She was the first person to surrender voluntarily to the War Crimes Tribunal for the former Yugoslavia. This factor, together with her guilty plea, led to a plea bargain in her sentencing that spared her from charges of genocide. Instead, she received 11 years for crimes against humanity. Given the extent of her crimes, the sentence seems light. A biologist by training, and former Dean of the Natural Sciences and Mathematics at the University of Sarajevo, she drew on genetic arguments to goad men into committing crimes in the war to overcome the impact of mixed marriages on the degeneration of the Serbian nationhood.[34] Women have also been perpetrators of sexual violence in other prominent cases, as seen in the abuse at Abu Ghraib in Iraq, where women were among the US troops who forced Iraqi detainees to masturbate and simulate homosexual relations in what constituted cultural humiliation, violation of Islamic law, and torture. They even took photographs as trophies.[35]

Many forms of abuse and torture accompany rape in war as integral to the campaign of terror. The atrocities include genital mutilation and other means of degradation directed against sexual organs or the body in ways that have sexual connotations to the rape victim and other members of the family and community.[36] Women are not the only targets. Four thousand Croat male prisoners were sexually tortured in Serb detention camps, according to estimates by the Zagreb Medical Centre for Human Rights. Such differential targeting of men versus women in the context of genocidal violence has been termed "gendercide" to draw attention to the fact that genocide is not gender neutral.[37] Likewise, in Rwanda, men, especially from the Tutsi, were sexually assaulted and targeted for extermination. The gendercidal degradation they faced included the mutilation of their genitals, which were displayed in public in some instances. Tutsi men and boys were also forced to rape Tutsi women. Alternatively, they were forced by Hutu women to have sex with them. Women and girls were not spared from a host of sexual atrocities and human degradation, either. They faced rape, gang rape, sexual slavery, forced incest, and forced marriage. Torture included the amputation or mutilation "of victims' breasts, vaginas and buttocks, or of features considered to be Tutsi, such as small noses or long fingers. Even pregnant women were not spared."[38] There were undoubtedly many cases of male rape of men in the civil war in Sierra Leone. For reasons of cultural stigmatization, documentation of these cases by Human Rights Watch was the exception rather than the rule.[39]

Rape may involve vaginal or oral penetration with the penis or hands, or with sharp instruments such as a gun barrel, swords, knives, sticks, bottles, or other objects. Very often women are badly injured by multiple rapes, gang rapes and various objects leading to a medical condition known as traumatic fistula. It results in the formation of a rupture, or fistula, between a woman's vagina and her bladder or rectum, or both. Women who suffer traumatic fistula lose the ability to control their bladder or bowels, resulting in urine or feces leaking from the tear. Affected women are often divorced by their husbands, shunned by their communities, and unable to work or care for their families.[40] Traumatic fistula, together with the effects of unwanted pregnancy and risk of sexually transmitted diseases and HIV/AIDs, amplify the psychosocial trauma of the rape. Adequate medical attention requires complex reconstructive surgery and long-term care that is not available to most victims around the world.

Like rape, mutilation of body parts communicates the (enduring) political power of the perpetrator over the victim. Whereas men use various emblems like heroic insignia or war paraphernalia to inscribe power on their own bodies as soldiers or heroes, the converse of this is the mutilation of enemy bodies. Mutilation may be inflicted on the living or dead: by removing clothes; leaving the body in sexually provocative positions as a symbol of the rape and power of the opponent; through various means of keeping body counts; or by using photography of the corpse as a trophy of war, and so on.[41] In Colombia, for example, a 2001 United Nations Special Rapporteur on Violence Against Women reported that a "girl was raped and killed, her eyes and nails then removed, and her breasts cut off."[42] Other kinds of violations include dismemberment, cutting open pregnant women, removing the fetus, and violating it, too. Sexual violence against men in conflict, as reported in the wars in Yugoslavia, for example, included castration of prisoners, including by forcing other internees to bite off a prisoner's testicles, use of electric shock to the genitals, or having their penis removed for having an erection when forced to view Serb women naked.[43]

Branding the victim is another method of torture encompassing sexual violence. Branding has been practiced in many historical contexts, including under colonialism and slavery as a means of inscribing the power of the colonizer or slave master over the subject. For example, slave owners sometimes branded their own initials on the foreheads of their slaves. Jews had numbers tattooed on their bodies during the Holocaust, sometimes in sexually provocative places. Because branding is both a lasting physical and psychological scar, it invokes and re-invokes the horror of the original violation, and preserves and communicates the power of the perpetrators over family members and others in the community. For a survivor, branding is a lifelong symbol of the suffering and defilement.

Whether or not it leaves visible physical scars, rape is itself a kind of branding. In many cultures, a rape survivor may be disowned by her husband, and ostracized by her family and community, as happened to Muslim women in Bosnia, or survivors in many African conflicts. In Afghanistan, under the Taliban regulations, a woman who was raped needed four male witnesses to prove her noncompliance; otherwise, she was at risk of punishment for fornication and adultery. Lacking any system for reporting abuse or receiving assistance, an unmarried girl exposed for having sexual relations could marry the perpetrator. Or the offended family might kill the girl and perpetrator to restore its honor. Human rights organizations continue to call on the Afghan government to differentiate between rape and adultery and to consider rape a heinous crime to be dealt with separately from Islamic adultery penal codes.[44]

Children born of rape in war also continue the stigmatization for the mother and her family. Finding ways for the child to be included in the family is often a challenge. A constant reminder of the rape, children are at greater risk when their origins are visibly marked by their features, such as happened with "Vietnamerican" children that resulted from US troops' sexual exploitation of Vietnamese women, or the half-Arab children in Darfur who are the offspring of Janjaweed gang rapes.[45] While infanticide or death through the neglect of a mother too ill to care for the infant is not uncommon in war rape cases, the children who survive infancy can face severe stigma within their communities. Children born of wartime rape have been vilified and defamed from birth: in Rwanda, they have been referred to as the "devil's children"; in Kosovo, "children of shame"; in East Timor, "children of the enemy"; in Nicaragua, "monster babies." Male babies are sometimes at greater risk than females, because they could become "fifth-column enemy combatants growing up within the community."[46] In the DRC, for example, shelters hold more boys than girls (unheard of elsewhere since boys are usually desired over girls in most cultures): there is a greater concern that they will grow up to turn against their own family.[47]

The horror faced by a victim of sexual violence does not end with the cessation of hostilities. They live with the physical and emotional trauma of their injuries. Women must continue to care for children, including those born of rape, and suffer because society and their husband and own family treat them as "damaged goods, living symbols of a nation's humiliation and bearers of 'enemy' children."[48] Women suffer from shame and devaluation for the tortures they have endured rather than gain treatment as heroes, which status is conferred on injured males.

Threshold 2: Taboo targets

Runaway norms can also be conceptualized in terms of the *intended targets* of the violence. Sexual violence is a runaway norm not only because of the type of violence perpetrated, but also in terms of the many categories of noncombatants that are targeted. Raping and mutilating pregnant women, breastfeeding women and elderly women are clearly violations both for the act itself and because of the special status of the victim. For example, women who have recently given birth are accorded special standing in many countries. In Sierra Leone, for example, according to cultural practice, women are not to have sexual intercourse until their children are weaned and can walk, which can take up to three years.[49] Children also have special standing in society around the world. As de Berry argues, "there is no doubt that children have a special status in any society, a status often closely aligned with their physical fragility and dependence."[50] Sexual violence against young girls is taboo across cultures. Yet young girls have been targeted for sexual violence in many conflicts, sometimes because of beliefs in the magical protections that violating a virgin provides the offender. For example, in what is known as the Rape of Nanking, Japanese soldiers raped virgins because they thought that it would make them more powerful in battle.[51] In the wars of the DRC, "some Congolese soldiers think that having sex with virgins conveys magic powers or can even cure AIDS."[52]

The abuse of the elderly is often ignored or is one of the violations taken least into account in conflict zones. Yet elder abuse has happened at different times and places across history in war. This topic is especially difficult to contemplate, not least because in many cultures and especially in societies that retain traditional mores, the elderly are held in special esteem. This can be seen in many Asian countries such as India, Nepal, and China.[53] The high status and respect society accords elders makes their sexual violation all the more reprehensible. A comprehensive study on the sexual violation of elders concluded that, in many countries around the world, older women are more vulnerable than men, especially in wartime when traditional support networks break down.[54] While contemporary conflicts seem to pose particular threats to girls and women, including elderly women, similar violence has occurred in previous wars. For example, an eyewitness to the Rape of Nanking recorded in his report that girls as young as eight years of age and women over the age of 70 were raped, beaten, and their bodies brutally displayed.[55] Similar spans in the age of victims were recorded in the Armenian genocide, and also documented recently in the ongoing wars in the eastern parts of the DRC.[56]

Threshold 3: Oppressed agency
Much can be said of agency and sexual violence in war. Indeed, fear, threat, coercion, and force are all at the core of sexual violence – acts committed under conditions or circumstances in which the perpetrators exercise nearly complete control over victims emotionally, physically, and sexually. Forced incest, sexual slavery, forced marriage, forced prostitution or survival sex, camp roles for boys or girls as "spies" using sex to gain strategic advantage, trafficking, and the child soldier all present conditions that limit agency under oppressive conditions encompassing great power differentials. The French sociologist Michel Foucault's work on power provides a lens through which to understand the "productive" effects of power in such contexts for disciplining, punishing and subjugating marginalized communities and also for locating opportunities to resist power with power, in spite of constraints on choice, freedom, and autonomy. Foucault argues that power is leaky, so there are always opportunities to resist. From a relational autonomy perspective, even oppressed

agents have "options to act against, around or with others."[57] However, in oppressive situations like sexual violence in armed conflict, options are greatly constrained, and the costs of resisting seem prohibitively high.

Oppressed agency has been a key element of sexual violence in conflicts in Europe throughout the twentieth century and elsewhere. For example, the Armenian genocide involved camps that functioned as slave markets. The most desirable females, those from the wealthiest families, were examined by local doctors for diseases and were made available to high-ranking Muslim officials. If the woman refused, she was detained until she accepted her life in slavery.[58] During World War II, Nazi concentration camps included camp brothels for forced sex labor in ten of the major concentration camps. Women were brought from female concentration camps, encouraged to opt for forced sex labor with the false promise of a release after six months of work. The Nazis' powerful paramilitary unit known as the "SS" or Schutzstaffel – German for "Protective Echelon" – ordered the camp brothels as part of a strategy to increase slave labor productivity, which it would not accept at 50 percent of the level of civilian labor productivity.[59] Within the concentration camps, women also faced various forms of sexual violence, including verbal abuse and humiliation as they passed through the "sauna" – the disinfection routine on arrival at the camp – to cases of physical abuse and rape, including in the gynecological exams that followed. This happened despite Nazi mythology of the pure race and prohibition against such "racial shame." For camp survivors, the horror did not end at liberation, as many Soviet Army soldiers raped (mostly) non-Jewish German women, as well as some Jewish women still in the concentration camps.[60]

Trafficking is another threat communities face in conflict zones, two prominent examples being Nepal and Afghanistan. Lucrative trafficking networks sell Nepali girls for US$2,000 or more for domestic and sex work to brothels in Mumbai, a top destination, and to other Indian cities including Pune, Delhi, Kolkata, and onto the Middle East and Asia.[61] Reports indicate that trafficking of Afghan women and children has been increasing rapidly, a consequence of 26 years of war, along with the poverty, cultural and political oppression that has accompanied it. A 2004 report of the International Organization for Migration indicates that "forced prostitution and prostitution of minors, forced labor, abductions for forced marriage for debt relief, and exchange of women for dispute settlement continue to thrive in Afghanistan."[62] Known as "bad," the exchange of women for dispute settlement is a mechanism for the perpetrator's family to recuperate its honor (over issues such as murders, elopements, intertribal animosities and land disputes). In Afghan society, abuses against women are a function of (superior) male honor in society.[63]

Children are also targets of sexual violence in war. They are especially at risk of capture and induction into the armed forces of government or rebel groups in many conflicts, given the widespread lack of security in their home villages, at schools, or in refugee and IDP camps.[64] Child soldiers are oftentimes abducted or "voluntarily" recruited into governmental or rebel forces in exchange for food, shelter or protection. As captives, child soldiers are by definition trafficked victims. For some armed groups, such as the LRA in Northern Uganda, child soldiers serve as a commodity: they have reportedly been trafficked into Southern Sudan and exchanged for weapons.[65] In Afghanistan, warlords have returned to a traditional practice of using young boys sold by their families for sex and entertainment, or taken as street orphans for *bacha bazi* (boy play), an exploitative practice previously banned by the Taliban. Boys as young as 11 years of age called *bacheh beereesh* (beardless boys) are selected for their height, size, and beauty. They are dressed in women's clothes to sing and dance and are traded for sexual favors among warlords, ex-commanders, and businessmen.[66]

Children are among the most vulnerable of civilian populations in war, and their recruitment and abduction has been a defining, even extreme feature of post-Cold War conflicts. Their numbers have been estimated at 200,000–300,000 just for the period 1988–2002. In 2002 alone, child soldiers "served in seventy-two government or rebel armed forces in about twenty countries."[67] These numbers indicate the pervasive violation of a growing body of international protocols, agreements, and declarations that work toward the protection of children from both forced and voluntary recruitment.[68] While there is some evidence of a decreasing number of armed conflicts using child soldiers – a drop from 27 to 17 between 2004 and 2007 – the trend seems to be more a function of conflict termination than the end of child recruitment per se. Active conflicts where child soldiers are involved include Afghanistan, Burundi, Central African Republic, Chad, Colombia, Cote d'Ivoire, the DRC, India, Indonesia, Iraq, Israel and the Occupied Palestinian Territory, Myanmar, Nepal, Philippines, Somalia, Sri Lanka, Sudan, Thailand, and Uganda.[69] Eighty-six countries in the world recruit or use children in the military and in hostilities.[70]

Such vulnerability among children raises many difficult questions: at what point do they stop being child victims and become perpetrators in conflict, responsible for their actions? When do they become child soldiers – when they are abducted or when they take up arms? Do they continue to merit protection as an IDP? How should they be treated in the aftermath of conflict? Another set of questions concerns the gendered aspect of the child soldier. More has been done to address the needs of the boy than the girl soldier. In addition, international campaigns to draw attention to child soldiers have failed to bring attention to the special plight of the girl soldier and the kind of sexual violence to which they are often subjected. For example, the Coalition to Stop the Use of Child Soldiers campaign focused on the age issue – raising the age requirement for recruiting soldiers from 15 to 18 years old. But this framing of the issue at hand diverted attention away from the effects of armed conflict on children, and especially the efforts to highlight the impacts on girl soldiers. As a consequence, "despite frequent mention of sexual violence against girls in articles and reports published by organizations involved in the Coalition, little was done to create inclusive international laws once the issue had been framed."[71]

Threshold 4: Loss of neutrality and safe space
Runaway norms also cross escalation thresholds by disregarding claims to neutrality and by targeting and eliminating safe spaces in society. The ICC enumerates the legal protections regarding questions of neutrality and safe space as war crimes. Under Article 8, War Crimes, the Rome Statute specifies that war crimes constitute grave breaches of the Geneva Conventions, meaning acts against person or property protected under the relevant provisions of the Geneva Conventions, such as willful killing, torture or inhuman treatment, willful causing of great suffering, or injury to body or health; extensive destruction and appropriation of property, not justified by military necessity and carried out unlawfully and wantonly, and taking of hostages.[72]

Article 8 also enumerates other serious breaches of laws and customs applicable in *international armed conflicts* that bear on the protection of neutrality and safe space, including intentionally attacking civilian populations, or civilian objects that are not military objectives; and "intentionally directing attacks against personnel, installations, material, units or vehicles involved in a humanitarian assistance or peacekeeping mission." Article 8 further encompasses prohibitions on actions that would cause severe and long-term harm to the natural environment; attacking or bombarding by any means towns, villages, dwellings, or buildings that are not defended and not military objectives, including buildings dedicated to religion, education, art, science or charitable purposes, historic monuments, hospitals and places where the sick and wounded are collected, provided these are not military objectives. Furthermore, Article 8 prohibits the improper use of a flag of truce, including the military insignia and uniform of the enemy or the United Nations, and distinctive emblems of the Geneva Conventions. Buildings, material, medical units and transport, and personnel using the distinctive emblems of the Geneva Conventions are also protected. Article 8 also specifically includes prohibitions on conduct in armed conflicts *not* of an international character – in other words, internal conflicts. Prohibitions on the willful destruction of safe spaces and persons in international armed conflicts covered under the Geneva Conventions are restated in paragraph 2(c) of Article 8 with respect to internal armed conflicts.

Despite these international standards, one of the alarming features of the "new wars" is the denial of neutrality and safe space. First, as political authority fragments, and the state's monopoly on the use of force breaks down as rebel groups take up arms, getting aid to civilian victims becomes increasingly complex and challenging. Second, for the most part, fighting in state-based conflicts is highly localized. In fact, ethnic cleansing and genocide are quintessentially forms of violence where safe space is eliminated in society and intimacy a hallmark of the killing and exploitation. Rwanda represents these realities with both the loss of life and the very public spectacle made of the mass rape of women. The loss of an estimated 800,000 lives in the Rwandan genocide during a three-month period is also "the most rapid genocide in recorded history."[73]

The killing was brutally rational and carried out in intimate, closed and even sacred quarters. As a witness explained,

> "where large numbers of people had to be killed, as happened where dozens or hundreds had sought refuge in churches, the death squads went about it methodically: phase one involved breaking the ankles so as to prevent the victims from running away; once the victims were immobilized, they worked on the wrists and arms, to prevent them from fighting back; the killers could then turn to the last phase, using clubs, sticks and machetes to break the skulls and necks."[74]

Infants were not spared, either, thereby eliminating the threat of a new generation seeking revenge. Lemarchand estimates that about 10 percent of the Hutu population was responsible for the genocide either as executioners, organizers, or unwilling accomplices. Ninety percent were not – that is 5.8 million Hutu. Many of the innocent Hutu were killed, or died as they fled the Rwandan Patriotic Front (RPF) that overtook the Hutu military and assumed control of Rwanda.[75]

Third, the juxtaposition of rebels, government forces, and civilians in an undifferentiated landscape puts people at greater risk than in conventional wars where battle lines were more clearly delineated through trench warfare and other means. The nature of new wars puts families and communities in the path of violence while the combatants from both rebel and government military flout international humanitarian law that proscribes the killing of civilians. Putting civilians in the crosshairs of the new wars is central to the political economy of violence. Rebel and government forces move among civilian populations seeking shelter, supplies and more (e.g. cell phones, livestock, food stocks, sex, cash). Further complicating matters, rebels and soldiers are often indistinguishable from the general population. In Sierra Leone, for example, some soldiers fought with the army during the day and joined the rebel forces at night. They were dubbed "sobels."

Fourth, whereas the superpowers used to exercise some leverage over proxies in the Cold War to rein in their excesses, in post-Cold War armed conflicts, discipline comes from the international community in a more diffuse manner: through the force of the body of international humanitarian law; and through the United Nations, regional organizations, and many NGOs that raise the flag of moral condemnation and standard setting, while the great powers still wield economic and other influences, if more subtly than before. The great powers may also raise moral and human rights questions, as Hillary Clinton did on her state visit to the DRC in April 2010, calling attention to the epidemic of sexual violence against civilians in Eastern Congo by government and rebel forces. But behind this cloak of humanitarian concerns lie deeper stakes in global economic and security issues. For example, Hillary's moral concerns voiced during her 11-country tour of Africa have to be weighed against the reality that the United States lags behind China and Russia in the scramble for African oil and other vital resources.

Fifth, carving out secure space for humanitarian operations is "an elementary struggle in the new wars."[76] Usually central government authorities negotiate with humanitarian agencies for legal entry to a country and access to victims. But the collapse of that authority presents challenges for a humanitarian system that is based on formal principles of state consent. As a consequence, "finding victims, securing access to victims, and delivering relief to victims has led to the creation of humanitarian space in law and practice – that is, room to maneuver and help in providing protection and relief to war-ravaged populations."[77] Srebrenica serves as an ignominious reminder of the failure to provide protection, even though the United Nations had designated it a "safe area" in response to the assault of the Serbs on the town as women and children attempted to flee. Lacking sufficient UN forces and mandate to protect the city, Srebrenica became a site of gendercide as thousands of men were killed *en masse* or hunted down in the forests around the city when they tried to get out.[78]

Sixth, adding to the political calculations of safe space, its definition also varies culturally and may change throughout the course of a war and in its aftermath, too. For example, the definition of safe places differed considerably even among Sierra Leoneans in the course of the civil war that unfolded in that country from 1991 to 2003, as interviews in the field suggest. Survivors variously pointed to the bush, hospitals, churches, and hometowns where people were familiar with the community and could expect support from it, particularly in the case of belonging to a special (ruling) family. Secret societies were also considered safe places. They functioned in the bush where initiation rites into puberty are administered, and brought a feeling of safety because most people from Sierra Leone are a part of secret societies and united through them. Therefore, if one member of a secret society is affected, others are, too. But there were many cases of violence in those institutions as well.[79] The definition of safety was also very dynamic throughout the war. Mainly, to be safe meant to be as far from the actual fighting as possible. At the beginning of the war, large cities were considered safe as rebels only had enough force to attack small villages. Later, after rebels attacked major towns like Makeni, Bo, and finally Freetown with great loss of life, people ran away to the bush, avoiding villages. Since the bush was considered to be safer, people started forming settlements far from roads and formerly existing villages. However, rebels killed many people during the war in those bush houses.

The seventh and final consideration concerns safe space for humanitarian aid workers and United Nations peacekeepers that once counted on protection under principles of neutrality and impartiality, and consent of the host government for their intervention. They have lost these protections in the new wars, too, while facing mounting risks. They consistently find themselves targets in the crosshairs of the fighting while aid workers maintain cell phone numbers and locations of key commanders and rebel leaders in the field to make security assessments and endeavor to ensure through these contacts (safe) access to local communities in urgent need of humanitarian aid. Despite precautions to enhance their own safety, from 1997 to 2006 there were over 500 acts of major violence against aid workers, involving 1,127 victims and resulting in 511 fatalities.[80] These findings are reinforced by a 2009 report from the Humanitarian Policy Group on aid in insecure environments: 260 humanitarian aid workers were killed, kidnapped, or seriously injured in violent attacks in 2008, the highest level the organization has recorded in 12 years of tracking these incidents.[81]

Both the civilian population and the humanitarian community assisting them face concerns for neutrality and the protection of safe space in the new wars. Since the end of the Cold War, the United Nations, agency staff, and humanitarian workers have found it increasingly difficult to carry out their operations without becoming targets in the conflict, whether as a means for belligerents to negotiate for some of the relief supplies in exchange for access to civilians, or as targets themselves in an attempt to force aid workers to leave and the UN Security Council to withdraw peacekeeping operations. In the Rwandan genocide, the killing of ten Belgian peacekeepers deployed on April 7, 1994 (one day after the crisis unfolded) to protect the prime minister had the desired effect: the United Nations withdrew the peacekeeping force instead of reinforcing it as General Dallaire, the UN commander, begged the Security Council to do.[82]

A "scorecard" from OCHA for the first eight months of

2009 for the conflict in Darfur, Sudan, gives alarming statistics that illustrate the erosion of neutrality and safe space that the humanitarian community itself faces, including the deaths of seven national humanitarian staff and three members of the African Union/United Nations Hybrid operation in Darfur (UNAMID). Other casualties included dozens and dozens of injuries to humanitarian and UNAMID staff; kidnappings, sexual and physical assaults, and abductions; carjacking, arrest, and temporary detainment of staff; theft or hijacking of humanitarian and UNAMID vehicles; and assaults and break-ins on humanitarian agency and UNAMID premises.[83]

Conclusions

Armed conflict encompasses many different kinds of violations of human rights, including those related to sexual violence. The international community has made progress identifying and prohibiting them in landmark court cases and legal instruments, especially through the establishment of the ICC. These initiatives provide legal recourse to end the silence and the impunity on crimes relating to sexual violence in armed conflict. Nevertheless, as the typology of sexual violence in armed conflict developed in this chapter illustrates, the range of challenges to provide relief and safety to civilian populations caught in the line of fire in internal conflicts is daunting. Sexual violence violates many thresholds on conflict escalation across the multiple dimensions of conflict, including types of violence, the targets of that violence, and the space and safety of persons who should be protected against it. Next, chapter 3 addresses the roots of these challenges by tracing the conditions of inequality and structural injustice that already make women and girls vulnerable in peacetime. It then examines how the social construction of hegemonic and aggressive masculinities in times of crisis and armed conflict exacerbates women and girls' insecurity and risk of violence, while putting at risk the safety and lives of subjugated or targeted males.

CHAPTER THREE

Sexual Violence and the Onset of Armed Conflict

The context of gender injustice is shaped by many political, cultural, social, economic, and religious influences. International and regional forces intersecting in the local context also impact on gendered injustice.[1] Nonetheless, it is in the local context that communities determine cultural norms regarding gender practices, such as the rites of passage through puberty, rituals, and rules for (forced) marriage, rights of inheritance, the responsibilities of women and men in the household and outside it, codes of family honor (such as the rules for honor killings), and the definitions of and punishments for prohibited conduct such as rape and adultery – including whether they are considered distinct.

While it is important to read each locality from the perspective of its particular historical and contemporary experiences, the social construction of gender and related expectations regarding inequality and gender-based violence shape risks women and girls face for structural violence. Cross-national studies indicate that improving indicators of gender equality bode well for the development of society, but in areas of the world where there are significant gaps in gender equality, or where gender inequality is already poor and deteriorating, there is a significant correlation with the outbreak of armed conflict.

Chapter 3 examines local-to-global patterns of structural violence that women and girls face, and how these structural conditions put them at greater risk of gender violence

with the onset of war. The slide toward open conflict reverberates in highly gendered ways, often quite differently for
men and women. As aggressive masculinities are mobilized
through propaganda by political leaders and the media, and
in-group homogeneity is intensified in the face of external
threats, safe space for women and girls collapses. Meanwhile,
enemy males are often rounded up in early stages of violence
for detention, torture, or executions, leaving women more
exposed. Ultimately, the collapse of safe space is reduced even
to the woman's most intimate space, her own body and control over it. These risks persist through war and its aftermath.
For these reasons, women's and girls' bodies are the first and
last battleground in war. They face intimidation and violence
well before violent conflict erupts and long after the formal
hostilities end. Their bodies are war's most intimate and
enduring theater of violence.

Gendered nature of structural violence

Despite progress in reducing the gender gap in some parts of
the world over the last couple of decades, women and girls,
especially those who are poor, have limited access to basic
human rights, including education and literacy, health care,
work and remuneration, inheritance, and property, such
as their own home and land.[2] In contrast to direct violence,
such as murder or rape, indirect, or structural, violence has
no particular subject as its target. Rather, it is the structure of
the system that deprives people of their human needs, thus
limiting each person's ability to realize his or her potential.
Examples of structural violence include malnutrition in countries where there is enough food for everyone, illiteracy or
lower rates of educational attainment within minority communities compared to the dominant sector, or high rates of
infant mortality among marginalized groups in a society

with otherwise adequate health services. As Norwegian peace scholar Johan Galtung puts it, "the violence is built into the structure and shows up as unequal power and consequently as unequal life chances."[3] In his later work, Galtung focuses on cultural violence embedded in many institutions and social contexts, such as religion, the law, political ideologies, science, and medicine, suggesting that cultural violence legitimizes both personal and structural violence.[4] The uneven distribution of resources, access to them, and the uneven distribution of power to decide how the resources are to be distributed are three elements that together with cultural violence shape structural violence.

However, feminists contend that Galtung's approach to direct, structural, and cultural violence would have more explanatory value by taking into account the power of gender in the social construction of violence.[5] Despite the focus in his work on systems of domination like imperialism, capitalism, or patriarchy, a more direct engagement with feminist theories would articulate more clearly the mechanisms that lead to structural violence, and how, indeed, structural violence is itself gendered. One strategy is to incorporate gender as a social construct that embodies relations of power. Gender is not just about women. Rather, "it generally refers to the socially learned behaviors, repeated performances, and idealized expectations that are associated with and distinguish between the proscribed gender roles of masculinity and femininity."[6] Gender may be related to sex (a function of biology and anatomical features), but not always. A second avenue for gendering structural violence is to examine the ways dichotomous thinking supports the production and reproduction of (gendered) violence. Dichotomies or binary thinking divide concepts into either/or categories that are paired and defined by mutually exclusive criteria or characteristics (such as friend/foe, victim/perpetrator, rebel/soldier, and so on). Such oversimplification limits understanding of the complexities of how violence is gendered, as well as possibilities for preventing it or transforming it. For example, child soldiers are at once both victims and perpetrators, not either/or. Likewise, not all soldiers are men, nor are women always the victims.

A third point of connection between feminism and the study of structural violence is the role of gendered language in terms of how it constitutes peace or violence. Feminist scholars Laura Sjoberg and Caron Gentry's study on women who commit acts of violence in armed conflict is titled *Mothers, Monsters, Whores*[7] because they want to draw attention to the social construction of women, and how different ways of framing women's roles open up or delimit understandings of them. A fourth possible area of connection between the study of structural violence and gender concerns differentiating masculinities, particularly the reproduction of hegemonic masculinity, and how it operates to create allies and marginalized men.[8] The social construction of hegemonic masculinity (through culture, ideology, language, art, media, and so on) provides a way to understand how the global political economy of violence is linked to armed conflicts in countries around the world through allied and marginalized masculinities, including in the production of aggressive masculinity.

Michel Foucault's work on power is also helpful here. For example, Foucault provides feminists with a framework for interpreting both micro and macro levels of power and abuse: micro-level practices work on local, minute force relations – like sexual harassment. In contrast, macro-level abuses of power work on large-scale social relations, such as the globalized "war on terror." At the macro level, power colonizes or circulates through cultural discourses, social practices, and institutional contexts within and across countries and globalization. Although some of the most important contributions that Foucault made to the social sciences include his study of discipline and punishment, he did not leave us with an account of how social practices discipline women, in particular. Nevertheless, it is apparent that many daily practices embody gendered forms of discipline, such as women dieting to remain thin (thus to take up less social space), or wearing high heels that limit mobility. These practices reinscribe the importance of female submission and its connection to making the female body pleasing to men and under their control.[9] These examples have their basis in cultural constructions of femininity in Western societies. Other cultures have different disciplinary mechanisms, such as bride dowry, honor killings, and forced marriage.

Feminist theories of intersectionality provide another perspective on structural violence and the social practices that constitute it. Intersectionality emphasizes how ethnicity/race/clan, class, sexuality, nationality, dis/ability, employment status, and so on crosscut gendered divisions of power. In other words, structural violence is also socially constructed through other identities, and not just gender. Hispanic men may be affected differently than white men, or Hispanic janitors may be affected differently than white janitors. Intersectionality also examines how identities are shaped by inequalities and reinforced systemically through interlocking mechanisms (like elite, white hegemonic masculinity versus low class or minority, subordinate males) that lead to insecurity, violence, and armed conflict.

In sum, the power of gender operates through mechanisms that normalize or depoliticize essentialized categories (such as the assumption that women are submissive); dichotomized categories (that naturalize oppositional terms like civilian versus combatant), and hierarchical arrangements (such as placing the father as head of household, or male authority figures at the head of most religious organizations).[10] Structural violence also operates through the disciplining

effects of gendered socialization. It produces ways of identifying, thinking, and acting that maintain gender hierarchy
through conformity, self-policing, and compliance. "In these
multiple and overlapping ways, gender is political: It operates
pervasively to produce and sustain unequal power relations."[11]

Gendered forms of structural violence and its consequences

Gender equality is closely related to social progress in a
number of areas, while the lack of equality is tied to social
harms. The *Global Gender Gap Report 2008* benchmarks gaps
between males and females cross-nationally in terms of the
magnitude and scope of the disparities along four parame-
ters: economic participation, educational attainment, political
empowerment, and health and survival.[12] The 2008 report
shows that the gap between the sexes is closing in some areas
of the world, with Oceania taking the top ranking, and Western
Europe and North America close behind. These regions have
closed the gap to 70 percent of female equality measured
against males. Latin America and Eastern Europe have closed
the gap to 67 percent, while sub-Saharan Africa and Asia are at
64 percent. In last place are the Middle East and North Africa
with the gap only 58 percent closed. Reducing the gender gap
has many benefits besides the obvious improvement of the
status and well-being of women. These include enhanced productivity and economic growth that is linked to investment in
girls' education, and the resulting reduction in female fertility
rates, lower infant and child mortality rates, and lower mater-
nal mortality rates. In addition, as women gain education and
income, they use these resources to invest in their children's
educational opportunities.[13]

Improvements in gender equality are also related to lower
levels of armed conflict in society. Melander measured greater

equality in terms of female representation in parliament and of the ratio of female-to-male higher education attainment, and found that they both are associated with lower levels of intrastate armed conflict. "The pacifying impact of gender equality is not only statistically significant in the presence of a comprehensive set of controls but also is strong in substantive terms."[14] Conversely, other studies report that gender *inequality* is related to collective rape in armed conflict.[15]

The majority of the women in the world face daily struggles to provide for their families and survive. Most of the world's population is poor, and women are the majority of the poor, with the poorest of the poor also being women. The gap between the wealthiest and poorest in the world has continued to increase: the income of the richest 1 percent of the people in the world is the equivalent of the combined incomes of the poorest 60 percent (!). Nonetheless, progress has been made in areas of education, literacy, and poverty reduction, bringing some momentum to the realization of the Millennium Development Goals adopted by the United Nations in 2000. For example, China has reduced the number of people living in poverty (defined as less than US$1.25 a day) by 600 million. The World Bank also reports that in the developing world outside of China, the poverty rate has dropped from 40 to 29 percent over the period 1981–2005, but the total number of poor remains steady at around 1.2 billion. However, sub-Saharan Africa in particular has seen little progress since 1981, with 50 percent living in poverty, and the actual number of poor nearly doubling from 200 million in 1981 to 380 million in 2005.[16]

In the family setting, women bear the brunt of austere conditions, forgoing nutrition for themselves so the rest of the family can eat. Likewise, women and girls are the first to forgo education. Of the billion people who are illiterate, two-thirds are women.[17] Lack of safe drinking water and fuel for cooking are daily household concerns for many of the world's poor women and girls. They invest on average about 6 kilometers a day fetching 20 liters of water. Not only does time spent on such household duties limit their opportunities for education: going long distances in search of water or firewood to bring home puts women and young girls at risk of assault, especially as communal tensions increase. Similar concerns arise when accessing insecure and faraway sanitation facilities. The majority of women in the global South face many other structural barriers: most do not own property, or have rights to land, inheritance or other forms of wealth, even though women and girls are responsible for the agricultural labor. These forms of inequality are particularly salient in most of Africa, the Middle East, and South Asia. Cultural practices together with civil, customary or religious laws create the structures for this inequality. These limitations have a number of ramifications, such as restricting women's access to credit and means of escaping poverty. The spread of globalization also increases these disadvantages as cash economies displace the importance of the use of land for the household or community.[18]

Even where women have ownership rights, the exercise of them may be limited in a number of ways. In Mozambique, for example, women have limited access to ownership of land and property because they are prohibited from signing contracts without their spouse's consent. In any event, husbands are considered the sole administrators of any joint property attained during marriage. Women's access to land is governed by two different systems. First, there is a traditional system that encompasses many customary laws specifying the right for women to use land as a right only acquired through marriage. In contrast, there is a state system that is based on the 1991 Constitution and the 1997 Land Law. These sources of law specify that land belongs to the state, although men

and women have equal rights to its use. In practice, however, women still face barriers to ownership rights because a
woman cannot sign contracts without the consent of her husband and because the joint assets she acquires in marriage
belong to him.[19]

The persistence of gender inequality is linked to a number
of serious social problems. The 2009 *Global Hunger Index*
(GHI) highlights the gender connection to hunger. It reports
that progress on tackling global hunger has been slow and has
made little headway especially in South Asia and sub-Saharan
Africa since the early 1990s. There are 29 countries with
alarming or extremely alarming levels of hunger, while the
highest 2009 GHI scores are Burundi, Chad, the Democratic
Republic of Congo, Eritrea, Ethiopia, and Sierra Leone. War
and violent conflict are behind most of these high GHI scores,
leaving societies with widespread poverty and food insecurity. "Nearly all of the countries in which the GHI rose since
1990 are in sub-Saharan Africa." The 2009 GHI report
compares its findings to the *Global Gender Gap Report 2008*.
There is a significant correlation: low literacy rates are linked
to higher levels of hunger, which in turn is associated with
health and survival inequalities between men and women.[20]
In South Asia, only Bangladesh and Sri Lanka have achieved
the Millennium Development Goals for gender parity in primary and secondary education enrollment but, in the rest of
the region, the gaps between boys and girls in educational
achievement correlate with increasing GHI scores. The finding in this region is consistent with the global trend in which
gender inequalities related to limited access to education are
linked to hunger and malnutrition.

The violation of women's social and economic rights has
a number of consequences. In Asia, for example, marginalization prevents women from escaping abusive domestic
situations or accessing justice, while inequality in property

and inheritance laws leaves women dependent on patriarchal systems.[21] Pakistan is a case in point: ranking 87th on the *Global Gender Gap Report 2008*, and 83rd for the education sub-index, Pakistan has one of the highest levels of gender inequality in the region, closely related to its high rates of hunger and malnutrition.[22] These circumstances are greatly compounded by the ongoing fighting between Pakistan government forces and the Taliban in Northern Pakistan, where an estimated 2.7 million have become internally displaced persons in 2009. Transportation in the region is extremely limited while costs of accessing food or vehicles have skyrocketed. A woman without education and without access to employment has few alternatives for accessing transportation to escape the fighting, for seeking shelter elsewhere, or independently maintaining a family income, and so on.

Violence against women and girls: Social and cultural practices

Gender inequality is one measure of structural violence. However, many cultural practices and forms of gender-based violence put women at further risk. The Geneva Centre for the Democratic Control of Armed Forces estimates that 1.5 to 3 million women and girls are killed each year through gender-related violence. The risk of injury or death from GBV for women between the ages of 15 and 44 is greater than from cancer, traffic accidents, malaria and war combined. One in five women will be the victim of rape or attempted rape in her lifetime. Approximately two million girls are genitally mutilated each year, and as many as 60 percent of the HIV-positive youth between 15 and 24 years of age around the world are females.[23]

The post-apartheid health and sexual violence statistics for South Africa are among the most alarming anywhere in the world. South Africa has the world's largest HIV/AIDs population – 5.5 million people, with the overall rate of infection for those who are over 2 years of age at 10.5 percent. Women between the ages of 20–34 are the worst affected with 33 percent carrying the HIV virus, although the rate of infection of teenagers and children has fallen off, and use of condoms has increased greatly throughout the population.[24] Rape is also at epidemic levels. Studies have found that one in four men raped someone at least once, while half of them had committed more than one attack. Three out of four participants in the study who admitted having committed rape indicated they perpetrated their first assault in their teens. Gang rape is common because it is seen as a form of male bonding. Professor Rachel Jewkes of the Medical Research Council who led the research acknowledged the imperative of changing the underlying social attitudes that created the norm that forcing sex on women is somehow acceptable.[25]

Traditionally, domestic violence has been considered a private matter of the home and outside the purview of other family members, neighbors, friends, community, or local or national government and its authorities. Yet domestic violence is one of the most pervasive manifestations of structural violence that women face. This is without exception as to region in the world,[26] but prevalence varies from country to country. According to a 2002 multi-country study by the World Health Organization (WHO), the prevalence of sexual victimization by an intimate partner against women ranged from 6.2 percent reported by a study group in Yokohama, Japan to as high as 46 percent reported by a study group in Cusco, Peru. In most of the countries studied, younger girls (between the ages of 15 and 19) were at greater risk of physical or sexual assault by a partner than older women.[27]

The 2002 WHO report includes a wide range of forms and contexts under the category of sexual violence from rape within marriage or dating relationships to rape by strangers; systematic rape during armed conflict; unwanted sexual advances or harassment; sexual abuse of mentally or physically disabled people and of children; forced marriage or cohabitation, including the marriage of children; denial of the right to use contraception or other measures to prevent pregnancy or spread of disease; forced abortion; violent acts against the sexual integrity of women, such as female genital mutilation; and forced prostitution and trafficking of people for sexual exploitation.[28]

The scope and context of these challenges and the relevance for conflict is best understood by looking at country-specific settings. In the case of Sierra Leone, the general law, customary law, and for some groups, Islamic law have all provided for highly discriminatory practices against women. Islamic law in Sierra Leone has to be understood within the context of local, cultural practices. For example, under Islamic law, four wives is considered the limit but in Sierra Leone some chiefs may have as many as 50 wives. This means before the outbreak of the more than decade-long civil war in Sierra Leone in 1991, many segments of the society already embraced a gender ideology that promoted a sense of male ownership of women's reproductive as well as productive capacities. Sexual violence was a "normal" part of the culture in Sierra Leone.[29] Physicians for Human Rights make a similar assessment in Sierra Leone, noting "domestic violence against women and children is common, though it is not generally recognized as a societal problem. Nearly 67% of urban women interviewed for a survey on AIDS knowledge, practices and behaviors revealed that they had been beaten by an intimate male partner, and over 50% reported being forced to have sexual intercourse."[30]

Likewise, sexual violence in the wars of Central Africa in the 1990s following the Rwandan genocide has roots in cultural traditions that have supported the exploitation of women. For example, the nature and scope of GBV in the DRC is widespread across the cultural practices within the family unit and society as a whole, and encompassed by the legal system. The situation for women has many reinforcing elements of structural violence. The DRC is a patriarchal society where violence against women is rarely reported. There are various reasons for this. The legal institutions and their enforcement are weak and provide little protection against domestic violence and discrimination against women. Moreover, in rural areas, a woman is constrained by the traditional interpretation of dowry and inheritance laws. They limit her opportunities to divorce or live independently. Domestic disputes are generally handled by a male head of household, or in serious cases, by local male officials or chiefs. Married women do not have a say when it comes to sex with their husbands. Forced sex is often considered the husband's right, which assertion the dowry tradition supports.[31]

The lack of safe space within the home is amplified by risks of insecurity women face outside it. Even in the workplace and in schools, sexual harassment and assault are problematic in many parts of the world. Girls face risks to their personal security while walking to and from school. Matters do not necessarily improve on reaching school. Research on Ghana, Zimbabwe, and Malawi has shown that schoolgirls face sexual propositions from older male students and teachers, and use of sexually explicit language and graffiti. Girls are often the minority in secondary education, and attend schools where their classmates are mostly boys and the teachers are males. This creates a male-dominated power and decision-making structure. For example, in India, Chad, Malawi, and Mozambique, less than 50 percent of the girls stay in school through grade five. In 16 countries of sub-Saharan Africa, women hold 30 percent or fewer of the teaching posts, and are usually concentrated in urban rather than rural settings. The

gender imbalance makes it difficult for girls to assert themselves in school, and their trust in authorities is often violated.
For example, in Botswana, 20 percent of girl students reported
teachers had approached them for sex. In Zimbabwe, 19 percent of the girls reported being propositioned by a teacher, and
63 percent knew of other girls who had been approached.[32]
Similarly, Mary Okumu raises the alarm in the magazine
Sexuality in Africa that women and girls in Africa are not safe
anywhere in the continent.

> They are not safe in the work place or in public places such
> as on the streets or in the markets. They are not safe in places
> of worship, some of which are no longer treated as sacred
> places. Girls are raped or sexually abused in educational and
> learning centres. They certainly are not safe in our homes
> as they are raped by strangers and relatives right within the
> "home" environment.[33]

Women's activism and advocacy for women's human rights
can place them at risk, too. For example, in Nepal where many
women do not know about their human rights, women activists play a vital role raising awareness. However, they have
been attacked for challenging Nepal's patriarchal divisions.
Amnesty International reports that human rights activists
there "have become social outcasts for raising the issues of
domestic and sexual violence and are targets of intimidation,
beatings and even death. The Nepalese police often refuse
to file a complaint or to fully investigate and offer no protection."[34] Rape victims may find it impossible to access justice
because doctors will not complete a medical exam without
a police report, and police will not issue a First Information
Report without the medical evidence.[35]

In some countries, if a woman becomes pregnant from
rape, that pregnancy is considered illegal. Even when seeking
assistance from the police, women find the tables are turned
against them, and they may be imprisoned, as Human Rights

Watch has reported for women seeking protection in Darfur and Chad. In some of those cases, prison guards then also raped the detained women.[36] Human Rights Watch reports similar circumstances in Asia, where women seeking justice were subject to sexual harassment and abuse by the police. Pakistan's Hudood ordinances place further limitations on women's access to justice. A woman faces the risk of being convicted of adultery if she does not have the support of four male witnesses to back her claim. Legal systems protect honor killings as a way of settling the claim, but the victim's interest is not at the center of considerations. Since the perpetrator of the honor killing is often a member of the same family, it is not uncommon for the victim's families to receive a pardon for the crime.[37]

Crimes of honor, typically based on traditional codes of social conduct that severely limit women's agency while justifying male violence, are another major category of violence against women and girls that diminish the control over their lives and bodies.[38] In many cultures, the family's honor is protected by the woman marrying her rapist, or by a woman in the other family being raped to settle the score. Typically, the woman's honor is never a consideration – it is her husband's or family's honor that has to be repaid. Men are treated relatively lightly for their offense. Women in Afghanistan and Aceh, Indonesia, may be stoned to death for committing adultery, while men receive light sentences, if at all.[39] The high value placed on girls' sexual purity and honor restricts their freedom of movement and control over their own lives. Families exercise surveillance over girls to prevent any actual or perceived promiscuity. In Nepal, Bangladesh, India, Pakistan, and Afghanistan, more than 50 percent of girls are married before the age of 18. Girls who resist these arrangements face vicious reprisals, such as disfiguring acid attacks or honor killings.[40]

For some women, the only solution is to leave the family home or be forced to leave it. Women who have the courage to fight against honor codes are the exception and do so at great risk. One of them is Mukhtar Mai, who has inspired women and girls' resistance against the brutal oppression they face in Pakistan.[41] She was ordered to be gang-raped by the local tribal council to avenge the supposed affair of her brother with a higher-status woman. Instead of killing herself in shame, as expected, she pursued the prosecution of her rapists and has taken money from the settlement of the court case to build schools for girls. Mukhtar Mai's father and other family members supported her intention to seek justice from the Pakistani court system for the gang rape she suffered, in defiance of tribal practices. Her home has become a magnet for other abused women in Pakistan. Anecdotal evidence suggests more than 1,000 women are victims of honor crimes in Pakistan every year.[42] Mukhtar continues to advocate for them, in spite of threats to her own life.[43]

Threats to activists are the pattern across the region. Women working in public in diverse professions are at risk, whether they are activists, journalists, or government officials. They face constraints on their freedom of movement, harassment and even physical assaults. In Afghanistan, for example, Human Rights Watch reports that "women who run female literacy projects, raise awareness about sexual and domestic violence, or work in the government have received death threats, visits from gunmen, and attacks on their homes and offices."[44] Afghan women's experiences also speak to the multiplicity of oppression women face from both internal and external sources. They confront competing patriarchies as they struggle to define their own lives through the multilayered intersections of history and geography. The list of factors ranges from tribal patriarchies to the position of Afghanistan in the Cold War between the superpowers; their subjugation to fundamentalist regimes who have used them as a symbol of their power; Western rhetoric on women's rights/issues that justified attacks on Afghanistan under the "war on terror"; global economic interests in the search for new oil reserves; and new rounds of violence and displacement after 9/11. The experience of war and external occupation has made Afghan women's bodies "globalized property" over which they have limited control.[45]

Gendered maneuvers in the pre-staging of armed conflict

Many studies acknowledge that the extent and type of gender inequality significantly shape women's diverse experiences in war.[46] Showing how this actually takes place is more challenging. The gender roles and sexuality in Bosnia during the communist period, the war, and aftermath also went through a number of transformations, indicating the pattern of gender polarization that war produces, and also opportunities for resisting sexual hierarchies. Participants in a research group indicated that during the communist era, women experienced a great deal of equality in education and the workplace in contrast to the private sphere of the home, where traditional gender roles and expectations were typical even across different ethnic communities, following a traditional patriarchal family structure. In contrast, during the war, the focus group participants reported that gendered relations within the communities varied significantly. This difference was related to the ways that discourse on gender relations was embedded in discourses on sociopolitical and cultural change that happened as the war ensued. For example, for the Bosniak women, the presence of the foreign mujahideen fighters in the war brought restrictions on their movements and interaction with men. The Croat participants saw an increase in young marriages in the rural population as something that was primitive – a throwback to the past. Serbian participants emphasized how the war impacted economic structures, leading to tensions between men and women. Changing economic conditions "altered notions of male and female sexuality through the issue of 'sponsorship.' Female sexuality became a commodity for sale, and men with cash or other material goods to offer had a new market for sexual outlet. The focus-group participants situate this as an ethnic phenomenon, because it started, they argue, when the international community implemented sanctions against Serbia."[47]

This example illustrates why it is imperative to understand the local circumstances of gendered insecurities and mechanisms for coping with them. However, there are some patterns of gendered violence that often emerge *across* cultural contexts as societies gravitate toward open violence. These patterns can serve as a framework for the deeper analysis of specific contexts. Six factors are particularly salient:

(1) gender polarization;
(2) rise of catastrophic- and hyper-masculinities;
(3) loss of safe space for the women both inside and
(4) outside the home;
(5) mounting pressures for women to be sole providers for the household while opportunities to do so (safely) are increasingly scarce; and
(6) the loss of safe havens, such as churches, clinics, or schools.

All these factors tend to work together, reinforcing the loss of women and girls' security with the onset of conflict, and are intensified by the proliferation of small arms and light weapons.

First, the intensification of gendered conflict is often seen in the amplification of nationalist ideologies (ethno-religious, racial) deployed to mobilize and polarize members of society.

These maneuvers draw tighter boundaries between in- and out-groups. They also reduce space for women to be engaged within their own communities and outside them. This results in gender polarization, but, as Skjelsbaek's focus group participants' account of the war in Bosnia illustrates, gender polarization is not only about who leaves to fight (mostly men and boys) and who stays at home (women and other family members they care for), but also about how gender polarization intersects with the political objectives of war, and with the economic, cultural, and other landscapes that are in flux as society disintegrates. Instead of pushing more gender polarization, this can lead to the subversion of the gender and socioeconomic hierarchies in society, either by men or women (as chapter 4 shows).

Second, in the midst of this mosaic of social upheaval, constructs of hyper-masculinity play a key role. The impact of natural disasters on masculine identities offers an important analogy. Natural disasters, similar to war, destroy and change the institutional supports of noncatastrophic masculinities. In a crisis, hyper-masculinity elevates an exaggerated male type, drawing on dominance, toughness, aggression, and violence, captured by the "Rambo" warrior image promoted by Hollywood and mimicked by soldiers and rebels in many conflicts, to restore the lost credibility and viability of hegemonic masculinity. Ismael Beah describes this yearning in his autobiographical account of how he came to be a child warrior in the government forces during the civil war in Sierra Leone. In *A Long Way Gone*, Beah writes about his indoctrination into a fighter, of the cocktail of alcohol and drugs he consumed with the rest of his comrades, and the movies at night: "War movies, *Rambo: First Blood*, *Rambo II*, *Commando*, and so on, with the aid of a generator or sometimes a car battery. We all wanted to be like Rambo; we couldn't wait to implement his techniques."[48]

Hyper-masculinity is legitimized by traditional patriarchal gender expectations that see the role of the woman in terms of satisfying the man and procreating, and also as the "mother of the nation," and carrier of the "purity" of the group. The assertion of hyper-masculinity greatly circumscribes women's autonomy, and sets them up for strict control by their husbands and family to serve as the carrier of the next generation, or to "breed" soldiers. It puts them at greater risk should they venture outside their own group to court men from the enemy community and betray their own by producing baby enemy warriors. Lesbian or bisexual women are also at risk for living outside prescribed gender expectations, and thus serving the interests of the enemy. Similarly, homosexual men also face violent forms of discrimination for failing to adhere to hyper-masculinity. In many conflicts, they are labeled unpatriotic or unrevolutionary or are accused of acting like foreign imports, polluting and weakening the culture.[49] Meanwhile, the emasculation of men in war, their sense of marginalization and disempowerment, often reverberates directly on their own wives in the form of increasing levels of domestic violence and insecurity.[50] As war reduces accountability, it also puts more pressure on males to conform to hyper- or militarized masculinity, which legitimizes aggression. Women and girls' claims to bodily integrity are gradually eroded.

War creeps up on its victims much like territory under assault. The early threats are often gendered, and thus represent different kinds of risks for men and women. In the early stages of conflict escalation, males face risks of demonization, discipline, and control that are preludes to genocide: detentions, torture, sexual violence, and selective killings. These risks are greatest for battle-aged men typically between 15 and 55 years of age.[51] "Eliticide" is one form of selective killing that disproportionately affects males. These are the educated and prominent cultural, political, and business figures who, in societies that have high levels of gender inequality for women, are mostly male.[52] The Rwanda genocide stands out not only for the organized propaganda against Tutsi women that fueled sexual violence against them and its level of brutality,[53] but also for the early pattern of systematic targeting of elite men, before Tutsi men, women, and children were targeted in general.

Third, for women, threats begin in public settings like marketplaces or public transportation, and move into the home and other places of refuge. Two stories from the former Yugoslavia illustrate this dynamic. Slavenka Drakulic tells of a Croatian friend's experience on the train going from Subotic to Belgrade when war was beginning to engulf Croatia. There were a dozen young Serbs on the train. "'The lady is reading a book in the Roman alphabet?' they sneered, spotting the book in her hands. 'Surely the lady must be a Croat. How about a nice fuck, you bloody bitch? Or would you prefer this?' one asked, sliding the edge of his palm across her neck, as if he was holding a knife."[54] Jennifer Rawlings relays the story of Emma, whose father taught her how to use a gun in the Bosnian war.

> "When he would leave the house, he would give me a gun with three bullets in it. If a soldier comes to the door, I was supposed to kill my mother, my sister and then myself. I would worry should my mother see my sister die, or should my sister see my mother die first, or what if I miss? I only have three bullets. And what if I make a mistake and it is someone else at the door?"[55]

At the same time tensions were increasing in the former Yugoslav Republic of Macedonia, where Albanian women expressed fears of abuse if they were to seek gynecological care from doctors, who were generally ethnic Macedonian.

Fourth, the onset of war increases women's risks outside the home in many ways, as conflict works to produce gender *and* intercommunal polarization. In both the former

Yugoslavia and Rwanda, the media played crucial roles in promoting hyper-masculinity, sanctifying their "own" women, and targeting the other's women for rape and extermination. In both cases, the context for gender violence was set by government authorities and communicated through official documents, plans, strategies, and the media. In the former Yugoslavia, President Slobodan Milosevic was at the head of vile propaganda that fueled violence between Serbs, Croats, and Muslims, and also Serbs toward Kosovar Albanians. He insisted the Albanians were systematically raping Serbian women in Kosovo, while Albanians "reproduced like rabbits."[56]

In Rwanda, due to the high levels of illiteracy at the time of the genocide, radio was a primary means of communication in society and for the government to deliver its messages to the public. Two radio stations played a leading role in inciting violence both before and during the genocide: Radio Rwanda and Radio Télévision Libre des Mille Collines (RTLM). The gender polarization of society was prepared well before the outbreak of the genocide, with such propaganda as the "Hutu Ten Commandments" that were already published in December 1990. This document included four commandments that portrayed Tutsi women as sexual weapons that the Tutsi would use to destroy weak and unsuspecting Hutu men. For example, Commandment 1 states: "Every Hutu must know that the Tutsi woman, wherever she may be, is working for the Tutsi ethnic cause. In consequence, any Hutu is a traitor who: Acquires a Tutsi wife; Acquires a Tutsi concubine; Acquires a Tutsi secretary or protégée."[57]

The role of hate propaganda is imperative to understand the rising tensions in Rwanda before the outbreak of the genocide. Both the written press and radio stations launched government-inspired propaganda campaigns that played on historical stereotypes used by the former Belgian colonizers (for example, that Tutsi have long noses and fingers, and are taller in stature) that were intended to identify the targeted group. Tutsi women were demonized as evil seductresses: their beauty made them dangerous. They would trick Hutu men into having sex with them, humiliate them, and diminish the Hutu people. "The existence of such extensive hate propaganda targeting Tutsi women supports the argument that the sexual violence was not a mere side effect of the conflict, but rather an integral part of the genocidal campaign."[58]

The dynamics of conflict work against women's safety outside the home. Familial protection, such as it may be, is diminished as men are mobilized to go on patrols at night, or join armed forces and leave home, while women face local male predators on their own property, and beyond as they seek work outside the home to sustain household needs. As conflict intensifies around them, they will need to seek alternative shelter for the family and face greater risks as they flee, usually while pregnant or caring for infants, the elderly, disabled, or sick members of the family. A survey of Albanian families fleeing the Serbian offensive on Kosovo in 1999 found that 45 percent of the extended family groups had at least one nursing mother; and 22 percent of them included pregnant women.[59] Women face difficulties gaining access to legal and administrative remedies for control of family assets, to report rape or other abuse, or to secure documents they may need to prove their identities when the family flees.[60] Women from ethnically mixed backgrounds and their children face particularly difficult situations in conflicts that target civilians. Many families ended in divorce in the former Yugoslavia, as the ethnic tensions and ethnic cleansing literally drove them apart.[61] Children of mixed backgrounds were forced to choose sides between their own and their parents' heritage. Serbian women married outside their ethnic group were seen as belonging to their husbands, in effect as traitors, by Serb authorities and local Serbs assisting international aid organizations who denied them aid or protection.[62]

Fifth, women's workload increases with the onset of conflict, as natural resources or basic goods, including livestock, crops, and foodstuffs, become scarce or are destroyed and prices skyrocket. The homestead becomes a focus of attack, with family wells poisoned by throwing animals down them, for example. In many conflicts, agricultural and pastoral land has been mined, rendering it useless and also dangerous (for years to come). Marketplaces are another familiar target of attack on civilian life and livelihood, while the accumulation of such destruction ultimately makes a deadly matter out of attending to daily chores, like collecting water, farming, or bringing goods to buy and sell in local markets.[63] Women are also less able to rely on extended family members for assistance because they may be experiencing the same difficulties. Women may be reluctant to tell others what is happening to them due to fear. Women may not be able to call on neighbors if they are from "opposing" ethnic or tribal communities. Friends soon become "enemies," despite years of sharing with each other and caring for each other's families. Stories of such polarization of communities from each other, even from one household to the neighbor's beside it, are told in conflicts in the Balkans and elsewhere. One Bosnian woman refugee explained that

> "we stayed [at home] for two years from the beginning of the war. We lived in fear but nobody touched us at first. I was alone in the house. My husband is an Albanian who works in Macedonia. We were afraid that if some people got killed, [the neighbors] would no longer say hello to us, as if we were the ones who did it."[64]

In addition, the available niches for women to find employment decrease as conflict intensifies. If already during peacetime poor, illiterate women are relegated to the marginal workforce, they are further displaced from those niches as men, also increasingly out of work, compete for those opportunities. Women are often forced to provide for their families through extremely dangerous economic endeavors, such as prostitution, survival sex, smuggling, or begging. The emergence of camp followers around United Nations peacekeeping operations or humanitarian camps is hardly a manifestation of "human nature." Women engage in such work out of extreme necessity and lack of alternatives. This also places them and their children at risk of trafficking. Networks that move illicit goods in war can also move humans.[65]

Sixth, another blow to the safety of women is the collapse of safe areas or safe havens. Clinics and hospitals or schools, as well as marketplaces, once considered safe, become targets of violence against civilians. The destruction of health facilities and schools during conflict places new burdens on women for caretaking and meeting basic needs. As food stocks dwindle, women suffer malnutrition first, as they provide the rest of the family with available resources. This is often done in highly gendered ways, with men and boys eating first, girls second, and women last.[66]

Conclusions

While some progress has been made around the world to reduce the inequality gap between the sexes (most notably in the global North), women elsewhere, and especially poor women, face great challenges to access basic human rights, especially of a gendered nature. Substantial patterns of inequality and injustice are still found especially in parts of South Asia and sub-Saharan Africa, areas that have seen many conflicts and extreme forms of violence against women since the end of the Cold War. The proliferation of small arms and light weapons has facilitated fighting among armed factions and rebel groups and increased the insecurity for women at home and in their daily lives, going to market, fetching water or fuel to cook, or working in the fields. The slide to war polarizes gender relations along with intercommunal ties in society, with severe repercussions on women and girls, and threats to males. This polarization collapses safe space for women and girls, already limited in societies marked by high levels of gender inequality. Hyper-masculinity becomes a dominating expression of manliness for many men in society, as traditional masculinities and contemporary alternatives fail to address the marginalization and emasculation of men dealing with increasing scarcity and facing the threats of war.

Chapter 4 examines the many gendered ways that armed conflict unleashes as sexual violence. It reveals especially how patterns of inequality and structural violence that existed before the outbreak of armed conflict predispose females to multiple risks of victimization and revictimization as war threatens to engulf their lives, and the different gendered ways these developments reverberate on males.

CHAPTER FOUR

Seeking Safe Space

Safe space is the most critical means to survival in the new wars, but it becomes increasingly scarce as localized violence consumes the most intimate theaters of life. Even in the safer spaces like the home, school, church, mosque, clinics, police stations, or villages and cities, women, men, and children are not out of harm's way. Fleeing to escape escalating conflict raises its own risks of being raped, abducted, or killed by prowling gangs, government troops or rebel forces setting up roadblocks and check points, or patrolling backcountry and mountain passes. Fleeing also risks separating family members from each other, relatives, and community, which in turn brings about the loss of their own safe circle or network. Then reunification also becomes one of the urgent needs for protection.

If family members are fortunate to reach the (presumed) safety of camps for the internally displaced or for refugees, they are not completely protected from perils there, either. Just leaving camp to fetch water or firewood hazards opening a new chapter in the war-torn lives of survivors. People are exposed to threats from all sides. The systematic collapse of safe space erases all distinction between the public and private realms where the private may have provided some protection before war's onset (domestic violence notwithstanding). For women and girls – the most frequent targets of sexual violence as conflict escalates – the possibilities of ensuring their own safety is increasingly threatened at the most intimate level: control of their own body from sexual assault.

Despite the grave dangers faced in war, the risk of gender violence does not disappear with war's end, but rather the nature of the threat itself is transformed. Women face gender backlash, increasing levels of domestic violence or rejection by their husband and/or his family (if they have been raped, or if they served with combatants, or were captured by them), homelessness, and perils of sex work and human trafficking if that is their only alternative. This chapter explores the political economy of sexual violence as it unfolds in armed conflicts. The analysis focuses on the elimination of safe space and the use of sexual violence as a tool to subjugate, terrorize, exploit, displace, and exterminate targeted groups. Insights are drawn from a number of recent and/or ongoing conflicts, including Nepal, Sri Lanka, the eastern part of DRC, Sierra Leone, Rwanda, the West Balkans and more where men, women, and children have pursued a wide range of coping strategies to survive war.

No safe space at home, school, work, or play

As Krisjon Rae Olson cautions, "the truth of war is always worse than what is expected."[1] Men, women and children, along with the elderly, infirm, and disabled, find few safe spaces in the new wars. They confront risks to their safety almost anywhere they go – whether they are at home, school, in a religious center, hospital, or at work. These risks also subvert the sexual order and hierarchies in society, putting great stress on families to find ways to cope. In Sri Lanka, for example, parents forced young girls, even teenagers, into marriage, believing that would provide them protection against increased sexual vulnerability during the 30-year insurgency that pitted the government against the LTTE who were defeated in 2009.[2]

In Afghanistan during the height of the Taliban regime

(1996–2001), women were forced to adhere to extreme forms of subjugation. When leaving the house, they had to wear a burqa – a full-length robe that only permitted a woman to see through a small, heavy mesh opening over her eyes, while they could be punished for wearing shoes that made noise or clicked on the sidewalk, or for not having a close male relative escort. Roving police enforced these and other restrictions, including prohibitions on women working outside the home, and rules against women being attended to by male physicians, preventing them from accessing medical care. Even while inside their homes, the windows of the house had to be painted over so the women inside would not be seen from the street.[3]

The Maoist insurgency that erupted in 1996 in Nepal in a struggle against a monarchical, single-party government provides another stark example of how people's freedom of movement and livelihoods are jeopardized in the new wars, while sexual hierarchies are subverted. Caught in the middle between insurgents and government forces, an estimated 100,000–200,000 Nepalese displaced civilians from rural areas have sought refuge with relatives or taken shelter in abandoned plots in district or regional towns or the capital. Moreover, Nepal has one of the highest rates of disappearances in the world, as reported by the UN Working Group on Enforced or Involuntary Disappearances. Displaced women live on the margins of existence, distilling alcohol or engaging in sex work to support their families. In addition, an estimated two million Nepalese have fled to India to escape insecurity, death threats, the impositions of taxes or "donations" to rebels, daily harassment, looting and destruction of homes that comes along with such banditry and lawlessness, as well as the lack of services, access to education, or health care, and especially, threats of abduction or child recruitment by the Maoist forces.[4]

To keep their children out of the hands of the Maoist insurgents, some Nepalese families pay a monthly "donation" to the rebels. Nevertheless, 40,000 children have been displaced by the conflict in Nepal, many of them illegally detained, tortured, sexually violated, abducted, and recruited for military activity. Even when released from abduction by the Maoists, government security forces often pursue them for intelligence on the insurgency. Nepalese children, like schoolkids in other conflict zones, face the greatest risk of capture at school, making it difficult for many of them to concentrate on their studies. In Nepal, the threat to their safety has exacerbated the already low primary and the very minimal secondary enrollments and resulting illiteracy which among adults is estimated at 42 percent and even higher among women. Nearly three-quarters of the children quit school before completing primary education, and many only manage to get two years of schooling. The Maoists have systematically targeted teachers and children in schools. Schools are central to the insurgents' indoctrination strategy and efforts to weaken government influence in rural areas. Schools provide a ready supply of children for abduction into the rebel movement, while school buildings can be used as garrisons and for recruitment.[5] Boys or girls of less than 18 years of age have made up as much as 30 percent of the Maoists forces in Nepal.

Join combatants or risk abduction?

During armed conflict, people are forced to negotiate complex social relationships riddled with dangers and, in the case of mistakes and miscalculations, tragedy. Whether abducted or striving to remain free of abduction, everyone in war zones has to navigate relations among a field of competing actors – a struggle to preserve one's own relational autonomy against threats of subjugation, sexual exploitation, and violence. The social field of navigation includes maintaining relationships among family members, boy- and girlfriends, husbands, commanders, co-wives, peacekeepers, NGO staff, neighbors, well-placed or marginalized civilians, political authorities, and so on. In Afghanistan, for example, the Taliban has pressed families to recruit young boys to serve as spies and scouts to report on the movements of US troops, while it also delivers "night letters" threatening the lives of any villagers who collaborate with the enemy. In the Liberian civil war, families sometimes sent young men or women to join different rebel groups as a form of protection, and also as a means of access to resources and "lootable" goods. Women and girls formed relationships with soldiers for protection for themselves and family members. They sometimes participated in war campaigns, carrying guns, killing, and looting.[6]

Vulnerability of children

Children face great risks, too, including abduction as child soldiers, forced labor, or sexual slavery. The sanctuary of an IDP or refugee camp does not guarantee protection for children against risks of abduction, either. Camps (like schools) are ideal recruiting grounds for combatants. They offer an ample supply of children in a concentrated location. Children are especially vulnerable for a number of reasons. In the new wars, children function as a commodity that supports the political economy of violence. While some child soldiers may voluntarily join an army or rebel force before the age of 18, more typically they are abducted and coerced into participation. Military groups, such as the LRA, are known for deliberately and systematically abducting children during their attacks and turning boys into fighters and girls into "army wives." In the Sierra Leone civil war, all parties to the conflict co-opted child soldiers. The forces of the Revolutionary United Front (RUF) treated children and youth especially badly, making them consume a cocktail of cocaine, gunpowder, and alcohol to increase their aggression, while numbing their minds. Altogether, the civil war in Sierra Leone affected the lives of an estimated 36,600 children by the year 2001, including "child soldiers, camp followers, street children and war-affected children in IDP camps," while 6,787 child soldiers went through the DRR programs in the post-conflict period.[7]

Children are highly vulnerable to the psychological process of induction into a combatant role and killing. In his memoir, *A Long Way Gone*, Ishmael Beah gives a child soldier's account of how the slide from victim to camp follower and perpetrator of atrocities unfolds almost seamlessly from one set of dire circumstances to the next. For Beah, the tipping point followed an appeal by the army lieutenant in charge of the garrison in the village where he had sought refuge from the RUF fighting. As Beah recalls, the lieutenant assured them the rebels were in the forest waiting to launch an attack. The village was no longer safe.[8] Gathering all the villagers, the lieutenant presented the mutilated bodies of a father and son who had attempted to leave the previous night. He then described in graphic detail the atrocities rebel forces had committed, concluding "they have lost everything that makes them human. They do not deserve to live. That is why we must kill every single one of them. Think of it as destroying a great evil. It is the highest service that you can perform for your country."[9] The lieutenant's speech had the desired effect, as the crowd chanted "kill them all." Beah and his other young friends (boys nearly all between the ages of thirteen and sixteen) lined up to join the army and avenge the deaths of their family members which had turned them into IDPs months earlier.

The psychology of abduction relies on many strategies, often in combination. These include magic rituals to indoctrinate the child into believing it possesses special powers (like being bullet proof); slowly numbing the child to violence through exposure to gradually increasing levels of brutality; forcing a child to kill or commit atrocities against a relative or friend (or fall to the same fate themselves)[10]; provision of a system of rewards or incentives (bestowing junior military "titles" or war nicknames); indoctrination (using war films, like *Rambo*); the provision and forced use of drugs; and certain death for any escapee caught.

Child soldiers typically perform a wide range of functions: participation in combat; laying mines and explosives; scouting, spying, acting as decoys, couriers or guards; training; carrying out drills or other preparations for combat; numerous logistics and support functions like portering, cooking, cleaning, washing clothes, and other domestic duties. By definition, child soldiers are trafficked individuals and, since their participation is forced, so is their labor. Girls or boys may be subject to sexual slavery and other forms of sexual abuse, although girls are probably at greater risk.[11] For example, during the civil war in Sierra Leone, thousands of girls and women were used as sex slaves by rebels and then were forced to "marry" their rebel husbands. Girls and women who faced forced pregnancies were often prevented from aborting them (even though they often tried by using traditional herbal medicines) because of the rebels' concern that the high rate of civilian killings required them to replace the population lost. The dangers the child soldier faces do not end with the termination of war. There are always risks of re-abduction/ re-recruitment, should the violence erupt again. Beah's memoir documents this with descriptions of some of his comrades who UNESCO took from the army to Freetown to rehabilitate, but many of whom escaped to the army again when the capital was engulfed in fighting.

The Sudanese People's Liberation Army Movement (SPLA/M), a rebel force active in South Sudan, recruited children as young as age 10 to fight for the independence of South Sudan. After signing the Comprehensive Peace Agreement

(CPA) between the Khartoum government and SPLA, and incorporating the SPLA as the legitimate part of the Sudan government, most of the children were demobilized from the army. Nevertheless, the South Sudan government argued against the reunification of the former army children with their families and instead requested UNICEF to build schools for these children in the South's capital, which, in effect, would afford the government an educated, young army, ready, trained, and loyal.

Strategies of survival

The lines between civilian and combatant often blur as people use all manner of coping skills to navigate complex relationships and dangerous challenges in war. Strategies of survival unfold while the moral community is tested to its limits and sometimes collapses. The necessity of navigating complex social ties under constant dangers and threats to life means that identities shift as different survival strategies become available and as opportunities for access to resources or social mobility materialize or evaporate. For some members of society, like warlords and associates linked to lucrative, illicit economies, war is an opportunity to accumulate wealth and power. For most people, it destroys livelihoods and assets and spreads impoverishment.

Mats Utas, a cultural anthropologist who has worked in West Africa, tells the gripping survival story of "Bintu," the fictitious name he gives to a woman he and his wife knew well from Liberia's civil war, but eventually lost track of. His account encompasses her vast repertoire of shifting identities and range of strategies she plied to stay alive and gain protection. This included negotiating with soldiers and commanders for protection through her personal relationships as the fortunes of one or another military faction rose and fell, whether

government or rebel. In this process, Bintu had to manage
her relationships with the other women who were also these
men's girlfriends. At one point, Bintu was abducted by rebels,
accused of being a spy and held captive for months as a sex
slave, but another camp woman with the rebels succeeded in
negotiating her release.[12]

Despite finally reaching the refugee camp where her family
was outside Liberia, Bintu returned to the region where she
was held by the rebels because of the dismal conditions of the
refugee camp. She then took up work in the "loving business"
to support herself and the camp woman who had liberated
her. Later, she formed a relationship with one of the rebel
commanders and eventually fought and looted with him, until
he was killed in battle. Later still, she made her way back to
Monrovia from where she had originally fled, but now with
a looted vehicle (thanks to her stint fighting alongside the
rebels), which she used as a cab to earn money in the capital.
From that point, she pursued efforts to reunite her family in
Sierra Leone, but then Utas lost track of her whereabouts.[13]
Bintu was a master at navigating social relationships in
war, and the few opportunities it presented for survival or
advancement. Despite her extreme circumstances, Bintu was
remarkably resourceful. She did not lose the capacity to resist
or rebound as needed, even when raped for months when the
rebels held her captive.

For marginalized youth especially (Bintu fits into this
category as a minority Muslim from rural Liberia), armed
conflict opens up opportunities to subvert male and female
gender roles, thus transforming conceptions of masculinity
and femininity.[14] Joining the armed forces or a rebel group
is one means of moving up the social ladder in otherwise
limiting circumstances. Young men can gain land, marriage, and power by joining an armed group, rather than
working through traditional structures that marginalize the

low-ranking among them. A Human Rights Watch report on the Congo documents such motivations among some of the Congolese soldiers who took girls to be their wives without having to pay any dowry.[15] Taking a woman from a man or a girl from her father's family is the ultimate humiliation and annihilation of the (patriarchal) male head of household with political, economic, social, and cultural ramifications. When men cannot afford to pay for the wife they want, war becomes opportune to implement "the logic of the philosophy of grabbing by force."[16]

In the civil war in Sierra Leone, one of the most notorious fighting units called the West Side Boys used cross-dressing, drugs, and the occult to intimidate the enemy and subvert traditional power structures. Their fierce reputation preceded any real fighting.[17] The WSB developed sophisticated strategies to operate economic networks in the formal and informal shadow state. They carved out strategic positions outside Freetown where they conducted "business" with ECOMOG soldiers, Lebanese diamond traders, transport owners, drivers, and petty traders. They also raised revenue by charging tolls to travel through WSB territory, and traded in arms, medicine, diamonds, food, and looted goods. They thought of themselves as a kind of extended family whose relations were based on social marginality and identity rooted in a youth revolution aimed at taking power from village elders, chieftains, and patronage-based elite. They also drew from images and ideals of the American rap artist, Tupac Shakur, to create a group mythology and "me-against-the-world" fashion. In this setting, they "adopted families," caught young boys and girls, and forced them to become part of their household, to carry food and ammunition, and to carry out military or other duties.[18] Drugs were used strategically to enable them to fight ultra-violently and also to allow them to relax in such extreme settings of terror and death, thus enhancing the WSB's image as "randomly murderous and brutal rebel soldiers."[19] Even though they appeared rag-tag, many of their members had substantial training, including at camps with the notorious South African mercenary organization, Executive Outcomes. The leadership came from educated urban settings, including military families in Freetown. The WSB were notorious for brutal, sexual violence.

Girls join militias or marry soldiers because they believe this will allow them to escape forced marriages and abductions, or at least because they will be safer already being a girlfriend of a soldier than not. Some women are compelled to "marry" their rebel husbands under dire and coercive circumstances, or they concede to it as a tactical necessity. In West Africa, most of the women who joined the rebels were given tasks related to female roles, but they sometimes thwarted these and fought as combatants. Some of the women were involved in planning and carrying out combat operations, although most of them did not attain leadership positions and command male fighters.[20] Nevertheless, new hierarchies developed among the camp women. They had to manage complex relationships among a host of women who would be the "lovers" of a particular commander, each woman having her place on the social ladder. The women on the bottom rung were used as mere sex slaves to absorb the impact of failed combat missions.[21]

In Liberia, estimates place women and girls as constituting anywhere between 2 and 4 percent of the fighters to as high as one in ten of the rebel movement, the National Patriotic Front of Liberia (NPFL). Women gained reputations as ferocious warriors, earning such monikers as "Colonel Black Diamond," or Ruth "Atilla" Milton, and sporting fashionable clothing, hairdos, and makeup to complete the glamorous, intimidating commando image. Civilians were often shocked to see female combatants whom they feared even more than men because "the female combatants' temper was very quick." However, as

Utas also notes, the role model of the young warrior exuding female authority and empowerment stood in sharp contrast to the "fragile positions in which most young women found themselves."[22]

Abduction is one of the most serious risks that adults, youth, and children face in armed conflict. Their capture for use as camp cooks or other camp duties, as sexual slaves or as child soldiers for armed combatants, is illegal under the UN Convention against Transnational Organized Crime, and its Protocol to Prevent, Suppress and Punish Trafficking in Persons. The Convention considers "trafficking in persons" as

> the recruitment, transportation, transfer, harbouring or receipt of persons, by means of the threat or use of force or other forms of coercion, of abduction, of fraud, of deception, of the abuse of power or of a position of vulnerability or of the giving or receiving of payments or benefits to achieve the consent of a person having control over another person, for the purpose of exploitation.

Exploitation includes prostitution of others, sexual exploitation, forced labor, slavery, servitude, or removal of organs.[23]

Captives and child soldiers are forced to perform a variety of functions that support government or rebel forces. They participate in combat missions and raids, search for water, food, and firewood; carry these and other camp supplies such as munitions; and perform other camp duties – from washing clothes and preparing food to caring for the wounded. Women and girls especially are prone to many forms of exploitation and abuse in captivity, for example, by being coerced to act as spies to gain information from enemy forces through sexual exploitation and carrying out other intelligence services. They are sometimes forced to have sex with one or many different combatants as a punitive measure (for a lost battle or whatever capricious reason), and often have to endure gang rapes. One Sierra Leonean survivor recounts the terror she faced: "One

rebel had sex with me several times. He said he was punishing me for not having shown him where the rice and palm
oil was hidden. I yelled for the commander and complained
saying, 'He wants to kill me, tell him to leave me!' but he said,
'We have killed others that are better than you.'"[24] Meanwhile,
by providing support for war operations, captives' labor frees
combatants to fight and plunder.

Captors who attempt to escape from sexual enslavement and
forced labor under rebel or government forces are also at risk
of being recaptured by the same or other factions. Going to the
police for protection is often not a viable strategy. Police can be
linked to one side of the conflict or another, and, in any event,
women may be vulnerable to sexual assault by authorities at
local police stations. Also, when pregnancy outside of marriage
is considered illegal under local cultural norms, regardless of
whether it was a result of rape, a victim presenting herself to
the local police for rescue may instead end up imprisoned for
having committed adultery.[25] Returning home is often not an
option for multiple reasons. The area may not be safe from
fighting; even if it is, a woman who has been raped may not be
accepted. Her husband and possibly entire family may shun
her, forcing her to leave the family compound entirely, or live
on its margins because she has "bad spirits."

Dangers in IDP and refugee camps

In the new wars, families face continual risks of attack if they
stay in their homes, if they take to the road to escape fighting, or if they are fortunate enough to find refuge in an IDP
or refugee camp. As families are forced to flee their homes
to find safety in other locations, their vulnerability increases
for becoming separated from one another, for being killed,
dying on the road from disease, malnutrition or mishap, or for
being targeted for sexual violence. A survey of IDPs in Sierra

Leone revealed that 13 percent of household members had experienced war-related abductions, beating, killings, sexual assaults, and other abuses, while 9 percent of them reported war-related sexual assaults.[26] Internal displacement or relocation to refugee camps still leaves individuals vulnerable to sexual violence for several reasons. First, if women flee with just children and elderly or infirm members of the family, they lack the protection of male family or community members. Without any male household members, lack of security within the camps also places them at risk of sexual violations from other camp residents.[27] For this reason, the placement of bathrooms and showers within camps, for example, is an important security consideration for the protection of women and girls especially.

The circulation of small arms and light weapons in armed conflicts is another security threat that spills over into IDP and refugee camps. In Darfur, Sudan, for example, a 2008 Amnesty International report indicates that the IDP camps are "flooded with weapons." Although the African Union's forces were supposed to provide protection to the Darfuris, the Janjaweed and other armed opposition groups attacked them, overwhelming them with fire and manpower. The Sudanese army and police, who are supposed to provide civilians protection, are seen by the IDPs as agents of the government and antagonistic rather than a protective force. They regularly arrest civilians outside the IDP camps on the grounds that they belong to the armed opposition groups.[28] Displaced women in Darfur report being raped by the Janjaweed militia, as well as soldiers in the Sudanese army, the police and other armed groups, including the Sudanese Liberation Army-Minawi soldiers.[29]

Refugees and IDPs typically have to leave the relative safety of a camp to collect water and firewood, or to sell goods at the marketplace, but these departures onto open roads and fields also place them at risk, especially women and young girls to whom these tasks traditionally fall.[30] To improve the chances of safety, they have attempted to travel in groups with other women or also with elderly women, and unarmed male relatives or other men from the camp, but these strategies have generally not proven effective against well-armed gangs, rebels, or government forces. Women in Eastern Congo have attempted to wear many layers of clothing in an effort to discourage sexual violence, but this strategy has not afforded much protection either. If a woman struggles when a soldier attempts to take her, he may simply call on other soldiers to assist him in detaining her, probably increasing her risk of gang rape.

Refugee and IDP camps can also place children in harm's way. The complexity of the political victimization of the child soldier often begins with the child's highly vulnerable status as a refugee or IDP. In their comparative study of child soldiers in Africa spanning 1975–2002, Achvarina and Reich focus on the degree of insecurity of refugee and IDP camps, and the practical reality that a high concentration of children is an ideal source of new recruits to armed groups. In refugee or IDP camps, armed groups infiltrate and blend in among the civilian populations. Adults and children alike can be taken or manipulated into joining – what is known as "refugee manipulation and militarization."[31] Of course, such activities put at risk the humanitarian nature of the enterprise. It led many aid agencies to abandon operations assisting Hutu refugees following the Rwandan genocide when the Interahamwe took over the running of the camps.

Lack of protection in the IDP camps in Sudan, the DRC, Sierra Leone, Uganda, and so on makes the most vulnerable groups of people targets for attacks, abuse, and recruitment for illegal activities, including the military. Children are vulnerable to recruitment in IDP or refugee camps for reasons other than lack of security, too. In some cases, refugee and IDP camps are well organized but restrictions imposed on refugees (and sometimes IDPs) prevent them from finding jobs, studying, or maintaining their traditional lifestyle. Other times, food rations and other support services in camps may be limited or sporadically available. Such circumstances push young people into illicit networks. One of the long-term Myanmar refugees living in a refugee camp in the south of Bangladesh explains, "living here is like a prison, but at least in a normal prison there are opportunities to do something. Here there is nothing. The only opportunity here is to be idle. Day by day, our lives are filled with nothing but darkness."[32] While many international organizations plan activities for children and youth in refugee/IDP camps, they face the risk of creating organized and well-connected groups of children and youth who can be collectively recruited by the military groups later.

When international aid workers become perpetrators

Aid workers play many roles in the new wars, not just as representatives of the international community or as victims of the violence, but some of them as perpetrators of sexual violence of those they are charged to protect.[33] The risks of sexual violence emerge from many factors. When peacekeepers work closely with local police or integrating rebel forces into army units as in the case of the United Nations peacekeeping mission in the Congo (MONUC), the local population may perceive them to be no different than the perpetrators of sexual violence in the groups they patrol with or train. Second, the international aid community is often implicated in the local political economy of violence. This can be as simple as their reliance on charter aircraft for humanitarian work with a company that smuggles guns or cassiterite (tin oxide ore mineral) on other flights.

Some international aid workers have taken advantage of their foreign posting to engage in sexual promiscuity taboo in their communities of origin,[34] while local and international officials have attempted to rationalize this conduct. For example, Dr Dennis Bright, former Sierra Leonean cabinet minister who served as Sierra Leone's Minister of Youth and Sports from 2002 to 2007, suggested that the alarming fall of the age of "kolonkos" (prostitutes) to include school-age girls in service especially to international aid workers and peacekeepers stationed there after the civil war "must be expected whenever men are plunged far from home into the ambiguities and uncertainties of a war/no-war situation that is not theirs; their conduct changes to levels of permissiveness that would never have been imagined at home."[35]

The presence of aid workers from other countries sets up a hierarchy of dominant and failed masculinities in the local context of the host-country setting. The men who constitute most of the personnel in a peacekeeping mission form an "international fraternity." They are the experts and the decision makers on a mission of goodwill. Owing to their standing as "saviors" or "rescuers," these men have higher status and more resources available to them than the local community or refugees they are charged to protect. Local men, both ex-combatants and civilians, view such spectacles of virility as an affront.[36] Meanwhile, women's human rights and dignity are on the line, entangled in the "multiple male power struggles played out as identity norms."[37]

In a multi-country study, Save the Children found a systematic pattern of sexual abuse and exploitation of children as young as 6 years of age, who traded sex with humanitarian aid workers or peacekeepers in return for such goods as food, money, soap, tennis shoes, T-shirts, or even cell phones and cash. Although forced sex was the least common offense reported, in all of the sites studied, Save the Children found that it was the principal concern of families. Verbal sexual abuse was reported to be the most common, with local women and girls vulnerable to peacekeepers or aid workers calling out to them on the streets. For example, a young boy in Southern Sudan reports that "although the peacekeepers are not based here, they have abused girls here. They come here a few days at a time where they stay in a local compound. This compound is near to the water pump where everyone collects water."[38] Similarly, boys from the Ivory Coast tell of being propositioned for sexual favors when they went to the peacekeepers' camp to sell sculpture and jewelry to contribute money to the family's income. The soldiers would invite them into their rooms to ask them to find them young girls their age. The girls would be promised cell phones and food rations. The boys understood their complicity in this exchange: "for us, we said to ourselves that even if it is bad, we are gaining something from it too. So we continue because we then get the benefits, such as money, new T-shirts, souvenirs, watches and tennis shoes."[39]

There have been many reports of sexual exploitation of women and children by male UN peacekeepers and other representatives of the international community.[40] Human Rights Watch has documented several cases of sexual abuse by peacekeepers with the UN force in Sierra Leone, UNAMSIL, and has documented reports of rape by soldiers from ECOMOG. Soldiers from both peacekeeping missions were referred to by locals as "beachkeepers" because of the time they spent at the beachfront bars in Freetown. They have also solicited child prostitutes and sexually exploited women while in Sierra Leone, the evidence of which is apparent in the features of their mixed race offspring visibly present in society long after their mission's end.[41]

Such abuses have led to international efforts to adopt and

enforce a code of conduct among aid workers and UN peace-keepers.[42] At the same time, victims and families are usually reluctant to report the crimes. Efforts to address these forms of exploitation tend to criminalize victims rather than offenders.[43] Families do not want it known that their daughters have been violated: in some cultures, they would never be eligible for marriage, and the loss of bride dowry may be seen as an unacceptable blow to the household income. Other times, the restitution for the abuse is negotiated through traditional practices to arrive at some form of compensation to the family and to restore its honor. Furthermore, local community members may discourage reporting to avoid losing aid from the presence of international aid workers or peacekeepers. Even when abuse is reported, the evidence suggests that these violations are rarely prosecuted after the accused individual returns home.[44]

Persistence of sexual violence in the aftermath

As a runaway norm, sexual violence casts a long shadow over the aftermath of armed conflict. It continues to limit safe space and options for recovering from war experiences and for rebuilding lives. The risks of violence continue, although in new ways. Peace agreements may fail, triggering a relapse of war. The exclusion of women and girls from demobilization, disarmament, and reintegration programs (DDR), even if they have been combatants, also limits their opportunities to restart their lives. Other challenges emerge as men and boys demobilize, reassert their authority in the home, and compete for a niche in the postwar economy.

Women and girls live (usually in silence) with the physical and emotional trauma of their injuries from the war. If they have been sexually violated during the war, revealing it can bring shame on the family and lead to honor killings, socially

condoned suicide, or abandonment by husbands and relatives. In contrast, the experiences of men and boys in war are
celebrated, although war rape and the sexual violation of men
(and boys) are silenced in most cultures even more severely
than with women. This translates into little documentation of
such gender violence, and few programmatic efforts for post-
conflict assistance for males. Women who have kept their war
babies (rather than abandoned or killed them) typically raise
them alone, often struggling to survive day to day. The fact that
women in many cultures do not have control over or rights to
inherit property – including their home or land – may also
compel them to stay with their wartime captor (rapist/father
of the war baby) or, if not, lead to their displacement after
fighting has ended.

The loss of a husband in war also has many ramifications
for women, including the likelihood of homelessness. In
many societies, local tradition and/or law dictates that male
relatives inherit the deceased husband's property. The widow
and her children are at the mercy of extended family members who may or may not take them in. For example, under
customary law among the Yoruba (located in the southwest of
Nigeria and encompassing both Muslim and Christian communities), "widows are considered part of the estate of their
deceased husband and, therefore, have no inheritance rights
themselves." Traditionally, either a brother or son (of a different wife) of the deceased husband was permitted to inherit the
widow as a wife – what is referred to as levirate marriage.[45]
The gendered challenges of resettlement were particularly
acute in post-genocide Rwanda: many of the men were killed,
imprisoned, and facing prosecution as perpetrators, in hiding
with Interahamwe factions in Eastern Congo or elsewhere in
the diaspora.

Another dynamic of the post-conflict gendered backlash is
the re-entry of demobilized men into the workforce, making

it difficult for women to defend economic niches gained in the informal economy during the war (such as petty trading, networking to supply and sell scarce, precious, or illegal commodities, including drugs and alcohol, or smuggling light arms). War affords a greater range of female roles than peacetime, including the involvement of women in tasks that men typically had performed. Women thus face pressure to return to a subservient role in the household after having assumed expanded (male) household duties in the husband's absence. The opportunity to remain engaged outside the household quickly diminishes at war's termination, as men reassert their authority over women and the public domain. Competition for scarce jobs in the formal marketplace drives women out, while DDR and other post-conflict humanitarian aid programs have traditionally overlooked the training of women for reintegration.[46]

The incidence of domestic violence surges in the aftermath of conflict as men are demobilized, return home, and reassert control. The high levels of circulation of small arms and light weapons left over from the fighting, and brought home by men despite incentives of disarmament programs to exchange them, increase risks of deadly violence in family and community quarrels. Habituation to resolving disputes violently shifts cultural practices and mindsets that cannot be easily transformed in the aftermath of conflict. The prevalence of drug use among combatants during war leads to drug addiction problems that exacerbate rehabilitation and integration into family and community life in the aftermath of war.

As countries move from conflict to development, the postwar economy develops out of the shadows of the illicit networks that funded the warring parties. Wartime profiteers emerge as peacetime economic and political leaders, while the illicit trade that brought them power and wealth during the war persists, usually with government or rebel support.

Initially, at least, these markets are the only means of development, as the persistence of the role of opium in Afghanistan
attests. Resource-rich states like the DRC or Angola tend to
have more political instability than states with fewer resources,
making these postwar transitions even more difficult.[47]

Such structural and cultural barriers drive many women,
girls, and males into prostitution or human trafficking.
Postwar human trafficking is a multifaceted and multilevel
phenomenon, exacerbated by the normalization of acute
levels of violence and subversion of traditional social relations
and norms. It is an important indicator of the continuing
disempowerment of women and extreme vulnerability of children,[48] linked to factors such as domestic violence, abuse of
women, and other human rights violations, the feminization
of transitional economies, and the feminization of (forced)
migration. There is a global political economy of human trafficking encompassing not only origin and destination but
also transit countries, in which many post-conflict zones are
clearly enmeshed.

Nepal presents such a case. Historically, the Nepalese have
been linked with trafficking networks into India and elsewhere
in Asia. A report from WatchList on Children and Trafficking
found that "trafficking of women and girls into India for
domestic servitude work in carpet factories, circuses, farms,
road construction and other purposes, as well as for sexual
exploitation, has likely increased due to the armed conflict;
displacement of children and their families emulating traditional migration patterns has also significantly increased."[49]
According to Louise Shelley, the rebels have taken over the
trafficking networks to fund their insurgency.[50]

Armed conflict has exacerbated high levels of child labor
in Nepal, estimated at 2.6 million children who toil in a variety of settings, including commercial sex work. A surge of
prostitution in Kathmandu Valley, the capital city of Nepal,

accompanied the conflict in such venues as "massage parlors, cabin restaurants and cheap lodges."[51] In Nepal, as in many other cultures, a girl or woman who has been raped brings dishonor to the family and is likely to be shunned. Altogether, these abysmal social conditions exacerbate the risk of spread of HIV/AIDS, especially among girls who are vulnerable to rape, sexual exploitation, and trafficking.

Similar to Nepal, numerous forms of sexual exploitation against women, girls, and boys have persisted in postwar Sierra Leone, typically among women and children displaced from their homes and with few means to support themselves and their children.[52] Although the Sierra Leone parliament passed legislation in 2004 which prohibited trafficking in persons, and the government took measures to prohibit children from nightclubs (havens for prostitution), closed brothels, and promoted public awareness campaigns on trafficking through radio and press statements, it remained a country of "origin, transit, and destination for international trafficked persons."[53] Children were trafficked within the country from the provinces to work either in the capital as laborers or commercial sex workers, or they were trafficked to the diamond areas where they were also used as laborers and sex workers. Trafficking was not only internal. It flowed both into and out of postwar Sierra Leone, with persons trafficked from neighboring countries in Sierra Leone for domestic and street labor and for commercial sex work, and out of the country to destinations in West Africa, including Nigeria, Cote d'Ivoire, Guinea, and Guinea-Bissau for labor and sex work. A US State Department report found that "persons were also trafficked to Lebanon, Europe, and North America. The country served as a transit point for persons from West Africa and possibly the Middle East."[54]

Human trafficking also quickly became a fixture of the postwar political economy in the West Balkans, emerging organically out of the criminalization of the economy under the UN-imposed international sanctions regimes together with the organization of sexual violence as a war strategy.[55] During the war, sexual violence was an integral part of the campaign of ethnic cleansing – a genocidal strategy used to create ethnically homogenous regions. In Bosnia-Herzegovina, Bosnian Muslim women were targeted by Serbian military forces for sexual violence as part of a strategy to destroy the Muslim community. Forced impregnation, for example, was a means of destroying and exterminating the Muslim community while strengthening the Serbians, since most Serbians accepted the nationalist claims that the babies were Serbs. Such genocide in Bosnia was planned at the highest levels by Serbian authorities in Bosnia and Serbia. An estimated 20,000–50,000 rapes were committed in Bosnia-Herzegovina during the war.[56]

The town of Foca was among the first cities to be captured by the Serbs, and the ethnic cleansing carried out there set a pattern for the rest of Bosnia in cities and villages across the countryside. The rapes in Foca lasted from April 1992 through February 1993. "Following the separation by age and sex, women were detained in various houses, apartments and motels throughout Foca. Quickly, a regime of torture and gang rape was instituted and participated in by Bosnian Serb soldiers, policemen, and members of various paramilitary groups."[57] Seventy-two Muslim prisoners were held at the Foca High School, fifty of them women and girls. These included girls as young as twelve years old. Victims were later moved from the High School to the Partizan Sports Hall that became the new rape camp from July 13 to August 13, 1992. Some of the women detained in the Partizan Sports Hall were released as sex slaves, including one 12-year-old girl who was kept at a number of houses-turned-brothels, and then sold to Montenegrin soldiers for 500 Deutschmarks.[58]

The signing of the Dayton Peace Accord in 1995 overlapped in the same year with the emergence of trafficking of women and girls for forced prostitution. In the postwar period, arms trafficking, drug trafficking, and human trafficking remain deeply intertwined and are "embedded in the pervasive culture of corruption" in the West Balkans region.[59] A Human Rights Watch investigation in 1999–2001 found conclusive evidence of widespread trafficking of women and girls into the sex industry in Bosnia-Herzegovina. Human Rights Watch cites experts and members of the United Nations Mission in Bosnia and Herzegovina (UNMIBH), who, as of October 2002, "suspected 227 of the nightclubs and bars that dot Bosnian cities and towns of involvement in trafficking in human beings."[60] Experts estimated that as many as 25 percent of the women and girls working in nightclubs and bars were trafficked. Traffickers faced few fears of criminal prosecution or punishment for their crimes. Trafficking laws were unenforced, while corruption in the Bosnian police force was an additional permissive factor. The collusion among police, bars, and brothel owners was tight and insidious, leading to tip-offs for brothel owners about pending raids and document checks from local police. Still more disturbing, Human Rights Watch's investigation also led to evidence of individual members of the International Police Task Force (IPTF) – UNMIBH's police monitoring force – being involved in trafficking-related offenses.[61]

The United States came under criticism for the conduct of its own nationals in postwar Bosnia involved in the Stabilization Force in Bosnia and Herzegovina (SFOR) and IPTF forces (responsible for international peacekeeping and policing operations respectively). SFOR civilian contractors from the security company DynCorp, employed on US military bases in Bosnia and Herzegovina, "engaged in the purchase of women and girls. Although these US employees enjoyed only 'functional' immunity (immunity only for acts related to their official duties), as of October 2002 not one had faced prosecution in Bosnia and Herzegovina for criminal activities relating to trafficking."[62] Instead, they were quickly repatriated to the United States, skirting the criminal investigation in Bosnia.[63]

Women and girls (and men and boys who are victims of sexual violence) are revictimized by the lack of adequate health care and support structures for assisting survivors of sexual violence. They also have mental health needs, and usually face multiple health complications from traumatic rape and sexually transmitted diseases, especially HIV/AIDS. The health consequences of sexual violence are both immediate and long term, and include physical and psychological impacts, ranging from sexually transmitted infections to abdominal and severe body pain, chronic gynecological problems, and unwanted pregnancy to longer-term problems that include permanent disability, traumatic fistula and severe damage to the reproductive health system, and even death.[64] Reports on the violence in Eastern Congo also reveal that many women who did receive treatment from Doctors Without Borders operating in that region returned only a few weeks later having suffered repeat assaults.

The shame and psychosocial stigma that survivors of rape suffer is another form of revictimization. Thus, simply reaching out for help is problematic. Programs to assist survivors of sexual violence have to be designed so that women and girls can access them without that very help serving as another marker of victimization. The Rainbow centers in Sierra Leone, set up to assist women, sought to circumvent these cultural issues in a number of ways, including by the name they chose for their organization and also by the array of services that they offer. Similar strategies were used in the former Yugoslavia.

Conclusions

Sexual violence in war knows no bounds. No space is safe from attack. Nothing sacred is left in society, not even centers of worship or surgical wards in hospitals. Sexual violence in war consumes the most intimate theaters of family and community life, even of the body itself. Rallying males whose identities align with fouled, catastrophic, and hyper-masculinity fuels their insecurities and anger and opens the door to sexual violence and atrocities that cross one threshold after another. As conflict escalates, sexual violence becomes normalized: war-formed models of masculinity come to shape the definition of masculinity. The widespread use of sexual violence corresponds to the calculations made by commanders and soldiers alike that this is rational.[65] In the post-conflict period, the horrors of sexual violence persist for vulnerable and marginalized women and girls in new forms as domestic violence, prostitution, and trafficking.

Sexual violence does not take place in the vacuum of lawlessness and chaos of the new wars. Rather it is one of the central organizing and disciplinary tools of these wars. Its functions as a weapon of war and method of governability are enmeshed in the larger context of local-to-global economic interests. UN Security Resolution 1325 together with Resolution 1820 has put attention on the gendered nature of violence, as concerns women and girls before, during, and after conflict, and strategies of remedying it. Despite these landmark achievements, they do not make the connection to the economic interests that drive sexual violence in the new wars, or the social construction of hegemonic masculinity on which the pursuit of these interests depend. Thus, we turn now to chapter 5 to uncover why and how sexual violence lies at the crux of the political economy of violence in the new wars.

CHAPTER FIVE

Sexual Violence and the Global Political Economy of War

Sexual violence in armed conflict is a multifaceted and complex criminal act. Trying to explain why it happens seems like answering a bottomless question. There is certainly no one, simple, definitive explanation for sexual violence in warfare. However, this chapter develops a framework of analysis to explore the multiple factors that lead to sexual violence in conflict and the ways they are linked. The objective is to identify the networks of power relations in the global political economy of war that connect warring parties to the global marketplace, entangling formal economies in the illegal exploitation of natural resources and other commodities. Clearing the land of local resistance through sexual violence and other atrocities against civilians opens the door to predatory practices that enrich militia leaders, political backers and their network of allies, while funneling the rest of the wealth up the chain and out of the country.

Chapter 5 opens with a case study of armed conflict in the eastern region of the DRC, exploring the networks that connect multinational corporations to the political economy of violence on the ground. The objective is to understand the power of hegemonic and allied masculinities, and the ways they subjugate others for plunder and profit, especially failed and marginalized masculinities. The last section of the chapter explores the impact of these power relations on communities that are the target of the violence. The focus is on the victim's loss of control and bodily integrity, and the symbolic meaning of such violence as it is perpetrated against women, men, and children.

Plunder, profit, and sexual violence in Eastern Congo

The eastern region of the DRC presents a sobering example of the conflicts that have erupted in much of central Africa, especially since the 1994 genocide in Rwanda, and illustrates the complex relationship between the global political economy and profit making in the new wars at the expense of marginalized people. The complex of conflicts in Eastern Congo features the collusion of multinationals together with neighboring states (including Rwanda, Uganda, Burundi, and Angola) and a multitude of rebel factions and militaries in the illicit extraction of natural resources that has become integral to local war and sexual violence. The DRC has 80 percent of the world's reserves of coltan, just one of the minerals in abundance in Congo that is vital for the global electronics, aerospace, defense, and nanotechnology industries. The DRC also has considerable deposits of other vital natural resources, including niobium, uranium, gold, tin, diamonds, and copper. There are likely substantial reserves of petroleum and natural gas, exploration of which has already begun in Lake Albert and Lake Tanganyika. Coltan is a key element in cell phones, computer chips, and PlayStations, and for nuclear reactors and the aerospace industry. The tech boom, such as Sony's rollout of the PlayStation, along with China's rising prominence in the global economy and increasing resource demands, caused the price of coltan to escalate from US$65 per kilogram at the start of the second Congo war in 1998 to as high as US$600 per kilogram in 2001.

Mining conditions are extremely hazardous. Mining in Eastern Congo is usually "artisanal," a term that sounds much finer than reality: miners work literally by hand, usually without protective clothing or gear, and at great risk to their safety from dust and poor structural conditions in the mines, or treacherous open pits. Some mines are so thoroughly mined that the roofs have collapsed, killing dozens of miners.[1] Rebel forces in the region, such as combatants associated with the Interahamwe (the group responsible for the genocide in Rwanda), along with Ugandan and Rwandan soldiers, and various DRC military units compete and fight for control over the extraction, sale, and transport of coltan, gold, tin, and other minerals and resources to the global market.[2] Many rich sources of minerals are located in Eastern Congo, especially in the provinces of North and South Kivu and Ituri, where sexual violence has been brutal and pervasive, and homes, schools, clinics and other infrastructure have been systematically destroyed. Clearing the region of inhabitants and the civilian infrastructure has opened the land for control by the shifting alliances of contending and colluding factions and their ties to intermediaries and multinational corporations.

The devastation throughout the region is widespread. Drawing on aerial photographs and on-the-ground investigations, Human Rights Watch reports that since early 2009 when the Congolese government launched military operations against the Rwandan Hutu militia – the Democratic Forces for the Liberation of Rwanda (FDLR) – in North and South Kivu provinces of Eastern Congo, over 9,000 homes and other structures such as schools, churches, and health centers have been burned.[3] The aerial evidence indicates that in just a 100-square kilometer region in North Kivu, 80 percent of all structures have been destroyed.

There is almost no safety for the region's inhabitants. "Whenever there is fighting, there are attacks on women. Those attacks reduce when the armies are actually in battle, but once that stops and they settle into their new positions, the rapes will start."[4] The sexual assaults follow a familiar pattern across Eastern Congo. A retrospective cohort study covering the period 2004–8 by Oxfam International and the Harvard Humanitarian Initiative at the Panzi Hospital in Bukavu, South Kivu, reviewed 4,311 intake reports of patients requesting services from the hospital's Victims of Sexual Violence Program. This study showed that victims identified 52 percent of perpetrators as armed combatants, although an additional 42 percent, identified as assailants only, carried the same signature pattern of attack. The pattern of military rape in South Kivu included a predominance of gang rape (almost 60 percent), often with as many as 7–8 assailants; attacks carried out in the home in front of other family members, accompanied by looting (leading to loss of cash, livestock, food, clothing, cell phones or other valuable items); or in the fields where women were tending to crops. Often women were forced to carry looted goods into the woods where they would then be raped, or taken as sexual slaves. Ransom demands were sometimes made to families to secure the release of a loved one from sexual slavery. Attacks took place in front of the husband or involved forced incest, and also cannibalism. Husbands and other family members were brutally beaten and/or killed.

In contrast, civilian rapes did not involve gang rapes or the encirclement and attacks on families, sexual slavery, or looting. Another finding of the study was that, while the number of reported assaults decreased over the period 2004–8, the number of rapes identified as committed by civilian perpetrators during the same period increased by an astonishing 1733 percent, or 17-fold, indicating the normalization of rape. Constructive mechanisms in society that would have protected civilians from such assaults, for example, intervention by local leaders or chiefs to halt such abuse, had totally broken down.[5]

Various localities in Eastern Congo have provided their own account of the extent of the sexual violence. For example, the UNFPA indicated that 7,500 cases of sexual violence were reported by health centers in North and South Kivu in the first nine months of 2009, at a rate that was practically double what had been registered the previous year.[6] The Congolese Women's Campaign Against Sexual Violence in the DRC reported more than 5,000 rape cases in the province of North Kivu in the first six months of 2008.[7] A doctor at the Panzi Hospital reported that girls as young as two years and women as old as 80 had been raped, while 30 percent of the rape victims treated at the hospital are HIV-positive.[8] A hospital that specializes in sexual violence in Goma, the capital of North Kivu, has admitted more than 18,000 victims, or an average of four a day, since it opened in 2003.[9] The United Nations reported 27,000 sexual assaults in 2006 in South Kivu.[10] These figures undoubtedly represent just a fraction of the cases, since the sexual assaults are so violent that many victims die immediately or before they reach medical help.[11]

The recent origins of the conflicts in Eastern Congo stem from the spillover of the 1994 Rwandan genocide into then Zaire, where remnants of the Interahamwe took refuge among Hutu refugees fleeing Rwanda. This has to be seen against a backdrop of a postcolonial region that was already plagued by instability, high population density, and competing land and citizenship rights (especially among the Banyamulenge of Hutu origin), all exploited by the former dictator Mobutu Sese Seko. The region was primed for insecurity. The spillover of the Rwandan genocide overwhelmed local capacity. The destabilization in Eastern Congo enabled local rebel leader Laurent-Désiré Kabila to push west with his forces into Kinshasa, the capital of Zaire, ending in 1997 the 31-year reign of Mobutu.

After Kabila assumed power, he tried to remove his backers,

Rwanda and Uganda, from the newly established Democratic Republic of the Congo. When they resisted, this opened the floodgates to even more violence, called the Congo's second war, and also African's first "world war" because of other African states' intervention. Eight of the DRC's surrounding countries became involved in a scramble that was a mix of military-security and illicit economic operations. While Uganda and Rwanda turned against him, Kabila found support from Chad, Libya, Sudan, as well as Namibia, Zimbabwe, and Angola. Instead of routing the Genocidaires who fled with the Hutu refugee population into Eastern Congo, the Rwandan army troops captured mines, such as the one in Kalehe, enslaving the local population to dig for them and teaming up with the Genocidaires in an operation that has taken millions of dollars of natural resources out of the DRC with the revenues flowing into Rwandan bank accounts.[12]

Uganda's involvement in Eastern Congo's first war stems in part from Ugandan President Museveni's support of Tutsi refugees in exile who helped him overthrow the Uganda dictator Idi Amin (who had ruled from 1971 to 1979) and later helped him ascend to the presidency in 1986. This came after Museveni toppled the short-lived military coup by Tito Okello against Milton Obote (Amin's successor), who had received support from Mobutu (something Mugabe would later "repay" with his support for the overthrow of Mobutu). He initially rewarded the Tutsi with prominent posts in his government, including in the military. Paul Kagame received one of these postings to serve as acting chief of military intelligence. Such posts allowed him and other refugee Tutsi to form an army within an army, which later became the Rwandan Patriotic Front that invaded Rwanda in 1990. The RPF eventually came under Kagame's leadership. After the failed Arusha Peace Accords and unleashing of the Rwandan genocide in 1994, the RPF forced the Interahamwe out of Rwanda. This cleared the way for Kagame to establish a post-genocide government, of which he became president.

With the collapse of Zaire, the Ugandan People's Defense Force (UPDF) has controlled mines in the Eastern Congo region intermittently in collusion with international mining corporations and also Rwanda. A UN panel of experts investigating illicit activities in the DRC by other countries and multinational firms included in its report an assessment of the UPDF's activities in 1998 in the DRC. The UPDF was found guilty of maintaining a monopoly of the area's natural resources through the physical control of areas containing coltan, diamonds, timber, and gold. The UPDF also participated in corruption through cross-border trade and the collection of tax revenues that enriched high-ranking members of the military and other leaders.[13]

The second Congo war began in 1998, and continues amid often bewildering complexity that encompasses the involvement of several neighboring countries (especially Uganda, Rwanda, and Burundi) still vying for access to and control of Congo's resources, along with shifting rebel alliances and other international players, including mining, petroleum, and natural gas companies from Western countries, China and Russia. In this respect, the wars in the Congo have had less to do with inter-African tensions and more to do with the global appetite for the Congo's resources. As host to approximately 60 percent of the world's mining industry multinationals, Canada has figured prominently among the countries examined in UN investigations of the illicit operations in Eastern Congo. For example, the 2002 *UN Report on the Illegal Exploitation of Natural Resources and other Forms of Wealth in the Congo* cites ten Canadian companies for violating the guidelines of the Organization for Economic Cooperation and Development, accusing some of them of bribing officials to gain access to land. According to Mining Watch Canada, the Canadian government has nonetheless failed to launch an investigation of the companies' roles in the Congolese wars.[14]

Challenges of reining in the violence

Since 1998, the violence in the Congo has been concentrated in the eastern part of the country. A bewildering array of rebel factions splintered off from each other. An attempt to identify all the factions in the region in 2010 yielded a list of 19 armed groups vying for control of resources.[15] Much of the insecurity and violence centers on Congo army efforts to quell the insurgency led by the former Interahamwe forces – the FDLR that continue to use Eastern Congo as a base of operations and shelter from the Rwandan army. The unrelenting proliferation of rebel factions and growing regional and international involvement in the conflicts in Eastern Congo (especially along the border with Uganda and Rwanda) are among the factors that have undermined efforts to end the violence. Following the Lusaka Accords in 2002 that put in place a peace process for the DRC and national elections, the Congolese government army – the Armed Forces of the Democratic Republic of the Congo (FARDC) – has been undergoing the process of "brassage" (the mixing of former Congolese army with various rebel factions) and their reassignment to areas different from their original deployment. This is one of the major initiatives to reassert central Congolese authority over the region and regain government control of the economic, political, and security issues that are fueling the violence.

Among the rebel factions involved in the brassage are the Congolese Rally for Democracy (RCD) from the Goma area of Eastern Congo, formerly under the command of Major Laurent Nkunda, who was fighting on the side of Rwandan, Ugandan, Burundian, and other Tutsi-aligned forces. On joining the Congolese army, he was appointed a colonel at first, and then a general by 2004. However, after the assassination of President Laurent Kabila and replacement by his son, Joseph Kabila, Nkunda withdrew his support from the transitional government, and retreated with some of the RCD-Goma troops to the Masisi forests in North Kivu. Nkunda, who previously fought with the Rwanda Patriotic Front to liberate Rwanda from the Hutu Genocidaires, claimed to be defending the interests of the Tutsi minority in Eastern Congo subjected to attacks by Hutu who had fled after their involvement in the Rwandan genocide.

In August 2007, Nkunda established the National Congress for the Defense of the People (CNDP), setting up operations in the Masisi and Rutshuru territories of North Kivu. There he led a force of an estimated 4,500 combatants ostensibly protecting the minority Tutsi in the eastern Kivu provinces, though UN and human rights groups indicate that the CNDP has uprooted hundreds of thousands of people and carried out massacres in villages. For his part,

> the former general ruled his own "mountain state" from his villa in Kitchanga in North Kivu. Nkunda raised road tolls, taxes on the sale of timber, coltan, gold and other natural treasures. But his small empire collapsed following the restoration of relations between Rwanda and the DRC after two wars and years of trading allegations of aiding each other's rebels.[16]

In September 2005, he was indicted for war crimes and desertion by the Congolese government. After unsuccessfully attempting to defeat the CNDP militarily, Congolese president Kabila made a deal with President Kagame of Rwanda to allow Rwandan soldiers into the DRC to uproot FDLR militants in exchange for Rwanda removing Nkunda. Rwanda subsequently detained Nkunda. According to The Hague Justice Portal, although Nkunda's defense team attempted to have his detention declared illegal, the Rwanda Supreme Court ruled on March 26, 2010 that "his case could only be heard by a military court, since the military had been responsible for his apprehension." This decision does not seem to entirely remove the prolonged uncertainty regarding his status, not least because the DRC continues to seek his extradition to face charges in their courts, while rumors persist that the ICC has a sealed warrant for his arrest.[17]

While the ICC in The Hague has not publicly indicted Nkunda, it has carried out investigations into the actions of his militia. Many human rights organizations and the UN have accused his CNDP of serious human rights abuses, including sexual violence and recruitment of child soldiers, during his five-year rebellion in Eastern Congo. The CNDP's current leader, Bosco Ntaganda, has been promoted to general in the Congolese army while he, in fact, is wanted by the ICC for war crimes and crimes against humanity and recruitment of child soldiers, offenses he committed in Ituri.[18]

Nkunda's defection is just one example of the strained process of the brassage of rebel factions into the Congolese army. While the objective of ending the violence is laudable, the brassage strategy has left soldiers in camps without food, shelter or payment of salaries, and consequently nearby residents without protection. The UN Group of Experts 2009 report on the violence in Eastern Congo acknowledges the difficulties of documenting which combatants have actually joined the brassage process (and stayed with it) to generate army payroll information. In contrast to the promised US$5 wage, militias offer the men as much as $60 a month to seize territory and rape and kill. The militia can afford the higher "salaries" because they still control most of the coltan, gold, and diamond mines, with Western and Chinese companies working out deals with them for access.[19] Thus, the army continues to be ineffective, underfinanced, unmotivated, and in many cases just as dangerous as various rebel factions (which in fact are now part of the army, in some cases like the CNDP as its own brigade).

The operations by various parties in Eastern Congo are facilitated through regional networks, including in Uganda, Burundi, Rwanda, the United Republic of Tanzania, and United Arab Emirates (UAE). FDLR has a tight gold smuggling operation with links to trading networks in Uganda, Burundi, and the UAE. Since the start of the second Congo war, the UPDF has continued to promote its own lucrative businesses through timber and mining operations and other illicit activities in Eastern Congo, including in the provinces of Equatoria and Ituri. As in other conflicts, opposing rebel forces partner with each other when expedient. The complex security situation is accentuated by efforts of various rebel groups and army units (Ugandan, Congolese, Rwandan) to make atrocities they commit appear to be the signature actions of one of the opposition. Meanwhile, Tanzania plays a role as a supply chain for weapons trafficking over Lake Tanganyika, and the FDLR gains support from its regional and international diaspora through fund-raising, propaganda, and money laundering coordinated by members living in central African countries as well as Europe, Africa, and North America. Some of these members are part of the FDLR military leadership and include suspected participants of the 1994 genocide in Rwanda.[20]

A further complication is the 2009 incursion of the LRA into Eastern Congo from its former base in Northern Uganda. Since its founding in 1986 and takeover by Joseph Kony, the LRA has captured as many as 10,000–14,000 children, turning boys into fighters and girls into "army wives." In fact, most of the estimated 3,000 LRA rebels are former abductees themselves who grew up in the movement. Forced out of Uganda and attacked by a coalition of Ugandan/Southern Sudanese/DR Congo armies in December 2008, the LRA "are accused of mass murder, rape and pillage in DRC and Southern Sudan."[21] While the ICC indicted Joseph Kony and four other LRA leaders in 2005 (on charges of crimes against humanity and war crimes, including murder, rape, sexual slavery, and enlisting of children as combatants), the leaders remain at large. Whether the LRA is aspiring to play a peace-spoiler role in the region can be debated,[22] but there is little doubt they have long since lost ties to the founding ideology of the group and have instead degenerated into a roving band of highly trained, brutally dangerous combatants, with criminal interests and disposition to terrorize civilians for the sake of doing so.

Besides issuing charges against the top LRA leaders, the ICC has focused indictments on other rebel leaders in Eastern Congo. The first case to go to trial, a watershed moment for the newly established court, concerns war crimes charges against Thomas Lubanga Dyilo, a rebel leader and head of the Union of Congolese Patriots (UPC), who faces war crimes for allegedly conscripting, enlisting, and using child soldiers to fuel Congo's brutal conflict during 2002 and 2003. Two other cases regarding the situation in the DRC are being heard before the Court concerning charges against Germain Katanga and Mathieu Ngudjolo Chui; and also against Bosco Ntaganda. While Katanga and Ngudjolo Chui are in the custody of the Court, Ntaganda remains at large. Lubanga's trial has received mixed reaction in the DRC. Live-screened in Bunia, capital of Ituri district where the alleged crime occurred and where the UPC has become a bona fide political party and still has many supporters, its acting president, Jean Baptiste Detsuvi, claims "all the images and what the court is projecting as child soldiers are a set-up; they are mistaken because in the DRC and especially in Ituri one [mis] takes someone of 20–25 to be a 14-year-old child."[23] Efforts to end impunity where violations involving child soldiers seem to be clearly founded from an international legal perspective nonetheless face local (political) opposition.

Multinational corporations' networks in war zones

Despite the investigations and ongoing trials at The Hague of indicted war criminals closely connected to the role of militia complicit in illicit mining and other operations extracting and smuggling natural resources out of the region, Eastern Congo has continued to attract the interest of a number of international mining companies. The July 2009 report by Global Witness, *Faced with a Gun, What Can You Do?*, indicates most of the international mining companies in North or South Kivu are not operational, but rather at the early stages of exploration. Nevertheless, access for foreign companies depends on networking with local parties to the conflict.[24] For example, a number of officials in Bunia, the capital of Ituri, maintain that Canadian executives from the Barrick Gold Corporation flew into the region with escorts from the UPDF and RPF to survey and inspect their mining interests.[25]

Some of the multinational mining companies operating in Eastern Congo, such as Anvil Mining Ltd, an Australian–Canadian company, have been accused of funding the fighting in Eastern Congo in exchange for lucrative contracts, assisting in routing rebels in areas near mining operations, and killing civilians. The 2009 Global Witness report also cites Rwandan, South African and Mauritius-registered companies, as well as the Canadian-based firms Banro and Shamika operating in Eastern Congo. The December 2009 UN Expert Group on Eastern Congo highlights the role of mineral exporting companies that trade with the FDLR, including such end buyers of cassiterite (tin) as the Malaysia Smelting Corporation and the Thailand Smelting and Refining Company, held by

Amalgamated Metals Corporation based in Great Britain and Northern Ireland.[26]

One section of the 2009 UN Security Council Report documents the multiple regional and international connections that make it possible for the export of gold through areas of Eastern Congo controlled by the FDLR. While government mining documents from the North and South Kivu regions show that only a few kilograms of gold are officially exported each year, a DRC senate report released in September 2009 estimated that US$1.24 billion dollars worth of gold are smuggled out of the country annually. Armed groups derive substantial income from this illicit economy: FDLR's trade in gold alone is estimated to be as much as several million dollars of revenue each year.[27]

The group of experts who authored the 2009 UN Security Council report (hereafter referred to as the Group of Experts) found that gold is trafficked through the region, especially through contacts in Uganda and Burundi. From there, it is sold to buyers in the United Arab Emirates. The networks that connect the operations in these countries are all interlinked. Glory Minerals is a main player. The company has a license from the Congolese government to export gold, although the UN investigation demonstrates that it does not operate in compliance with government regulations (in spite of direct ministerial oversight). Local traders confirm that a local general acts as an intermediary between FDLR and traders in Butembo (a city in North Kivu), while the laundering and smuggling of the gold is overseen by two key families in Kampala, Uganda, led by Rajendra Vaya and J. V. Lodhia. They pre-finance cash through trusted intermediaries for the purchase of gold in Butembo at slightly higher than market price to secure their supply of gold that is smuggled to Kampala by road or moved by commercial flight to Entebbe and from there to Dubai, where it passes into the hands of another associate, Mr Kumar (relative of Mr Vaya). Mr Kumar is also linked to a prominent gold dealer in Bujumbura, who is thought to trade in FDLR gold. The UN Group of Experts verified the existence of these networks through conversations with local gold traders in Butembo, investigations in Burundi, Uganda, and the United Arab Emirates; review of cell-phone and satellite-telephone records of the major players; and other import/export documentation.[28] The UN Group of Experts 2009 report similarly documented local-to-global networks for coltan and other minerals.[29]

For their part, international mining firms have encountered serious challenges, given "the widespread presence of armed groups and military in the mines; local disputes over control of resources; and tensions between the companies and local populations, sometimes resulting in violence."[30] To extract valuable commodities from some of most blood-soaked, war-torn and sexually violent regions in the world means that mining companies must have adequate security. Besides cooperating with various warring factions (including the armies of Uganda, Rwanda, or the DRC), mining companies also have their own private security services. A key company operating out of South Africa for mining interests through-out the African continent is Overseas Security Services (OSS). Its personnel draw on their experience working for the largest security firm under former Zaire dictator Mobutu. "Providing mine security, body-guard and protection services, OSS oper-ates in Burundi, Ivory Coast, Rwanda, Dubai, South Africa, Republic of Congo (Brazzaville) and Belgium, placing them in cahoots with all sides warring and plundering Eastern Congo today."[31]

The OSS concedes to potential clients that mining com-panies working in Africa face many security challenges, including the size and accessibility of sites, the extreme value of the products exploited, and equipment used. These all require strict security measures. OSS claims on its website that its "highly skilled personnel have extensive experience in the field . . . have established solid relationships and have acquired an excellent reputation in the African milieu." Among the security services offered by OSS are security auditing, the setup and managing of security units and escorts, transit of valuable goods, and training and development. OSS ensures its clients receive quality service so "they can focus on their activities with confidence."[32]

Summarizing the Eastern Congo situation before a US Senate Hearing on May 13, 2009, American playwright and feminist activist Eve Ensler (best known for her play *The Vagina Monologues*) contended that "corporate greed, fueled by capitalist consumption, and the rape of women have merged into a single nightmare . . . Women's bodies are the battleground of an economic war." Ensler emphasized that "international mining companies with significant investments in Eastern Congo value economic interest over the bodies of women by trading with rebels who use rape as a tactic of war in areas rich in coltan, gold and tin."[33] Similarly, in his Senate testimony, author/human rights activist John Prendergast stressed his concern with the ongoing escalation of sexual violence in Eastern Congo, arguing that the "conflict minerals power our entire electronic industry."[34]

Social construction of hegemonic masculinity in shadow economies

Across many arenas, such as foreign policy making, the neo-liberal marketplace, or global media, globalization in the twentieth and twenty-first century is gendered. As Australian sociologist of gender Raewyn Connell argues, "if we recognize that very large-scale institutions such as the state and corporations are gendered, and that international relations, international trade, and the global markets are inherently an arena of gender politics, then we can recognize the existence of a world gender order."[35] For example, Barrick, whose corporate vision is "to be the world's best gold mining company by finding, acquiring, developing, and producing quality reserves in a safe, profitable and socially responsible manner,"[36] has counted among its advisers and directors such quintessential symbols of hegemonic masculinity as George H. W. Bush, Brian Mulroney, Edward Neys (US ambassador to Canada), Howard Baker (US senator) and J. Trevor Eyton (Canadian senator).[37]

Hegemonic masculinity is a gendered concept that helps to articulate how power is socially constructed and deployed by elites through global institutions and policy making. Allied masculinities come from the ranks of government agents, including politicians, customs officers, police, and military whose complicity enables criminal networks to operate. The new socioeconomic and power relationships between state and nonstate, licit and illicit authorities have materialized as a "successful" strategy for hegemonic and allied masculinities under neoliberal globalization. Chaos in hollowed-out or collapsing states is functional from the perspective of multinational corporations that shape factional struggles and consolidate the political power of preferred groups among those vying for control of natural resources.[38]

These gendered power relationships have not typically been the focus of study in traditional approaches to international political economy (although feminist scholars have raised these concerns).[39] Scholars of international relations theory and international political economy have instead put their attention on the "upper circuits" of capital relations, like capital flows, foreign direct investment, transnationalization of production, and trade relations. The "lower circuits" or the underbelly of globalization remain in the shadows. In these reaches flow circuits of capital through migration, human and sex trafficking, domestic laborers moving to other countries to work in the household or care for the elderly, or tourists traveling to remote parts of the world to engage in sex tourism. As feminist political economist Anna Agathangelou puts it, the conventional focus on globalization obscures the global political economy of sex. It fails to identify "the asymmetric sexual division of labor based on racialized sex and the institutionalization of desire with millions of women, primarily, paying the price of such exploitation and violence with their labor and their bodies."[40]

While Agathangelou's work focuses on these relations in the context of the transnational sex industry, similar observations can be made about the investment and extraction practices of multinationals in war zones that are closely tied to strategies of sexual violence. The failure to give these relations of exploitation sufficient attention has allowed socially irresponsible multinationals to pursue profit margins without regard to human rights, the impact on the environment and other "negative externalities." This is evident in the sale of war zone commodities, whether conflict diamonds in Sierra Leone, Angola, Zimbabwe, or DRC; petroleum in Sudan, Chad, Angola, and other places across Africa, Central Asia and beyond[41]; the illicit sale of timber from armed conflicts in countries like Cambodia (via Thailand), Myanmar/ Burma, Zimbabwe, and Liberia; endangered species in parts of conflict-ridden Asia and Africa; or minerals from Eastern Congo.[42] There are other illicit economies that form part of militarized globalization, including drug trafficking, gun smuggling, and human and sex trafficking, that also connect to conflict zones.

Such profiteering takes place through black markets. Carolyn Nordstrom, an ethnographer specialized in the study of war zones, refers to these as shadow networks or shadow sovereigns to capture the extent of the power relations and capacity to govern (coercively) that rebel and other forces (including the army in the case of the DRC) have over the regions they control. She defines the shadows as "complex sets of cross-state economic and political linkages that move outside *formally* recognized state-based channels."[43] She uses "shadow" instead of terms like illegal or criminal because the trading, smuggling, laundering and other transactions that go on in the shadows cross lines between licit and illicit. As Nordstrom puts it, "there is no biological imperative marking crime from legitimacy; borders between the world of the licit and the illicit are conceptual."[44] As borders change, so do concepts; and as our concepts change, so do our ideas about the functions of borders, and where they lie. The shadows pull many people, even ordinary people, into their operations. They get involved as truck drivers, pilots, human "mules" or porters carrying contraband, forced laborers, the local supplier whose goods end up provisioning rebel forces, sometimes with humanitarian aid, and so on. One report tells of a taxi driver who made many trips as a primary intermediary during October 2001 to mines located near Kamituga, Maniema Province, exchanging raw fish for raw ore (coltan). He detailed how he then sold the ore to a Rwandan businessman in a purchasing house, who made arrangements for him with customs. The ore eventually went from an airplane at Bukavu airport to a truck to Kigali, and then on to South Africa.[45]

MONUC, the United Nations peacekeeping force in the DRC, has not remained outside the shadows, either. Besides the involvement of Moroccan troops in sexual abuse and other crimes committed by MONUC members (including rape, pedophilia, and human trafficking), Pakistani members of MONUC stationed at Mongbwalu were found trading gold with militia in exchange for providing them with weapons

to guard the perimeter of the mine; and Indian peacekeepers were found trading gold and buying drugs from militia
and flying a UN helicopter into the Virunga National Park to
exchange ammunition for ivory. Another report found that
one UN officer responsible for dealing in gold had allowed
traders to use UN aircraft to fly into town, and even put them
up on the UN base.[46]

The shadows of war function as an extra-state economy
and play a role in brokering political power and creating and
challenging hierarchies of power and deference (hence there
are social principles governing relations in the shadows). A
prime example is the town of Bisie in North Kivu, described as
a "state within a state," where FARDC involvement in mining
and other illicit activities is blatant and widespread. The army
controls the local cassiterite mines, whose value skyrocketed
with the rise in the price of tin in 2004. From 2006 to 2009,
Bisie was under the control of the 85th brigade of FARDC
headed by Colonel Sammy Matumo, who often oversaw per-
sonally the mining. The mine has attracted 10,000–15,000
civilian miners, women, men, and children searching for
work. To boost their revenues, the military watch which mines
produce the most, and then push out the civilians working
them. In addition to gaining resources by this means, civilians
are also forced to work some days of the week for the military
as community service (salongo), and concede daily a portion of
what they have mined.

The military have many other ways of collecting rent,
including at numerous armed checkpoints along the road
into and out of the mines where they charge for portions of
cassiterite that civilians have mined, and confiscate portions
of their food and other goods. The military also charges a
commission on cassiterite traded in Bisie and US$200 for
each plane that comes into Bisie to take cassiterite out of the
country. A couple of dozen to as many as 32 planes make

the round-trip daily. Commission on cassiterite sold in Bisie could net the army commander as much as US$120,000 a month, while the taxes assessed at road blockades result in an additional US$100,000 a month. Global Witness reports that the revenues are shared up the chain, first among the military commanders, then with FARDC at the provincial level, and finally with senior military and national government officials in Kinshasa. Local chieftains may also collect rents, while different groups of civilians have attempted to organize cooperatives to compete for control of mines, including against the military, rebel groups, or outside mining interests.[47]

By such means the shadows branch out from the local context to encompass regional, national, and international networks, thus defying any discrete notions of economies operating within nation-states, or within ethnic, tribal or other boundaries. Ultimately, the shadows are not the informal, low-scale economic activities they appear to be on the ground where day laborers, even children, toil in hazardous and, in this case study, arduous mining conditions. While the operations are highly fractured at their source, they add up to large-scale enterprises central to the functioning of the global political economy.[48]

As the example of Bisie shows, the benefits of the plunder and profit model are unevenly distributed at the expense of the majority poor, whose coerced participation is a survival strategy on the margins of the system. Macklin reflects on these ethical questions regarding her participation in a Canadian commission charged with investigating the role of the Canadian company Talisman working in Southern Sudan. Talisman's operations were particularly questionable from a humanitarian perspective because of the collaboration it carried out with the Sudanese government and security forces in order to extract oil. While Talisman worked on drilling and removing oil, the Sudanese government ensured unhindered access by orchestrating a campaign of terror, killings, and sexual violence that led to the displacement of hundreds of thousands of inhabitants from the region.[49]

Along with multinational corporations, private security firms are found within the array of allied masculinities that support shadow operations. Besides the role of OSS in much of Africa (taking the place of the now defunct Executive Outcomes that was prominent across the continent in the 1990s), security companies are deeply enmeshed in war zones elsewhere in the world. These include Halliburton, Kellogg, Brown and Root, and Blackwater (renamed Xe) in the war/reconstruction of Iraq and Afghanistan.[50] The symbiotic use of foreign investment coupled with private security firms is probably the cheapest indirect means of managing disorder in collapsing states, and helps solidify linkages between the formal markets of the productive global economy and the operations in the shadows.

Postcolonial scholars contend this has produced an Africa based on private, indirect government, where sovereignty has been privatized through international controls and regulations in a struggle that overlaps with concentrating and privatizing the means of coercion. As Mbembe puts it, "one characteristic of the historical sequence unfolding in Africa is *the direct link that now exists between, on the one hand, deregulation and the primacy of the market and, on the other, the rise of violence and the creation of private military, paramilitary, or jurisdictional organizations.*"[51]

Such masculine dominance in the African experience can be traced to colonialism and the slave trade and the ways they were inextricably linked in an economy of exploitation and concentration of wealth in the colonial centers. Mbembe refers to this history of colonial domination and its aftermath as "phallic" because the subjective mobilization of masculinity and femininity are rooted in phallic power, and they have a close relationship with the "general economy of sexuality." That is, "the phallus has been the focus of ways of constructing masculinity and power."[52] Similarly, sociologist Joan Acker argues that the masculinities of empire have constructed the male colonizers as more virile than the colonized, thereby emasculating the subject men, while legitimizing violence in the interest of empire. The spread of global capital under economic globalization has continued to reproduce many of these colonial relations of power.[53] In Eastern Congo, it even echoes the forms of Belgium colonial brutality in the same localities of a hundred years earlier.[54]

In some ways, it seems less of a new war (in the sense of Kaldor's work) than an overlay and compilation of old wars. As Jackson writes, "it might seem that all this analysis argues that there is something radically new to be observed in the Congolese war economy, something which alters forever the reality in which humanitarians must operate." Rather, he suggests the political economy of Eastern Congo manifests "longstanding contours and mechanisms of inclusion and exclusion, created and reinforced through violence." These are the legacy of predatory economics under Mobutu's dictatorship and King Leopold's Congo Free State. For Jackson, what *have* changed are the technologies and techniques of predation.[55] Surely, one aspect of this is the highly weaponized use of sexual violence to generate profits for the global market, and this despite decades of work since King Leopold II lived to establish humanitarian laws of war and human rights protections.

Hyper-masculinity in war

Sometimes sexual violence in war is called "collateral damage," opportunistic, or anomic (that is, an expression of alienation or purposelessness in life), or other times a weapon, or strategy for genocide and domination. Soldiers themselves give many different reasons for sexual violence in war in interviews with them. Some suggest it happens because of the war itself, claiming they would live a normal life and treat women naturally if there was no war. Congolese army soldiers felt that the civilian population lacked an understanding of their difficult situation and respect for them, treating them as "worthless people." They typically come from the poorest section of society, and their salaries, if they get them, are hardly enough to exist on. Many joined in expectations of career advancement and opportunities for education (including for their children), but mortality among the soldiers' children is very high, and school enrollments zero. Thus, soldiers also feel victimized and experience severe deprivations and suffering, which influences how they try to make sense of the violence that they have committed. Soldiers also imply they are unaccountable for the acts they commit because of their lack of control over their situation, whether it is from poverty, injustice, neglect, suffering, or frustration. They connect their crimes, such as stealing, sabotage, rape, killing, and injustice, to these deprivations.[56]

In his study, *Killing Civilians*, Hugo Slim connects hyper-aggressive violence to a number of psychological and sociological mechanisms, including authority, obedience and conformity; bureaucratic and euphemistic distancing; altered states; pleasure, power, and bonding; practice, repetition, and contagion; hurt and hatred; and denial. He notes in particular how violence itself is closely connected to the erotic. In personal accounts of their experience in Vietnam, US soldiers told that killing was like "'getting screwed for the first time'"; it turned men on. Slim argues that, in war rape, "power seems to be the main source of pleasure – complete power over the female body which is usually so proscribed."[57] The rush of power and violence comes with the subversion of hierarchies of war, and through gratuitous acts of violence. The scope of self-aggrandizement is considerable: roadblocks, checkpoints, in village raids, in the control of subordinates, including sexual slaves and child soldiers who can be made to carry out vicarious acts of violence, and so on. Slim considers such cruel treatment "is almost limitless in some of today's wars as it has been in many previous periods."[58]

Nevertheless, sexual violence in war is not unorganized. For example, gang rapes are inherently performative, encompassing elements of staging that cross cultural differences and time. Indeed, various kinds of staging terms have been used to refer to the places where rapists carried out their crimes. In the Philippines, it was called the "production room;" in South Vietnam, the "cinema room"; and in China, the "blue lit stage."[59] In many accounts, the rapists have used sedatives or pills to enhance their performance, and have called on their victims to remain silent about what happened (or else). Behind his drug usage are the perpetrator's deep fears of his own annihilation by other men, misgivings that he might be wrong in what he is doing, a hatred and fear of himself, and a sense of lacking personal qualities as he submits to the power of the tyrant. "That self-hatred is externalized and projected on to the victim who becomes at once both the instrument of and the scapegoat for his degradation."[60] In psychological terms, scapegoating emerges from a sense of powerlessness that leads to displacing fear and anxiety onto others. As Lisa Price notes, Frantz Fanon references a similar process of projection in his work, *The Wretched of the Earth* (1967). He describes the tolerance of the colonized person for the insults and physical degradation at the hands of the colonial powers and agents. However, this same subjugated person will with little provocation attack another colonized person with fury and murderous intent. It is a means to preserve one's own shattered self by denying it to another oppressed person.[61]

Taboo violation

Taboo violation is the fundamental source of power behind hyper-masculinity and its link to sexual violence in armed conflicts. The power that (failed) men (and sometimes women) obtain through sexual violence in armed conflict is a function of the disavowing of customary rules and codes of conduct to subvert social hierarchies and the sexual order in society. It is the nature of runaway norms that previously established boundaries, limitations, rules, or prohibitions are violated. Taboos are at the core of these violations, especially sexual ones. Feminist scholars suggest that taboo violation is central to the culture of patriarchy itself. That is why the social construction of hyper-masculinity is aimed at surpassing all limits. Whether this is to the final frontier in outer space, seizing "virgin lands," or unlocking the inner secrets of physics, "patriarchal men routinely disregard any notion of taboo or limitation and continually give themselves permission to 'boldly go where no man has gone before.'"[62]

Taboos can be understood as lying outside of social order, something that does not fit within a system of categories. A taboo is anomalous, existing in a liminal or undefined space between one category and another, like the juxtaposition of things that are "clean and unclean."[63] Entrances to the human body represent such liminal spaces, both in terms of what is clean and unclean and what is at the margins of the body and the world.[64] Taboos blur and challenge boundaries because breaking taboos engenders disorder. Under patriarchy, taboo violation becomes sexualized. Patriarchal culture functions around eroticizing the forbidden, pushing past established boundaries, going in without invitation, whether in a military campaign or through incest or to claim manifest destiny. Doing something that is prohibited and getting away with it demonstrates one's power much more fully than doing something acceptable. For this reason, "taboo-violation by powerful groups and individuals – particularly when it takes the form of officially proscribed abuses against those less powerful – serves to reinforce, extend, and reinscribe their power."[65]

In the film *The Greatest Silence*, producer (and rape survivor) Lisa Jackson captures on camera a number of extraordinary interviews with soldiers and rebels who she risked meeting in remote locations in Eastern Congo to ask them questions about why they rape. The following exchange between Jackson and combatants (facilitated by an interpreter) reveals the ways that the soldiers attempted to justify their breach of cultural taboos:

> *Jackson*: Tell me what you have done.
> *Soldier 1*: I've raped women in the forest.
> *Jackson* (to interpreter): Does it make him feel more like a man when he rapes?
> *Soldier 1*: I rape because of the need. After that I feel I am a man.
> *Jackson*: Is it about power or sex?
> *Interpreter*: These are complicated questions he cannot understand.
> *Jackson*: If there was a law that would put him in jail for raping a woman, would he stop raping?
> *Soldier 1*: Yes. But we have been suffering in the forest. That is why we rape women.
> *Jackson*: So he has to make the women suffer because he is suffering?
> *Soldier 2*: Ah, that's the problem. I have no time to negotiate; I have no time to love her. I am in need. If I ask and she says no, I will take her by force. They were afraid and when they resisted I told them I would use my gun to get what I want and most of the time they ended up accepting.
> *Soldier 3*: Because God said that man is superior to woman. The man must command, must give the orders, and must do whatever he wants to a woman.

Soldier 4: If she says no I must take her by force. If she is strong, I'll call some friends to help me. Yes, she is a human being but when I feel I want a woman and she is there, and my wife is not there, I must do it.

Soldier 5: Here you have educated people who have gone to university, construction workers, carpenters, and all kinds of workers. We could all make a good living if there was no war.[66]

Taboo violations that result in sexual violence face the same paradoxical limitation of other runaway norms: Once borders have been breached, taboos shattered, new thresholds of previously unimaginable violence established, it becomes more difficult to exercise power with the same impact. "One cannot break a boundary that is already broken, nor defile what has already been defiled,"[67] as radical feminist Rebecca Whisnant notes. There remain two other strategies. The first is to exercise even more cruelty, more extreme forms of defilement of the victim, more forceful penetration. Thus, violations are increasingly sadistic and multiple to achieve similar effects. This is evident in the FDLR assaults on civilians: Most victims have been gang-raped, often by as many as seven or eight soldiers. Sometimes the FDLR have tied their victims to trees to violently assault them in that position. They have shoved objects like gun barrels, sticks, or broken glass into the victim's vagina, and cut them with machetes and knives. Many have been brutally beaten and then shot in the vagina. If they resisted, they would be killed. Often victims have bled to death, while survivors suffer debilitating and chronic injuries, like traumatic fistula, that are difficult to repair even with highly technical surgeries (which are rarely available). The psychological damage is incalculable.[68] Nonetheless, women are unlikely to report rape to officials because judicial systems are weak, more so in war than previously in peacetime, and police officers can be bribed by those accused of carrying out rapes. Furthermore, women fear the stigmatization of being recognized as a rape victim.

The second strategy presents itself when violence reaches seemingly unsurpassable levels, that is, the level of taboo violations is so great there are practically no other means to escalate it. Then violence turns to special categories of victims such as babies, children, pregnant women, grandmothers, and so on. The indoctrination of child soldiers is often also an intensification of taboo violation. Strategies of indoctrination play on the psychological processes of powerlessness and displacement. For example, forcing children to commit acts of sexual violence against their own family members ensures they will have no one to return to in their own home or community, while also programming them psychologically to commit heinous crimes. For such reasons, initiation rites involve violating the most intimate, unspeakable taboos, like committing incest, or killing a childhood friend. Surely these crimes invite self-loathing and self-hatred in the young victim/perpetrator. It may be for such reasons that the soldiers and rebels in Eastern Congo, with perhaps as many as the majority of them originally child soldiers, speak so much about their own suffering as a reason for raping women, and also in the search for justifications for their own acts. Perhaps pointing to others, such as the FDLR, as the ones who commit the "bad rapes" is also a means of moral reasoning in an amoral universe of runaway violence.

A further manifestation of the runaway violence in Eastern Congo in 2009 is the increasing number of male rape victims. At a legal clinic for sexual violence in Goma, 10 percent of the cases in June 2009 were rape of men. This figure is likely to underestimate the extent of the assaults throughout the region, since men there, as in most cultures, are extremely reluctant to report such violations because of the shame and humiliation they suffer. The United Nations and several aid agencies attributed the escalation of rape of men to the joint Congolese–Rwandan military operations against rebel forces, unleashing new levels of horror against civilians. However, sudden escalation of sexual violence to include the rape of men also adds new elements of shock and humiliation.

Shifting the focus to the rape of men is a means to regain the edge on terror when the effects of other taboo violations and their intensification have been exhausted. A male survivor gives his perspective: "it was horrible, physically. I was dizzy. My thoughts just left me."[69] The taboo nature of violating men is also in itself multiple. It is tied to the shame of homosexuality and feminization of men. In Eastern Congo, male victims who self-identified faced ridicule in their own villages for no longer being a man and for having been turned into a "bush wife." Men have great difficulties recovering psychologically from rape. In Congo, as many other cultures, it directly challenges the connection of their identity to power and control. Sexual violence against men can be life-threatening, but many men forgo medical treatment and die rather than face such humiliation.[70]

Women and girls' loss of bodily integrity

The roots of women and girls' loss of bodily integrity in war lie in the prevalence of preexisting gender-based violence in society. In the DRC, as in many other countries examined in this book, women and girls have little standing before the law, or before their family and society. Until only recently, a female was considered an "eternal minor" under Congolese family law. She is still sometimes considered socially inferior. This low valuation is inscribed in part by the bride dowry system that signifies she is a chattel – property to be paid for by her future husband. The lack of women's physical integrity is where her subordination in society begins. This casts the existence of women's bodies for the use and benefit of others, especially for men, for reproductive purposes and the rearing of children. Around this central working of patriarchy other gendered institutions function, such as the sanctity of virginity that makes the woman's body a territory for someone else to conquer and annex; sell through the dowry system; control through forced marriage; preserve under the rites of honor killings; or to exploit through prostitution (and this despite cultural taboos on sexual promiscuity). All of these patriarchal institutions legitimize and normalize the subordination of women in their own, and often overlapping, ways. Sexual violence in warfare attacks women and girls through the very essence of being, in this case, "non-being," denying that they really exist at all. This denial echoes the domination that hegemonic masculinists have exercised over colonial peoples. Writing on Africa's colonial and postcolonial experiences of exploitation, Mbembe argues "more than any other region, Africa stands out as the supreme receptacle of the West's obsession with, and circular discourse about, the facts of 'absence,' 'lack' and 'non-being,' of identity and difference, or negativeness – in short, of nothingness."[71] The denial of women's bodily integrity, like the denial of colonial subjects as void of sovereignty, is not the only object of control under hegemonic masculinity. However, denying women's bodily integrity is at the heart of patriarchy.[72]

Even prostitution, which some feminists argue should be allowed as a free market option for women, is really a function of oppressed agency when it is a woman's last resort. Whether in red light districts or in war, women are bartering their sexual autonomy for other goods. In war, when a woman sells off the right to choose with whom and when she will have sex, it may be the last thing she can sell – all other means have been lost or closed off to her.[73] Based on field research and interviews with UN staff in the DRC, Paul Higate reports that girls as young as twelve were involved in prostitution with peace-keepers, using the money to pay for school fees while they had boyfriends on the side. His study criticizes the gender fram-ing by the UN staff and peacekeepers interviewed that cast the liaisons in these power relations in a context that ignored the "starkly contrasting opportunities between peacekeepers and local women."[74] When women and girls are exchanging sexual acts for food, assistance, protection, security, shelter, and so on, it may appear that they are exercising a sense of control over their own body and how they use it. In fact, under such exploitative conditions, these are not free choices.[75] This is especially problematic when it involves children. But even for adult women, such circumstances denote severely limited possibilities of relational autonomy. The options available are embedded in the reality of oppression.

Conclusions

The global political economy of sexual violence operates at multiple levels of power and depravation. Hegemonic mas-culinity and hyper-masculinity shape the power relations of those who dominate and exploit economic opportunities in marginalized parts of the world, taking advantage of chaos in war zones that serve their economic interests. The exercise of such power is only possible, however, because of the collabo-ration of allied masculinities. The tangled web of relationships that connect local factions with diasporas in neighboring countries and elsewhere in the world is part of the complex operation that make it possible to exploit natural resources in armed conflicts and move the goods onto the international market. The system is a mix of formal and violent markets, making it difficult to differentiate where one system begins and the other ends. Sexual violence is a key tool for empower-ing otherwise marginalized men and for motivating them to fight and to clear the land for economic interests. The coercive organization of social chaos is highly functional for generating profits from plunder – sexual and otherwise.

Such troubling insights still leave many questions to answer in the concluding chapter of this book. Central among them are issues of disciplining and punishing in a global political economy which profits from violence. What are the productive effects of this system? How are gender identities disciplined? What kind of new boundaries are drawn through sexual violence and the power relations behind it in the new wars? What kinds of strategies are possible and effective against such systemic and pervasive forms of aggression? Chapter 6 takes up these questions and examines the possibilities and limitations of practical steps to address them.

CHAPTER SIX

From Protection and Accountability to an Ethic of Caring

Hegemonic masculinity is the preeminent disciplinary mechanism undergirding the global political economy of sexual violence. It relies heavily on networks of allied and subordinate masculinities to bring valuable resources from war zones into the global marketplace. Like other variations of sexual violence in war throughout history, the militarized capitalist system has operated with impunity. But this is changing. Finally. Silence is giving way to the voice of survivors, the documentation of sexual violence, the creation of national and international laws against the use of sexual violence as a weapon of war, and accountability for the perpetrators. The day of impunity is over. However, points of contention remain, especially over how to hold perpetrators accountable: Should it be under the terms of international law or through alternatives to formal justice, such as truth and reconciliation approaches? Other aspects of accountability are gaining momentum. New measures are being introduced, such as mechanisms to stop multinational corporations from trading in conflict commodities similar to the Kimberley Process that governs blood diamonds – a joint process among governments, industry and civil society to verify the provenance and certify diamonds as "conflict free."[1] Establishment of these kinds of regimes also gives tools to consumers to advocate for corporate social responsibility.

Chapter 6 concludes this study with an assessment of the toll of sexual violence in contemporary armed conflicts across a wide field of power relations. This discussion draws from feminist approaches to Foucauldian analysis to uncover the effects of sexual violence in armed conflict. The analysis opens with a critique of neoliberal globalization, especially its political economy of violence, and how this relates to the disciplining and subjugation of marginalized identities. The discussion examines how the political economy of sexual violence exploits both the formal economy where profits are made by mining and international trade, for example, and the unpaid reproductive economies of (women) working in the household, agriculture, and fulfillment of community needs. The exploitation of these two economies in the new wars is often tightly interconnected: pillaging the reproductive economy clears civilian resistance for shadow networks to monopolize local resources (gold, tin, timber, rare species, and so on) and to channel them to the global markets of the productive economy. As there are many mutually reinforcing factors that lead to sexual violence in war zones, strategies to remedy it have to account for that, too. Thus, the book concludes by assessing the strengths, limitations, and possible unintended consequences of various strategies to remedy sexual violence in armed conflict, whether focused on protection, accountability, or the debate between retributive justice versus reconciliation. This final chapter argues for the importance of building an ethics of caring into the multifaceted frameworks of action that are needed.

Disciplinary functions of sexual violence and its paradoxes

In the organization of globalization, an aggressive, ruthless, competitive, and adversarial model of hegemonic hypermasculinity has emerged, driving profit making in violent markets.[2] States in the global south have been particularly vulnerable to this brand of unbridled capitalism for a number of reasons both historic and contemporary. Historical causes stem from the colonial legacy, whereas more proximate causes date to the end of the Cold War, when the West intensified its promotion of export-led growth and foreign direct investment in the global South. Many of these countries were also struggling with other policy requirements of the so-called Washington Consensus, including social and economic dislocations from structural adjustment. At the same time, they faced pressures to democratize and hold multi-party elections. Imposing from above such a destabilizing cocktail of social transformation resulted in failed transitions and war in many states. Indeed, the number of state-based conflicts peaked at 52 in 1992, and then began a steady decline through 2003 when it hit a low of 29.[3] As states like Sierra Leone or DRC became hollowed out and descended into armed conflict, multinational firms used the opportunity to maneuver for access to their resources. In many of these wars, the combination of state failure and aggressive ambitions of multinational firms merged into symbiotic relationships linking domestic and transnational criminal enterprises, politicians, and corporate interests.[4] Their collusion has enabled the functioning of violent markets: while politicians gain funds to mobilize political support, the criminal networks gain the protection, information, and support they need to operate.[5]

Even though sexual violence against subordinated men, women, and children is the fulcrum on which the political economy of violence in the new wars turns, this relationship is not the focus of most economic theorizing. The leading economic field of neoliberalism is concerned with the ("legitimate") hegemonic control of resources in the productive or formal economy, but is mostly silent about what goes on in its underbelly, such as the ties between the formal economy and war making, and its deep entanglement in illegal, exploitative enterprises. These are two parts of the dark side of the global economy that are intermeshed especially in the context of the new wars and violent markets. NGO-watch groups like International Alert, Global Witness and United Nations expert groups provide the investigatory work to map these relationships and advocate for corporate social responsibility. Strategies of shame (aiming at reputational costs), public accountability and socialization are the repertoire of these advocacy bodies, relatively weak instruments compared to the vast power and resources of multinational corporations.[6]

Violent markets consist of multiple, competing layers of rule within the weak state and beyond as contenders clash or create new alliances with each other amid changing geographic spheres of authority. In Eastern Congo, the trade in conflict minerals has contributed to the informal integration of regional economies in the Great Lakes Region, and "indicates a clear separation between politics (within the framework of national sovereignty) and economics (within the system of integrated trade in East Africa)."[7] The fluctuations in authority create volatile conditions and uncertainty that both enable and constrain agency as individuals struggle to survive in the midst of the political economy of violence and appropriation.[8] Soldiers, rebels, traders, agents of private security firms, foreign intermediaries, multinational corporations and their representatives, transporters, governmental officials, administrators, and local residents whose daily existence is at stake are engulfed in markets of violence, willingly or not. Although these markets are informal, they are not unstructured. The system of production is predatory. The involvement of the most marginalized members of society is under oppressive and often coerced conditions (such as forced labor, sexual slavery, child soldiering), while the profits coalesce in the hands of the networks of elite that "illustrate the criminal nature of relationships between business, politics and violence."[9] Despite encircling the lives of so many different players, including diggers, shovelers and pedestrian transporters of the ore, war zones work most effectively to magnify the power of hegemonic (hyper-)masculinity – the most desired and admired form of being a male, with its ties to myth, historical images of ideal manhood, and influential political leaders.[10]

The collapsing state in Zimbabwe under the authoritarian leadership of Robert Mugabe is a relevant example. A regime that emerged from a nationalist struggle for independence from the British in 1980, Mugabe brought to power a vision of masculinist authority that "prized physical toughness, the ability and willingness to use violence, loyalty to the cause and protection of dependants." He feminized his enemies and used violence as a test of manhood, and built a state that "reinforced and reshaped patterns of gendered domination, paternalism and violence that had existed throughout the colonial period."[11] The gradual erosion of his authority and attempts to reimpose it has opened the floodgates in Zimbabwe to human rights atrocities on a vast scale, unimaginable levels of hyperinflation (in November 2008 estimated at an annual rate of 89.7 sextillion percent), spread of preventable contagious diseases, and collapse of many core state functions, including sanitation, health, and education. Corruption includes police and army operations involving forced labor and sexual violence as strategies to pursue the extraction of diamonds in the Marange diamond fields that subsequently find their way onto the international market via South Africa. It is a chain of command, political control, and illicit wealth accumulation that leads back to President Mugabe himself, and the elite in the global diamond industry.[12]

From the strategic perspective of the oligopolistic system, sexual violence in the new wars is a low-cost, imminently available and highly efficient tool of war. It appears to have many kinds of useful, productive effects. Sexual violence is a cheap means to humiliate, dominate, or instill fear. For example, US military personnel and private contractors at Abu Ghraib used sexual violence in the "war on terror" to soften up prisoners for interrogation. Choreographing the rape *in front of women guards* as *spectators* may also have been intended to further the emasculation and demoralization of the male prisoners and their community.[13] Armed groups also use sexual violence to quell resistance. In many cultures, women's bodies are perceived as symbolic of the community; sexual violence perpetrated against them sends messages to their communities about the power and domination of the attackers, while humiliating, dehumanizing, and emasculating the victims and especially the male members of the target group. Sexual violence is a powerful and expedient means to send symbolic messages to the civilian population or through them to the government or other opponents; to forcibly remove people from their home area and disperse them; to drive away the international aid and peacekeeping community; and to accumulate wealth by controlling and subjugating local populations for forced labor, taxes, and other purposes that enrich elite patronage networks.

Sexual violence also plays an instrumental role for its effects on the perpetrators of the violence. For the ordinary, destitute, thin, ragged combatant, who sometimes has no food or shelter and no pay for months, rape and pillage afford what few means of power and control he can wield in his life, except for what he can do behind a gun. This point underscores the widely observed connection between masculinity and military weaponry and the phallic symbolism assigned to nearly every class of weaponry from the bullet to the bomb, a point encapsulated by the basic-training chant: "This is my rifle, this is my gun/This is for fighting, this is for fun," whereupon the male soldier points in turn to his weapon and his crotch.[14]

For some soldiers, rape is a way to take out their suffering on women, so that the women will suffer, too. For others, rape is a way for them to have sex when the situation affords them no opportunity for a regular family life or chance to date a woman. Thus, sexual violence may serve as a reward for participation; a means of building in-group solidarity, of establishing and fueling political identity and destinies, and of enhancing one's own power or status. It can also be used as a form of retribution. In all these ways, the instrumental use of sexual violence helps solidify the identity of militarized or hyper-masculinity. This identity is predicated on the opposition of self and Other, so that "I am because you are not." These maneuvers circle around social processes of dehumanization, treating the other as evil, subhuman or object of revulsion.

Sexual violence serves many instrumental purposes but may become an end of its own when it is used for ethnic cleansing or genocide. Then eliminating the "Other," the enemy group and its reproductive economy, *is* the target of the violence. The destruction of civilian infrastructure, including homes, schools, religious institutions, and health centers accompanies the sexual violence committed on site, even on hospitalized patients recovering from surgery. As one report puts it, "the shame and humiliation inflicted by these crimes is intended to prohibit recovery and re-integration into society, and to thereby destroy the victims' families and communities."[15]

In many of the new wars, sexual violence has been used instrumentally to weaken the reproductive economy so warring factions can more readily control assets in the productive economy, like diamond mining (Sierra Leone, Angola), tin, coltan and gold mines (DRC), or oil (Angola, South Sudan). When the productive economy is exhausted and the state collapses into anarchy, such as Somalia since the early 1990s,[16] then the only resources left to exploit are found through pillaging what is left in the reproductive economy. In that sense, the bodies of women, girls, and sometimes men may be the last lootable goods.

Whether instrumental or an end in itself, the terrorizing effect of sexual violence is driven by the escalation and multiplication of taboo violations. The litany of atrocities repeats itself in conflict zone after conflict zone and over the centuries: young and elderly, men and women, as well as pregnant women are targeted for rape. One family member is forced to commit incest on the others; the father is forced to watch. Family members are killed. Bodies are mutilated – anything from ears, nose, mouth, to limbs, women's breasts, and men's sexual organs. Cannibalism and the drinking of body fluids are forced. In some conflicts, combatants retain body parts as war trophies, while photographs and videos serve similar purposes. Fetuses are forcedly aborted; babies are mutilated and killed. Family members are burned alive while the others are forced to watch. Girls and boys are abducted into child soldiering, and forced to kill their friends or family members to become battle-hardened, and so on. The dynamics of mobilizing failed, catastrophic and hyper-masculinities drive sexual violence and atrocities across one threshold after another. Cultural taboos and norms of civil conduct are flouted in increasingly debased forms and combinations of violent and cruel assaults.

The performance, repetition, and routinization of sexual terror lead perpetrators to commit ever-greater spectacles to sustain the shock value and power of control it confers. In the Eastern region of the DRC, this has translated into the normalization of rape, leading to a stunning and perplexing increase in the numbers of civilian rapes. Experts offer various explanations: it is the result of the poor rehabilitation and re-integration of former combatants who have left rebel groups; or rape was like a gun during war, but the mindset has not shifted as the armed violence among warring factions has diminished. Alternatively, at the same time that society is burdened with the re-integration of battle-hardened soldiers, its most crucial social structures for violence prevention and resolution have broken down. The displacement or killing of many civilian leaders leaves the leadership structures in shambles, and further limits the capacity of society to cope with new aggressive norms of civilian violence.[17]

Gendered backlash or the unsettling of hegemonic masculinity?

The social construction of hegemonic masculinity contains its own logic of discipline and punishment, and mechanisms for silencing resistance to its abuse of power. By traditional masculinist values, men are called to fight and/or be killed. Those who do not are feminized, at risk of being labeled homosexual, and/or become potential targets of rape, castration, and death in war.[18] Meanwhile, women are expected to cook, fetch water, care for and teach the children, plant the fields, collect the crops and run the household, while filling in the gaps the absence of the men leaves in their families. In reality, this stereotypical image is disrupted in war, and especially in the new wars, by several turns of events.

First, instead of staying home to care for the family, many women serve as combatants, often valiantly. As the Liberian civil war illustrates, women combatants may even carry out their duties more ferociously than men. Even while some women keep the fires burning at home, they increasingly assume male duties (of necessity, if not also of choice), whether inside the household or outside of it in order to raise the funds to keep the family going. This exigency may bring women to sell their own bodies for sex as the last resource they have to barter. This is a dangerous and desperate option since war gives armed men extraordinary authority, and increases the vulnerability of anyone considered working outside the law.[19]

Women peace activists of Liberia took another strategy. They pledged to withhold sex from their male partners until the civil war ended. They also raised funds to send their representatives to the peace negotiations and eventually camped out on the negotiating grounds at a critical juncture. They refused to leave and threatened to strip naked (invoking an African curse for shaming men that would make them go mad or become impotent at the sight of their naked mother) unless the men returned to the table to reach a peace agreement.[20]

Women have used their bodies as a form of nonviolent protest in many parts of the world. Females stripping naked is a symbolic act that is powerful across cultures. Twelve women of the Meira Paibi women's movement in Northern India stripped naked at an historic military fort to protest the brutal rape and killing of Thangjam Manorama who they believed wrongfully accused of participating in the armed struggle for Metei independence. Naked, the mostly elderly women held placards saying, "we are all Manorama's mothers."[21] In Nigeria's conflict-torn, oil-rich Delta State, a group of 600 unarmed women peace activists occupied the ChevronTexaco oil terminal in Escravos (a seventeenth-century slavery collection point, its name bearing the Portuguese word for slave!). For ten days, they surrounded 700 Western oil workers and forced oil officials into negotiations for electricity, schools, clinics, town halls and other basic services for their village communities. "Despite reinforcements of 100 police officers and soldiers armed with assault rifles, oil officials agreed to hire five people a year over the next five years, to install water and electrical systems in the villages, and to build schools and a town hall."[22] Women's political use of their bodies is powerful because of the incongruity it invokes, challenging inhibitions and cultural codes of public decorum. Using women's bodies for peaceful protest is a way of putting their bodies in a physical relationship with male power. It is also ironic and paradoxical because of the way that women's bodies are commodified and sexualized and, in war zones especially, horrifically violated.

By taking such alternative paths during war, women subvert gender hierarchies. However, bending gender roles and using women's bodies for political leverage creates risks of backlash at war's end when men are demobilized and arrive home to reassert authority. The dramatic escalation of civilian rape in Eastern DRC is one manifestation of this. Another major factor in post-conflict backlash is the continued circulation of small arms and light weapons. When small arms and light weapons are not removed after a conflict, they become the tools for domestic violence, widespread criminality in society and an arms stash for the relapse into war. They also replace traditional mechanisms of dispute settlement and increase overall levels of violence in communities, family member on family member, neighbors on neighbors.[23]

Activists promoting human rights and bringing to light sexual violence in war are also often at great risk, another manifestation of gendered backlash. The DRC's most preeminent human rights activist Floribert Chebeya was murdered on June 2, 2010, shortly after his organization, Voice for the Voiceless, had taken on the issue of sexual violence. Advocating for the protection of survivors and calling for the end of impunity, his investigation named specific perpetrators and cited the involvement of many government agencies, including the national police, army, immigration police, and national intelligence.[24] Nepalese women's human rights activists face similarly high risks and also death. Uma

Singh, a young woman journalist and activist, was murdered on January 11, 2009 for raising the issue of violence against women in Nepal. Besides the risk of death, challenging patriarchy in Nepal and its high levels of sexual and domestic violence puts women human rights activists in danger of intimidation, beatings, and stigmatization as social outcasts.[25]

A third problem arises from traditional hegemonic expectations that legitimize war through the image of women taking care of the home and family while men are called to fight. This image assumes that, by fighting, the man protects his family and secures the (peaceful) future for his children. Through this division of labor, women come to represent stability and hold the keys to future prospects for rebuilding, reproduction, and peace. But rape against women *or* men in war ultimately undermines possibilities of present and future family formations – the very essence of the male estate (as Brownmiller would put it). Thus, the effects of sexual violence in war put into question the legitimacy of the patriarchal tradition of men committing themselves to fight. A man's departure for war amounts to a declaration of open season (as far as other men are concerned). While the Geneva Conventions and the 1977 Additional Protocol should mitigate such barbarity against noncombatants,[26] they seem to have little purchase in the new wars. The fighting is limited to relatively small areas of a country, and the violence is localized and intimate, directed as much against civilians or more so, than any other of the (often numerous) armed factions.

Marginalized, low-ranking men use the occasion of war to subvert traditional power hierarchies in their villages or communities to take women they otherwise could not. Combatants take other men's wives as an ultimate means of emasculating the husbands, fathers and other male authority figures in the family of the women. This reality is also exasperated in the new wars when combatants like the LRA have no ideology and support of civilians is utterly irrelevant to their banditry. Violence against civilians is committed for the sake of violence. The reproductive economy bears the full brunt of war. No one is safe.

From such paradoxes emerges the fundamental taboo character of sexual violence and of war itself. It also clarifies why silencing the perpetration of sexual violence in war is one of the most crucial disciplinary mechanisms of the masculine estate. The solution to the crux of the problem is to deconstruct aggressive, militarized, and hegemonic masculinities and reconstruct them in positive sociocultural terms. As gender is not biologically determined but socially constructed (as our understanding of sex is, too), there is hope for social change. Moreover, power is never absolute, and hegemonic power, like other forms of power, is leaky, and it can be challenged by other mechanisms to control its excesses. Some of these have already been put in place, while others are coming into play: maintaining discipline in the ranks of military organizations through military codes of conduct; ensuring civilian control of militaries under democratic institutions; human rights training for organized militaries and militia on the Geneva Conventions and Additional Protocols limiting the excesses of war; the creation and enforcement of national and international laws (with the establishment of the ICC) against rape and other forms of sexual violence; and so on. Thus, militarized masculinity does not have to inevitably lead to sexual violence in armed conflict. In most conflicts studied in this volume, sexual violence was committed more systematically, more brutally by some parties to the conflict than others. And some combatants do not commit sexual violence when their comrades do, effectively resisting group pressures. Understanding why these variations occur is an important area for future research.

The militarization of the global marketplace presents

another challenge for confronting the persistence of the new wars. Journalist Johann Hari underscores the moral implications with the words of 29-year-old Congolese human rights activist Bertrand Bisimwa whom he talked to in Bukavu:

> "Since the 19th century, when the world looks at Congo it sees a pile of riches with some black people inconveniently sitting on top of them. They eradicate the Congolese people so they can possess the mines and resources. They destroy us because we are an inconvenience . . . Tell me – who are the savages? Us, or you?"[27]

As a point of departure for peace-building, taking on structural change at the macro level seems daunting. However, practical steps can begin to dismantle the most obvious connections between plunder and profit. The Kimberley process began this work in the context of blood diamonds. Although challenges remain to make this regime more comprehensive and enforceable,[28] there are initiatives to extend this approach to cover conflict timber and other conflict minerals and commodities.[29] This is where citizens around the globe also have a role to play: mobilizing action to challenge the militarization of their own lives and communities, including when it affects the most mundane but valuable everyday objects like cell phones and laptops. In a reply to an e-mail from a concerned iPod buyer, Apple CEO Steve Jobs said, "We require all of our suppliers to certify in writing that they use conflict few [sic] materials"; however, he admitted there was no way to be certain unless the provenance of the minerals could be traced chemically to their source mine.[30] This hedged assurance will not satisfy a number of grassroots organizations, such as Raise Hope for Congo, the ENOUGHproject and its YouTube video, "I'm a Mac . . . and I've got a dirty secret." By protesting at the opening of the first Apple store in Washington, DC, and through such initiatives as the introduction of the Conflict Minerals Trade Act in the US Congress by Congressman Jim

McDermott (Washington State), activists have started to pressure the electronics industry to clean up their supply chain. "Blood phones" are becoming the new "blood diamonds."[31] Creating a greater awareness of the linkages to sexual violence in war zones like Eastern Congo is an important step to ending such atrocities and standing in solidarity with the people who have suffered the most from them. Their voices need to be lifted up in global actions of solidarity.

Another key element in the militarization of the global economy is the widespread accessibility and illicit transfer of small arms and light weapons. In fact, most studies of small arms and light weapons in the African context and other regions have approached the problem as if it only affected male members of society – women were not even interviewed. The presence of small arms and light weapons also increases the dangers of domestic violence as a long-term consequence of war. As Farr notes,

> the gendered effects of these wars are significant. Not only do levels of gender-based violence increase in public spaces, but those who are traumatized by war and then demobilized frequently carry on the fight inside their own homes, turning the violence they have witnessed or perpetrated inwards and expressing their rage and pain in attacks on those who are nearest to them.[32]

The ownership and utilization of arms becomes attached to perceptions of hyper-masculinity in many cultures, although women have also participated in light weapons smuggling during wartime, including in the civil war in Sierra Leone and in the liberation struggles in Namibia, South Africa, and Zimbabwe.[33] The illegal flow of small arms and light weapons across borders also fuels regional instability and conflict, as happened in West Africa in the 1990s and beyond. However, the United Nations has embarked on negotiations for an Arms Trade Treaty that would be the first to cover conventional arms transfer (aside from the Ottawa Treaty banning landmines). It is to be concluded at a UN conference in 2012.

Such signs of progress notwithstanding, the steps taken to date through international law, UN Security Council resolutions, and international peace-building strategies tend to aim at mitigating the protection problem that emerges from assumptions about hegemonic masculinity, rather than challenging its social construction and ties to war. Thus, UN Security Council Resolution 1325 and 1820 do not deconstruct the problem of sexual violence in war nor its ties to global economic interests. The word "economic" does not even appear in 1325 or 1820. Nor do the statements offered by members of the Security Council on the day of the adoption of 1820 make any connection between global economic interests and sexual violence.[34] In spite of several years' work of the United Nations Expert Group investigating the illicit networks behind the economic exploitation of the DRC's resources, the ongoing work of the Kimberley Process on conflict diamonds, and the growing realization of the prevalence of sexual violence in these conflicts, the only context within which the Council members considered the economy is either the devastating effects of war on women and their community's economic situation, or the need to ensure economic opportunities to them in the course of reconstruction. The most important dots have not been connected concerning the *global networks of economic interests behind sexual violence in war zones*. While ignoring this, Resolutions 1325 and 1820 try to find palatable (and palliative) solutions to the risks by emphasizing methods of protecting women and children in particular (while the men are away?), by including women more systematically in the search for solutions (to the mess the men created?), and by holding perpetrators accountable for their crimes.

The protection problem

The great suffering caused by sexual violence in the new wars has compelled the urgent and systematic organization of actions that address accountability for the perpetrators of atrocities and bring greater security to victims or populations at risk. The establishment of the ad hoc international criminal tribunals on the former Yugoslavia and Rwanda laid the groundwork for the protection/accountability approach. Radical and structural feminists succeeded in substantially influencing the courts over other, more liberal approaches to the law (such as feminist individualism).

However, the way the laws have developed raises some questions about the legal instrumentality of international humanitarian law in the context of crimes of sexual violence versus the unintended effects the rules may have in the real world. Feminist legal scholar Janet Halley sketches out several possible ways unanticipated effects could engender a backlash, rather than extend protection for women through legal methods of accountability. First, the principle that the victim does not need to prove consent/nonconsent in sexual violence cases in war (because coercive circumstances, threat of force, or detention vacate all questions of consent) could invite over-enforcement of the law. Perpetrators who *could* prove consent will not be afforded an opportunity to do so. This may very well stimulate resistance to legal prohibitions on rape in war.

Second, while radical and structural feminists argue that the source of the problem of sexual violence is male dominance, in the Yugoslav case (*Kunarac*) that established precedent for the nonmateriality of consent/nonconsent for conviction, dominance of men was not referred to as the larger context of the problem, but rather that rape was occurring within a given territory under control of one of the armed factions in a conflict. Because the Yugoslav conflict was defined along

ethno-nationalist lines, instead of male dominance, the deter-
mining factor decided in this case was ethno-national conflict.
If this logic is applied to the development of national laws
on rape, it could lead to the inference that international laws
govern sexual violence where there is no consideration of consent, but any rape committed *outside* a war zone will come to
be seen as implying the possibility of meaningful consent by
the victim. As Halley puts it, "structural/radical feminism
would then have won a battle but lost the war."[35] This formulation tends to void women of agency in war, while it could
suggest they are complicit in sexual assaults on their own
bodies in peacetime.

A third dilemma emerges in the context of prosecuting rape
as constitutive of an act of torture. In the former Yugoslav
tribunals, the feminist victory was showing that rape per se
always causes intense suffering. This meant also that women
victims did not have to testify about their suffering. While protecting the identity of victims, it can also be disempowering
and may limit their agency. Feminist legal experts raise other
concerns since it is possible that, if women *were* to testify,
they might actually say that what really caused them the most
intense suffering was seeing their children killed or violated,
or other family members tortured or disappeared. In other
words, they might focus on "the destruction of their worlds"
– not the rape itself – as the ultimate source of their intense
suffering.[36] The law presumes a certain definition of the situation, rather than enables survivors to articulate their suffering.

This dilemma is reinforced by the per se nature of the rule
that makes rape a form of torture. The per se formulation
means that the element of intrinsic harm in rape is established without requiring the proof of the damage or reference
to extrinsic circumstances. This approach could backfire by
actually *increasing the value of rape as a weapon of war*. Now the
suffering of rape victims has achieved real legitimacy. It can

no longer be dismissed with a wave of the hand and a cava-
lier "boys will be boys" what-does-it-matter attitude. Instead
of treating rape as mundane, routine, as what happens in war,
combatants may now see rape as a much *more* valuable tool.
They can exploit the rapes perpetrated by the other side to gain
the moral high ground for themselves and to consolidate control over their own people, while assured the gravitas of their
grievance will be acknowledged under international law. Now
part of war crimes, crimes against humanity, torture, and
genocide, rape has achieved an undisputed *weaponized* status.
Whether this will make rape more valuable as a tool of war
or less (assuming the courts enforce the law and its deterrent
value is thus established) remains to be seen.[37]

The role of the Security Council in the protection problem
The legal precedents and normative groundwork laid by
the ad hoc tribunals on Rwanda and the former Yugoslavia,
together with the 1998 Rome Statute, added to the political
momentum of the international campaign to end violence
against women and laid the groundwork for the adoption
of the landmark UN Security Council Resolution 1325 on
October 31, 2000.[38] Resolution 1325 embraces a number of
initiatives that address violence against women, including in
the context of armed conflict. It recognizes for the first time
the role of women in conflict – not only as victims but as
actors in the prevention and resolution of conflict and equal
participation in peace-building and decision making. It calls
for the full implementation of international humanitarian
and human rights law during and after conflicts to protect
women and children, and calls on conflict parties to protect
women and girls from gender-based violence, especially rape
and other forms of sexual abuse. It also calls on states to put
an end to impunity and prosecute those responsible for genocide, crimes against humanity, and war crimes. It also sets

new standards to overcome the gendered aspects of conflict during its intensification, escalation and de-escalation phases, and in the context of peacekeeping and reconstruction of societies.

The resolution sets out a broad agenda for addressing the gendered context of violence against women in relation to war, although it remains largely rooted in conceptions of the victimization of women, and creates a single category of women and children which it frames as the victims and the ones needing protection. This perspective is limiting in a number of respects: it tends to infantilize women (by placing them in the same category as children); and it limits the understanding of women's agency and relational autonomy, along with their many identities and roles in conflict (they may be combatants, or intermediaries moving smuggled goods like coltan, and thus not only the innocent mother-caregiver). At the same time, the male noncombatant is left out of the category of civilians needing protection.[39]

United Nations programming for women or girls in the aftermath of conflict has been introduced only recently, partly as a result of heightened awareness stemming from UN Security Council Resolutions 1325 and 1820 and gender mainstreaming efforts in the UN in these and other humanitarian contexts. However, there remain a number of challenges to ensure that DDR programs adequately address women's and girls' needs. The DDR process in post-conflict Sierra Leone serves as an important example of the inconsistencies in programming, particularly regarding the treatment of male and female soldiers.

The prevailing framework for post-conflict initiatives in Sierra Leone was based on the assumption of armed male soldiers versus peaceful female subjects. Even female soldiers were recategorized as wives, camp soldiers, or sex slaves, rather than questioned about the unit they fought with and the rank they held. Nor were women treated as a security concern in the same way that male soldiers were, even though they carried out many command responsibilities. For example, the "wives" of RUF commanders were in charge of small boys' units. To take another case, 72 percent of girls in the LRA in Northern Uganda reported that they had received weapons and military training. The LRA considered their support and service so critical that the girl combatants were the last to be released, and sometimes only a few were let go. Similarly, in Sierra Leone, the RUF made a goodwill gesture at one point during the conflict of releasing child soldiers, but of the 1,000 they let go, only 15 were girls (even though they represented one third of RUF forces).[40]

The failure to recognize the prominent role of women and girls in many armed units has prevented DDR programs from effectively addressing the needs of females. In the postwar period in Sierra Leone, women were skeptical of the limited resources available to them (the boots and clothes provided were for males) and avoided participating in DDR programs for a variety of reasons: they thought that the DDR was a tool to screen antigovernment combatants; they avoided it because it appeared that the funds were misused and the process corrupted; they did not have guns and believed DDR was about men with guns; alternatively, commanders took their guns away from them before they demobilized so they would not be eligible for the programs. Some women escaped from the armed forces and did not want to go through DDR because of the stigmatization it would give them with their communities and families. This could be from assumptions about loss of virginity, fear of retaliation from a community member of a different faction, or because they wanted to start a new life and break ties with their past as soldiers. Some women refused to participate in DDR for reasons of pride: higher-ranking female combatants did not want to be demobilized and channeled through a process with lower-ranking comrades they had previously commanded. By failing to include women in the DDR process, post-conflict programs strip them of agency, essentialize women's roles, push women to return to normal gendered expectations in war's aftermath, and reinforce the exclusion of women from policy discourse and societal rebuilding initiatives.[41] More recent DDR programs have attempted to address some of these shortcomings. For example, in 2009, ex-combatants in Goma, a city in the eastern Democratic Republic of the Congo that lies on the northern shore of Lake Kivu, were provided tents arranged for couples, single individuals, pregnant women, and child soldiers.

More innovative strategies also need to be implemented during conflicts to provide as much protection as possible to targeted populations while efforts to secure peace are under way. This means prioritizing security for women and girls in areas experiencing gender violence in armed conflicts, emergency medical assistance, HIV/AIDs prevention, and long-term psychosocial support in war zones. This is a tall order where there are already many legitimately competing demands for emergency assistance, beginning with the most basic – water, food, and shelter. Meanwhile, there are ample reasons to prioritize preventive action as an important component of the Responsibility to Protect. Introduced in the 2005 World Summit Outcome document, it commits the international community to intervene when states cannot or manifestly refuse to protect mass populations threatened or already experiencing grave harms. Since armed conflicts redound early and comprehensively in gendered ways that impact women and men often in different ways, focusing preventive action around gendered categories for conflict early warning and prevention should also be a priority, as Margot Wallström, the Secretary-General's Special Representative on

Sexual Violence in Conflict, has advocated. In remarks before the United Nations Security Council, she acknowledged that she "is haunted by what she heard in the DRC – that women are still not safe, under their own roofs, in their own beds, when night falls. 'Our aim must be to uphold international law, so that women – even in the war-torn corners of the world – can sleep under the cover of justice,' she stated."[42] The early targeting of women and girls is like the canary in the mine: a warning of much more danger to come.

UN Security Council Resolution 1820 takes the gender initiatives introduced in 1325 a step further to stress overcoming impunity for crimes of a sexual nature in armed conflict.[43] Resolution 1820 builds on a series of international precedents that include the annual follow-up discussions in the Security Council on the anniversary of Resolution 1325 (the only Security Council resolution with an annual review and anniversary recognition); the 2005 World Summit Outcome Document to eliminate all forms of violence against women and girls;[44] the Convention on the Rights of the Child and optional protocols; and the inclusion of a range of sexual violence offenses in the Rome Statute of the ICC and the statutes of the ad hoc international criminal tribunals.

Resolution 1820 notes that:

> rape and other forms of sexual violence can constitute a war crime, a crime against humanity, or a constitutive act with respect to genocide, *stresses the need for* the exclusion of sexual violence crimes from amnesty provisions in the context of conflict resolution processes, and *calls upon* Member States to comply with their obligations for prosecuting persons responsible for such acts.

It also calls on member states to ensure equal protection under the law and equal access to justice for all victims of sexual violence, particularly women and girls. Here, it again "*stresses the importance of ending impunity for such acts as part of*

a comprehensive approach to seeking sustainable peace, justice, truth, and national reconciliation."[45] While ending impunity is laudable, finding the right methods of overcoming the legacies of sexual violence in armed conflict are more complicated than this goal might seem at first glance. Many times victims are themselves forced to become perpetrators. This is especially problematic in the context of child soldiers.

Resolution 1820 also calls for measures to improve UN peacekeeping operations capacity to protect civilians and prevent sexual violence in conflict and post-conflict settings. One strategy the UN has implemented that aims at addressing some of these goals centers on a "cluster" approach. Its goal is to improve the effectiveness of humanitarian response and the UN commitment to the Responsibility to Protect principle through building partnerships and increased coordination within the UN system and between UN agencies and their NGOs partners during their response to emergencies across the world.[46] For example, in 2006, the protection cluster in the Kivu region of the DRC was developed with the intent to operationalize the Responsibility to Protect principle by providing protection to civilians that has been lacking in the past in the region and during the still ongoing conflict. Part of the problem was a lack of detailed institutional rules or guidelines for how the international community should protect civilian populations, and how international efforts that tend to take regional perspectives on conflict processes can be linked and relevant to local efforts.[47] To improve outcomes, the Inter-Agency Standing Committee (IASC) was called on to provide the cluster with an official protection mandate, develop guidelines on how and which different UN agencies should lead which groups/issues, define what activities to undertake, and commit staff to adequately support the cluster.[48] However, a 2010 evaluation of the cluster approach in the DRC still indicates many problems with coordinating the international community along with national, regional, and local level initiatives to address the multifaceted problems relating to security, IDPs, pressing nutritional needs, disease, and other matters to end the conflict.[49]

Yet another avenue for advocating gendered perspectives on sexual violence in armed conflict comes with the establishment of the new UN Entity for Gender Equality and the Empowerment of Women. Known as UN Women, it doubles the resources currently available to the four main UN agencies dealing with women's concerns: UN Development Fund for Women (UNIFEM), the Office of the Special Adviser on Gender Issues and Advancement of Women, the Division for the Advancement of Women, and the International Research and Training Institute for the Advancement of Women (INSTRAW). With six out of every ten women in the world experiencing physical violence, challenges to tackle are not lacking for the new entity. UN Women will open its doors in January 2011, headed by Michelle Bachelet, former president of Chile. It will begin its work with an annual budget of US$500 million (to increase to $1 billion annually within five years), focusing on programming to directly benefit the world's most vulnerable women. This will improve previous funding levels for gender initiatives in the UN budgetary context that had garnered less than 1 percent of the total UN funding previously.[50]

Gendered advocacy must be both moral advocacy and policy advocacy.[51] The moral advocacy needs to identify and raise consciousness about the structural forms of injustice and the networks of power relations that enable sexual violence as a weapon in the new wars. Foucault calls such work the "unblocking" of our own history or escaping our own occupation. This alternative discourse for social justice has to contend with many challenges. These include the close ties between the hegemonic leadership of states and multinational corporations which push policies that hollow out weak states in the global South and collude in the exploitation of natural resources in vulnerable communities. The downsizing of the functions of the state through structural adjustment, outsourcing, and privatization closes down the public sphere where debate, contestation, and dialogue should take place under conditions of transparency, accountability, and democracy. This is difficult if not impossible where markets of violence and international networks of profit making have overwhelmed the social organization of the state. Resistance to this depends on raising awareness outside the oppressed communities and supporting the vital work of social and human rights activists in these societies whose very lives are on the line. Consumers are part of the international community that needs to stand in solidarity with those who cannot raise their voice, or those who do at great risk. They are part of the sources of capillary power that can confront other forms of power, like the social construction of hegemonic masculinity for aggression and profit making through violence. Transnational social movements working in solidarity are needed to bring moral and policy advocacy to challenge corporate nonresponsibility and collusion in the production of social harms that result from supply chains that exploit violent markets.

Such a campaign has also to put forward an alternative vision of leadership rooted in an ethics of caring. As the well-known philosopher of care ethics Virginia Held has argued, the market has to have its own boundary. The ethics of care, with its emphasis on the interrelated values of "sensitivity, empathy, responsiveness, and taking responsibility," provide a means for judging where that boundary should be set. Advocates of the ethics of care have argued that these values pertain not only to the private, reproductive sphere of social life, but are also applicable to political, social, and economic life in the public sphere. The ethics of care requires that we care about each other as fellow members of a community and also of the global community.[52] In contrast to the individualism that underlines rationality and masculinist thinking in hegemonic approaches to international relations, an ethics of care emphasizes persons as "relational and interdependent." This approach understands the interests of self and other as intermeshed, and of trust as crucial. An ethics of care in the global as in the local context balances understandings of the reproductive and productive economies and the mutual responsibilities of all members of society to both spheres. This approach argues against the mainstream normative approach to international relations that has resulted in cultures of imperialism and neglect, partly by systematically devaluing interdependence, relatedness and the positive involvement in the lives of others distant from ourselves. Raising human rights and ending violence against women and sexual violence as a tool of war against all members of society are all part of a campaign aimed at ending a culture of neglect under hegemonic constructions of aggressive masculinity while in its place bringing into the forefront a local-to-global ethics of caring.[53]

Dilemmas of accountability

While the Rome Statute and other international legal instruments, such as UN Security Council Resolution 1820, have emphasized accountability over amnesty for perpetrators of sexual violence crimes in war, the difficulty of bringing rebels (or a head of state) into custody undermines the possibilities for finding timely remedies to conflicts. One major limitation that the ICC has faced is its lack of policing powers to enforce the warrants it issues. The ICC has recently issued the first indictment of a sitting president, Omar Bashir of Sudan; however, detaining him is another matter. Members of the LRA similarly have little incentive to give themselves up to the ICC for prosecution.

Among the issues at stake in such situations are shutting down the violence, sorting out different visions for restoring community relationships, and, at the same time, averting future cycles of violence. However, the international push to prohibit immunity runs counter to many local practices that work toward reconciliation. The debate over different legal and restorative justice systems is complex. At stake are Western practices that emphasize retributive justice as found in the mandate of the ICC versus customary practices that prioritize restorative justice and reconciliation.[54] Critics argue that the merits of local rituals as a means for traditional justice are oversold and the limitations and dangers underappreciated.[55] This debate is also challenging because it juxtaposes universality in international law that aims at creating equal opportunities as well as common standards on human rights around the world to cultural relativism where justice is relative and has to be situated in the context of local practice and tradition. There is always a danger in claiming universality because it can be a cover for imperialism, a claim to knowing all for everyone at all times, while showing insensitivity to "cultural texture and difference." Yet there is also a place for rhetorical power for claiming universal rights, obligations, and prohibitions, as long as it is possible "*at the same time* to interrogate and to use the terms of universality."[56] Strategies that combine international and national approaches to justice and reconciliation are positioned to engage in this dialogic process to keep the possibilities of how the future is to be shaped open to other views, to other ways of seeing the polity and the subject (war criminals) as well as the members of the affected society.[57]

Another complication is the assignment of guilt when there are many perpetrators. That raises questions of individual versus collective responsibility. Nearly every national legal system is set up on the principle of an "individual" approach to whether the suspected criminal is guilty or not. But criminal approaches that work on principles of individual autonomy and responsibility have many limitations for dealing with situations of collective and organizational massacre.[58] No national justice system has the capacity to deal with all the perpetrators of genocide on an individual, case-by-case basis. Nor are there "one-size-fits-all solutions" that can be merely "plugged into" each conflict setting. The cultural background, conflict background, and individual circumstances of each victim are special. These factors likewise vary among perpetrators and affected societies as a whole.

A number of countries have aimed at regional/country-specific solutions instead of generic formulas for action, drawing on traditional methods of disciplining and forgiveness that have been practiced for centuries. In Uganda, Sierra Leone, Mozambique, Rwanda, Peru, and many other countries, there are traditional community structures and rituals dedicated to cleansing and "readmission" back to the community for those members that violated cultural norms or committed crimes. As a consequence of complex humanitarian crises, in many countries some of these rituals have been forgotten, and elders familiar with traditional practices of conflict management have been killed or displaced. Nevertheless, given the reality of the virtual lack of formal legal systems in societies emerging from armed conflict, the recovery and modification of traditional practices might be more relevant than the application of international approaches, or at least they can be implemented in tandem and in mutually reinforcing ways.

Rwanda's experiment with adapting the traditional practice of Gacaca alongside formal legal approaches to the exigencies of justice and reconciliation in the aftermath of the 1994 genocide has been a widely studied model. Uganda has attempted its own effort along similar lines. With assistance from the International Organization for Migration, Uganda is working through the National Amnesty Commission to facilitate the return of former LRA combatants in Northern Uganda by means of a traditional cleansing ceremony held for them by the community. One method, Mato Oput, involves:

> the ex-combatants stepping on an egg placed between a reed called Opobo and a granary stick. The egg between the reed and stick symbolizes the cleansing of bad omens that one might have gotten while in abduction or rebellion. The granary stick symbolizes the opening of the food granary for the ex-combatants to share once again with the family.[59]

This is just one of several methods for justice and reconciliation that are proposed for ending the violence with the LRA in Northern Uganda.[60] A June 29, 2007 accord states that "Culo Kwor, Mato Oput, Kayo Cuk, Ailuc and Tonu ci Koka and others as practised in the communities affected by the conflict shall be promoted, with necessary modifications, as a central part of the framework for accountability and reconciliation."[61] In addition, there are three other mechanisms that may be called on separately or in combination with these traditional practices: Uganda's former legal and judicial system; the international justice process already under way through the ICC in The Hague with arrest warrants for four top LRA figures, including the movement's leader Joseph Kony; and the amnesty provisions of the Uganda Amnesty Act of 2000, which offers rebels a chance "to come out of the bush voluntarily if they renounce violence."[62]

In Sierra Leone, traditional methods of reintegration and restoration of community relations, such as spiritual cleansing ceremonies, also had beneficial functions. Participants reported that it had an immediate effect, lifting the veil of their suffering, clearing their heads, and opening the way for them to return to their family and community, who would say, "Yes, now these girls can eat off the same plate as us." Such ceremonies lifted the stigma of being spiritually contaminated (as carrying bad spirits) and ended the social isolation that kept them physically apart from their families and prevented them from marrying or becoming involved in business or education. Such practices had a dramatic psychosocial, transformative impact.[63]

The establishment of comprehensive health centers, like Panzi Hospital in Bukavu and the Rainbo Centers in Sierra Leone, is another example of an approach that facilitates the rehabilitation of survivors of sexual violence. Through the set up of Rainbo Centers, the International Rescue Committee (IRC) aimed to respond to GBV in Sierra Leone through the provision of immediate services (medical, psychological, and legal) and through outreach activities. Communities with many victims were a primary focus of awareness-raising. Transferring this short-term response into the longer-term structure, in 2006, the IRC handed Rainbo Centers over to the government, along with strengthening the government by setting up a "national sexual assault network, joint advocacy and shared learning."[64]

The Rainbo Centers' approach to postwar recovery is significant in at least one other respect. By offering multifaceted services, individuals seeking assistance from them would not automatically be stigmatized as a "rape victim" or former "child soldier" just for walking through its doors. This strategy is important for avoiding jealousy and invidious comparisons, especially when perpetrators benefit from DDR and other types of specialized services but the community survivor lacks such support.[65] All these efforts have to be accompanied by reform of national laws, police, and court systems to enforce prohibitions on sexual violence, and to overcome gender-based violence and discriminatory practices. This imperative

is underscored by the finding that the majority of the women
sexually assaulted in Eastern Congo, 59 percent of them, are
illiterate, while only 9 percent attended secondary or post-
secondary school. They are the rural poor: 74 percent of the
women said agriculture was their main source of income,
and 10 percent reported they were unemployed.[66] Much can
also be learned from women in countries such as Colombia,
Afghanistan, Bosnia, Haiti, Liberia, Nepal, and Rwanda, who
have created community-based approaches for peace-building
and conflict resolution, mechanisms for reconciliation, initiatives to facilitate access to support services, campaigns for
awareness-raising and attitudinal change, the development of
conflict monitoring systems, and programs to reduce small
arms and light weapons.[67]

The story of the reconciliation and reintegration of fighters from the former Maoist-inspired armed group Shining
Path (Sendero Luminoso) into local Andean communities in
Peru offers an inspirational cultural perspective on traditional
community practices for healing, and ways of promoting
this in relationship to formal modes of justice. Ethnographer
Kimberly Theidon provides a penetrating account of how conflict in the 1980s with the Shining Path (which also involved
the use of sexual violence as a weapon of war) marked the
descent into inhumanity of the Ayacucho communities that
brought them into "intimate violence" with their own community members, relatives on relatives, neighbors on neighbors.
As the communities were reconfigured and strengthened with
the easing of the war, they returned to their traditional emphasis on rehabilitation rather than execution as the means for
dealing with transgressions. This was especially the approach
they used with those Senderistas who emphasized they had
been forced to kill, or tricked into joining and fighting for the
Senderistas, or duped by them.[68] Local communities developed strategies to reincorporate these lost, "wandering souls"

who had suffered much. Together with their families, they were given communal lands and mutual obligations in new communities, thus establishing the *recogiados*, a Quechua term blending the Spanish *refugiados* (refugees) and *recogidos* (the ones gathered up), in the local social networks. Then they were allowed to become *runa masinchik* ("people we work with, people like us"),[69] that is, part of the moral fabric of village life that often depended on communal labor. In these ways, the *recogiados* could also be watched. These concepts and practices of communal justice both served as mechanisms of rehabilitation and measures of security and protection for the community itself.

Conclusions

Sexual violence in war as in peace is one of the ultimate taboos, and yet its prevalence begs for analysis, explanation, understanding, and remedy. This concluding chapter has focused on difficult issues that arise in the aftermath of the most intimate violence in war and the daunting obstacles communities face to rebuild lives. There is no one right approach for every community. While international law and especially the establishment of the ICC provide universal standards, mechanisms of accountability and redress where none existed before, these efforts can be fruitfully supplemented by community-based practices for justice and reconciliation.

The use of sexual violence in contemporary armed conflicts as a weapon to destroy reproductive economies in order to profit from plunder is one of the most troubling aspects of militarized globalization. Remedies have to tackle root causes of gender inequality and GBV within communities and around the world to transform both the direct and structural causes of this violence. This also requires a combination of macro and local efforts to dismantle the aggressive foundation of the social construction of hegemonic masculinity to promote leadership that cares for community instead of exploiting it. Challenging hegemonic masculinity is thus the ultimate taboo, but the only way to end the silence that gives license to so much atrocity in the most intimate theater of war.

Notes

PREFACE

1 Ervin Staub, "Breaking Cycles of Violence: Conflict Prevention in Intrastate Crises," *Political Psychology*, 22(4) (2001): 866–70.

CHAPTER 1 ENDING THE SILENCE

1 As quoted by Nancy Rose Hunt, "An Acoustic Register, Tenacious Images, and Congolese Scenes of Rape and Repetition," *Cultural Anthropology* 23(2) (May 2008): 225.
2 United Nations Development Fund for Women (UNIFEM), "Violence against Women – Facts and Figures," November 2007, available at www.unifem.org, accessed on November 9, 2009.
3 International Rescue Committee, "Special Report: Congo, Forgotten Crisis, 2008," available at www.theirc.org/special-reports/special-report-congo, accessed September 13, 2009.
4 United Nations Office for the Coordination of Humanitarian Affairs (OCHA), "Sexual and Gender-Based Violence in Conflict: Operationalizing Advocacy," p. 13, September 2009, available at http://ochaonline.un.org/News/InFocus/SexualandGenderBasedViolence/tabid/4753/language/en-US/Default.aspx, accessed October 2, 2009.
5 Lisa S. Price, "Finding the Man in the Soldier-Rapist: Some Reflections on Comprehension and Accountability," *Women's Studies International Forum* 24(2) (2001): 211, emphasis added.
6 See Hilary Charlesworth, "Feminist Methods in International Law," in Steven R. Ratner and Anne-Marie Slaughter (eds), *The Methods of International Law* (Washington, DC: American Society of International Law, 2004), pp. 159–83.

7 This definition of GBV and more information on it is available at www.humanitarianreform.org/Default.aspx?tabid=429. See also Beth Vann, "Gender-Based Violence: Emerging Issues in Programs Serving Displaced Populations," *Reproductive Health for Refugees Consortium* (Reproductive Health Response in Conflict Consortium, 2002): 8.

8 See Commission on National Security in the 21st Century, *Shared Destinies: Security in a Globalized World* (Institute for Public Policy Research, November 2008).

9 Joan Acker, "Gender, Capitalism and Globalization," *Critical Sociology* 30(1) (2004): 17–38.

10 V. Spike Peterson, *A Critical Rewriting of Global Political Economy: Integrating Reproductive, Productive and Virtual Economies*, 2nd printing (New York: Routledge, 2006), p. 79.

11 Acker, "Gender, Capitalism and Globalization": 24.

12 One of the classic works on this divide is Susan B. Boyd (ed.), *Challenging the Public/Private Divide* (Toronto: University of Toronto Press, 1997).

13 Bert B. Lockwood (ed.), *Introduction: Women's Rights: A Human Rights Quarterly Reader* (Baltimore: Johns Hopkins Press, 2006), p. xvii.

14 See Hilary Charlesworth and Christine Chinkin, *The Boundaries of International Law: A Feminist Analysis* (Manchester: Manchester University Press, 2001).

15 Carol Cohn and Cynthia Enloe, "A Conversation with Cynthia Enloe: Feminists Look at Masculinity and the Men Who Wage War," *Signs* 28(4) (Summer 2003): 1192.

16 Jean Ward, *Broken Bodies – Broken Dreams: Violence against Women Exposed* (United Nations, OCHA/Integrated Regional Information Networks – hereafter IRIN, 2005), p. 54.

17 This book follows these conventions. See World Health Organization (WHO), *World Report on Violence and Health* (Geneva, 2002); and Jeanne Ward, *If Not Now, When? Addressing Gender-based Violence in Refugee, Internally Displaced, and Post-Conflict Settings. A Global Overview* (Reproductive Health for Refugees Consortium (April 2002).

18 See Mats Utas, "Victimacy, Girlfriending, Soldiering: Tactic Agency in a Young Woman's Social Navigation of the Liberian War Zone," *Anthropological Quarterly* 78(2) (Spring 2005): 403–30; Rahel Kunz, and Ann-Kristin Sjoberg, "Empowered or

Oppressed? Female Combatants in the Colombian Guerrilla: The Case of the Revolutionary Armed Forces of Colombia – FARC." Paper presented at the International Studies Association's 50th Annual Convention, New York City, 15 February 2009, available at www.allacademic.com/meta/p310466_index.html.

19 Human Rights Watch, "We'll Kill You If You Cry: Sexual Violence in the Sierra Leone Conflict," *Sierra Leone* 15(1) (A) (January 2003).

20 See Adam Jones, *Writings on Violence, Men, and Feminist International Relations* (New York: Routledge, 2008), especially ch. 10.

21 Elizabeth Odio Benito, "Sexual Violence as a War Crime," in Pablo Antonio Fernandez-Sanchez (ed.), *The New Challenges of Humanitarian Law in Armed Conflict* (The Hague: Martinus Nijhoff, 2005), p. 166; Allison Ruby Reid-Cunningham, "Rape as a Weapon of Genocide," *Genocide Studies and Prevention* 3(3) (December 2008): 280–1.

22 See R. Charli Carpenter, "Women, Children and Other Vulnerable Groups: Gender, Strategic Frames and the Protection of Civilians as a Transnational Issue," *International Studies Quarterly* 49(2) (2005): 295–334.

23 Jennifer Lynn Green, *Collective Rape: A Cross-National Study of the Incidence and Perpetrators of Mass Political Sexual Violence, 1980–2003*, Dissertation (Graduate School of the Ohio State University, 2006); Michele L. Leiby, "Wartime Sexual Violence in Guatemala and Peru," *International Studies Quarterly* 53(2) (2009): 445–68.

24 Robert M. Hayden, "Rape and Rape Avoidance in Ethno-national Conflicts: Sexual Violence in Liminalized States," *American Anthropologist*, New Series 102(1) (March 2000): 27–41.

25 See Elizabeth Jean Wood, "Variation in Sexual Violence During War," *Politics and Society* 34(3) (2006): 307–42.

26 Jacqueline Novogratz, *The Blue Sweater: Bridging the Gap between Rich and Poor in an Interconnected World* (New York: Rodale, 2009).

27 See Tara McKelvey (ed.), *One of the Guys: Women as Aggressors and Torturers* (Emeryville, CA: Seal Press, 2007).

28 Wood, "Variation in Sexual Violence During War."

29 See V. Spike Peterson and Anne Sisson Runyon, *Global Gender Issues in the New Millennium* (Boulder, CO: Westview Press, 2010, 3rd edn), p. 27.

30 Jonathan Gottschall, "'The Odyssey' and 'The Iliad' are giving
    up New Secrets about the ancient World," September 28,
    2008, available at www.boston.com/bostonglobe/ideas/
    articles/2008/09/28/hidden_histories.
31 Susan Brownmiller, *Against Our Will: Men, Women, Rape* (New
    York: Simon and Schuster, 1975), p. 17, emphasis added.
32 Brownmiller, *Against Our Will*, pp. 17–18.
33 See Cynthia Enloe's critique of the gendering of war in *Bananas,
    Beaches and Bases: Making Feminist Sense of International Politics*
    (Berkeley: University of California Press, 1990); and Cynthia
    Enloe, *Maneuvers: The International Politics of Militarizing Women's
    Lives* (Berkeley: University of California Press, 2000); and Cynthia
    Enloe, *The Curious Feminist: Searching for Women in a New Age of
    Empire* (Berkeley: University of California Press, 2004).
34 See the discussion on Catherine Mackinnon and Beverly Allen's
    works on rape in the former Yugoslavia in Inger Skjelsbaek, *The
    Elephant in the Room: An Overview of How Sexual Violence Came
    to be Seen as a Weapon of War*. Report to Norwegian Ministry
    of Foreign Affairs (Oslo: Peace Research Institute Oslo, 2010),
    p. 34, available at www.prio.no/Research-and-Publications/
    Publication/?oid=57565085.
35 Skjelsbaek, *The Elephant in the Room*, p. 35.
36 See Laura Sjoberg and Carone E. Gentry, *Mothers, Monsters,
    Whores: Women's Violence in Global Politics* (New York: Zed
    Books, 2007).
37 For an overview of constructivism, see Michael Barnett, "Social
    Constructivism," in John Baylis and Steve Smith (eds), *The
    Globalization of World Politics: An Introduction to International
    Relations*, 3rd edn (Oxford: Oxford University Press, 2005),
    pp. 252–70.
38 See Susan J. Brison, "Relational Autonomy and Freedom of
    Expression," in Catherine Mackenzie and Natalie Stoljar (eds),
    *Relational Autonomy: Feminist Perspectives on Autonomy, Agency,
    and the Social Self* (New York: Oxford University Press, 2000),
    pp. 280–99.
39 Christine Beasley and Juanita Elias, "Situating Masculinities in
    Global Politics," Second Oceanic Conference on International
    Studies, University of Melbourne (July 5–7, 2006), p. 5,
    available at http://digital.library.adelaide.edu.au/dspace/
    handle/2440/36063, accessed on January 18, 2010.

40 Duke W. Austin, "Hyper-Masculinity and Disaster: Gender Role Construction in the Wake of Hurricane Katrina." Paper presented at the American Sociological Association Annual Meeting, Sheraton Boston and the Boston Marriott Copley Place, Boston, MA (July 31, 2008), available at www.allacademic.com/meta/p241530_index.html, p. 4, accessed on January 18, 2010.

41 Jane Parpart, "Masculinity/ies, Gender and Violence in the Struggle for Zimbabwe," in Jane Parpart and Marysia Zalewski (eds), *Rethinking the Man Question* (London: Zed Books, 2008), p. 182.

42 Charlotte Hooper, *Manly States* (New York: Columbia University Press, 2000), p. 39.

43 See Dubravka Zarkov and Cynthia Cockburn, "Demilitarization – or More of the Same? Feminist Questions to ask in the Postwar Moment," in Dubravka Zarkov and Cynthia Cockburn (eds), *The Postwar Moment: Militaries, Masculinities, and International Peacekeeping* (London: Lawrence and Wishart, 2002), pp. 22–31; Enloe, *Maneuvers*; and Enloe, *Bananas, Beaches and Bases*.

44 Hooper, *Manly States*. See also Enloe, *Bananas, Beaches and Bases*, pp. 2–3.

45 R. W. Connell, *Masculinities* (Berkeley: University of California Press, 1995), p. 68.

46 Hooper, *Manly States*, p. 55.

47 Enloe, *Bananas, Bases and Beaches*, p. 4.

48 Hooper, *Manly States*, p. 54. See also Dagmar Herzog (ed.), *Brutality and Desire: War and Sexuality in Europe's Twentieth Century* (New York: Palgrave Macmillan, 2009), which includes several chapters on European colonialism, racism, sexuality and the construction of masculinities and femininities in relation to the colonized.

49 Austin, "Hyper-Masculinity and Disaster," p. 5.

50 An example of this approach is found in Laura Shepherd, *Gender, Violence and Security: Discourse as Practice* (New York: Zed Books, 2008).

51 Brownmiller, *Against Our Will*, p. 30.

52 See R. Charli Carpenter, *Born of War: Protecting Children of Sexual Violence in War Zones* (Bloomfield, CN: Kumarian Press, 2007).

53 Reid-Cunningham, "Rape as a Weapon of Genocide": 282.

54 Utas, "Victimacy, Girlfriending, Soldiering": 407.

55 Human Security Report Project, *The Shrinking Costs of War: Part II of the Human Security Report* (forthcoming, Oxford University Press, 2010). The pre-publication version is available at www. hsrgroup.org/human-security-reports/2009/text.aspx), p. 2, accessed on June 10, 2010.

56 Human Security Report Project, *The Shrinking Costs of War*, p. 1.

57 Human Security Report Project, *The Shrinking Costs of War*, p. 2.

58 See *2009 Global Trends: Refugees, Asylum Seekers, Returnees, Internally Displaced and Stateless Persons* (United Nations High Commissioner for Refugees, 2010), available at www.unhcr. org/4c11fobe9.html. Another 50 million have been made homeless by natural disasters and experts predict that the effects of climate change, population growth, and poverty could increase that number to 200 million by 2050. See IRIN, "Global: Defining the Rights of the Internally Displaced" (October 16, 2008), available at www.irinnews.org/Report.aspx?ReportId=80942, accessed on June 16, 2010.

59 See the UNHCR's *2009 Global Trends*, pp. 2–9.

60 Odio Benito, "Sexual Violence as a War Crime" in *The New Challenges of Humanitarian Law in Armed Conflict*, pp. 164–5.

61 Iris Chang, *The Rape of Nanking* (New York: BasicBooks, 1997).

62 Odio Benito, "Sexual Violence as a War Crime," in *The New Challenges of Humanitarian Law in Armed Conflicts*, p. 167.

63 United Nations International Criminal Tribunal for Rwanda, "Jean-Paul Akayesu, summary of the Judgment," ICTR-96-4-T, delivered on September 2, 1998, available at http://docs.google. com/gview?a=v&q=cache:WV4-WsPM-08J:www.amnestyusa. org/events/western/pdf/AmnestyConference_BalthazarSitaCLE. pdf+general+paul+akayesu&hl=en&gl=us&sig=AFQjCNFL-qQhVFAoPyCTSMW-yoQyBbnJsg, accessed on June 8, 2010.

64 Odio Benito, "Sexual Violence as a War Crime," in *The New Challenges of Humanitarian Law in Armed Conflicts*, p. 168.

65 Odio Benito, "Sexual Violence as a War Crime," in *The New Challenges of Humanitarian Law in Armed Conflicts*, p. 169.

66 "Celebici Case: The Judgement of the Trial Chamber." Press release (The Hague: November 16, 1998), available at www.icty. org/sid/7617.

67 For the full text, see "The 1998 Statute of Rome," available at www.icc-cpi.int/Menus/ICC/Legal+Texts+and+Tools/, accessed on August 26, 2009.

68 See Natalie Florea Hudson, *Gender, Security and the UN: Security Language as a Political Framework for Women* (London: Routledge, 2010). See an annotated discussion of exploring the meaning of 1325 at www.womenwarpeace.org/1325_toolbox/1325_annotated, accessed on July 15, 2010.

69 See Shepherd, *Gender, Violence and Security*.

70 UN Security Council, "Security Council Resolution 1820 (2008): On Acts of Sexual Violence against Civilians in Armed Conflicts," June 19, 2008, S/RES/1820 (2008), available at www.un.org/Docs/sc/unsc_resolutions08.htm, accessed on September 3, 2009.

71 Graça Machel, *The Impact of War on Children* (New York: United Nations Publication, 2003); Yasmin Tambiah, "Sexuality and Women's Rights in Armed Conflict in Sri Lanka," *Reproductive Health Matters* 12(23) (2004): 78–87.

CHAPTER 2 DIMENSIONS OF SEXUAL VIOLENCE IN CONFLICT

1 Zaki Laïdi, *Norms over Force: The Enigma of European Power* (New York: Palgrave Macmillan, 2008), p. 42.

2 Martha Finnemore and Kathryn Sikkink, "International Norm Dynamics and Political Change," *International Organization* 52(4) (1998): 892.

3 For example, see Christopher J. Coyne and Steve Davies, "Nineteen Public Bads of Empire, Nation Building, and the Like," *The Independent Review* 12(1) (Summer 2007): 129–32; Cornelia Beyer, *Violent Globalisms in Response to Empire* (Aldershot, UK: Ashgate, 2008).

4 Jeffrey Z. Rubin, Dean Pruitt, and Sung Hee Kim, *Social Conflict, Escalation, Stalemate and Settlement*, 2nd edn (New York: McGraw-Hill, 1994), p. 93.

5 Rubin, Pruitt and Kim, *Social Conflict, Escalation, Stalemate and Settlement*, p. 108.

6 Michel Foucault, *Discipline and Punish: The Birth of the Prison*, 2nd edn. Translated by Alan Sheridan (New York: Vintage Books, 1991).

7 George H. W. Bush, "Address Before a Joint Session of Congress" (September 11, 1990). Miller Center of Public Affairs,

University of Virginia, Scripps Library, Multimedia archive, full text available at http://millercenter.org/scripps/archive/speeches/detail/3425, accessed on July 16, 2010.

8 Murray Edelman, "The Construction and Uses of Social Problems," in William Stearns and William Choloupka (eds), *Jean Baudrillard: The Disappearance of Art and Politics* (New York: St Martin's Press, 1992). See also Janie Leatherman (ed.), *Discipline and Punishment in Global Politics* (New York: Palgrave Macmillan, 2008).

9 Matthias Bjørnlund, "'A Fate Worse than Dying': Sexual Violence during the Armenian Genocide," in Dagmar Herzog (ed.), *Brutality and Desire: War and Sexuality in Europe's Twentieth Century* (New York: Palgrave Macmillan, 2009), p. 24.

10 Vanessa Farr, "Women, Men and the Struggle to Disarm," *Conflict Trends*, ACCORD 3 (2003): 27.

11 For example, see Laura Sjoberg, "Gendered Realities of the Immunity Principle: Why Gender Analysis Needs Feminism," *International Studies Quarterly* 50 (2006): 889–910. Sjoberg deconstructs the civilian immunity principle in just war theory to show that it essentializes women and links protection to women and children while, in effect, excluding men from the civilian category and hence protection.

12 Hugo Slim, *Killing Civilians: Method, Madness and Morality in War* (New York: Columbia University Press, 2008), pp. 187–8.

13 See Alexander B. Downes, *Targeting Civilians in War* (Ithaca, NY: Cornell University Press, 2008); Slim, *Killing Civilians*.

14 Recent research on targeting civilians in interstate war finds a strong positive correlation with victory, but the efficacy of civilian targeting in interstate wars has decreased over the last two hundred years. This finding raises important questions about possible correlations and trends for intrastate conflicts. See Alexander B. Downes and Kathryn McNabb Cochran, "Targeting Civilians to Win? Assessing the Military Effectiveness of Civilian Victimization in Interstate War," in Erica Chenoweth and Adria Lawrence (eds), *Rethinking Violence: States and Non-State Actors in Conflict* (Boston: MIT Press, 2010).

15 See Human Security Report table, Number of State-Based Conflicts, 1946–2007, available at www.hsrgroup.org/our-work/security-stats/State-Based-Armed-Conflicts.aspx, accessed on June 10, 2010.

16 See Tarak Barkawi, *Globalization and War* (Lanham, MD: Rowman and Littlefield, 2006); Michael Brzoska, "'New Wars' Discourse in Germany," *Journal of Peace Research* 41(1) (2004): 107–17.

17 Leatherman, *Discipline and Punishment in Global Politics*.

18 Vanessa Farr and Kiflemariam Gebre-Wold (eds), *Gender Perspectives on Small Arms and Light Weapons: Regional and International Concerns* (Bonn International Center for Conversion, 2002), p. 19, available at www.iansa-women.org/node/71.

19 See William Reno, *Corruption and State Politics in Sierra Leone* (New York: Cambridge University Press, 1995); William Reno, *Warlord Politics and African States* (Boulder, CO: Lynne Rienner Publishers, 1998).

20 B. M. Koroma, "Food Insecurity in Sierra Leone: Overcoming the Challenges in Post-Conflict Reconstruction," *Regional Development Dialogue*, 23(2) (2003): 157–76.

21 See Slim, *Killing Civilians*, pp. 244–5.

22 For a further exploration of his argument about the "unwars," see "Jeffrey Gettleman, Reporting from Mogadishu," *Fresh Air on National Public Radio (NPR)*, July 1, 2010, available at www.npr. org/templates/story/story.php?storyId=128222247&ft=1&f=100 1&utm_source=twitterfeed&utm_medium=twitter, accessed on July 1, 2010.

23 UNHCR, *2009 Global Trends*, pp. 6–9.

24 Catharine A. Mackinnon, "Crimes of War, Crimes of Peace," in Stephen Shute and Susan Hurley (eds), *On Human Rights: The Oxford Amnesty Lectures 1993* (New York: BasicBooks, 1993), p. 90.

25 Sandra Ka Hon Chu and Anne-Marie de Brouwer, "Rwanda Genocide Victims Speak Out," *Herizons* (Winter 2009), available at www.herizons.ca/node/334.

26 See United Nations, Report on the Situation of Human Rights in Rwanda submitted by Mr René Degni-Ségui, Special Rapporteur of the Commission on Human Rights, under paragraph 20 of resolution S-3/1 of May 25,1994, (E/CN.4/1996/68); Anne-Marie de Brouwer, *Supranational Criminal Prosecution of Sexual Violence: The ICC and the Practice of the ICTY (International Criminal Tribunal for the former Yugoslavia) and ICTR (International Criminal Tribunal for Rwanda)* (Antwerp: Intersentia, 2005), p. 11.

27 Ka Hon Chu and de Brouwer, "Rwanda Genocide Victims Speak Out."

28 Laura Sjoberg and Carone E. Gentry, *Mothers, Monsters, Whores: Women's Violence in Global Politics* (New York: Zed Books, 2007).

29 De Brouwer, *Supranational Criminal Prosecution of Sexual Violence: The ICC and the Practice of the ICTY and the ICTR*, p. 13.

30 Jacqueline Novogratz, *The Blue Sweater: Bridging the Gap between Rich and Poor in an Interconnected World* (New York: Rodale Books, 2009), p. 161.

31 Also accused in the genocidal killing in Butare is Pauline Nyiramasuhuko, the former Rwandan Minister for Family and Women Affairs (the only woman indicted by the UN tribunal for genocide and first woman ever to be tried for genocide) – along with her son.

32 Novogratz, *The Blue Sweater*, p. 168.

33 Novogratz, *The Blue Sweater*, see especially pp. 161–8.

34 See Sjoberg and Gentry, *Mothers, Monsters, Whores*, pp. 151–5.

35 See Seymour M. Hersh, "Torture at Abu Ghraib: American Soldiers Brutalized Iraqis. How Far up Does the Responsibility Go?" *The New Yorker* (May 10, 2004), available at www.newyorker.com/archive/2004/05/10/040510fa_fact, accessed on July 16, 2010.

36 Roland Littlewood, "Military Rape," *Anthropology Today* 13(2) (April 1997): 9.

37 See Adam Jones's writing on gendercide in *Gender Inclusive: Essays on Violence, Men, and Feminist International Relations* (New York: Routledge, 2008).

38 Ka Hon Chu and de Brouwer, "Rwanda Genocide Victims Speak Out."

39 Human Rights Watch, "We'll Kill You If You Cry: Sexual Violence in the Sierra Leone Conflict," *Sierra Leone* 15(1) (A) (January 2003): 22.

40 See UNFPA (United Nations Population Fund), Fact Sheet, "Traumatic Fistula," 13 November 2006, available at www.unfpa.org/16days/documents/pl_traumaticfistula.doc, accessed on September 3, 2009.

41 Littlewood, "Military Rape": 10.

42 Jeanne Ward and Mendy Marsh, "Sexual Violence against Women and Girls in War and Its Aftermath: Realities, Responses, and Required Resources," Briefing Paper, *United Nations Population Fund* (2006), p. 4.

43 Kelly Askin, *War Crimes against Women: Prosecution in*

International War Crimes Tribunals, 1st edn (The Netherlands: Martinus Nijhoff Publishers, 1997), p. 271.

44 IRIN, "Afghanistan: 'Differentiate Rape from Adultery' – Rights Groups," September 3, 2009, available at www.irinnews.org/ Report.aspx?ReportId=85978, accessed on September 3, 2009.

45 R. Charli Carpenter, *Born of War: Protecting Children of Sexual Violence Survivors in Conflict Zones* (Bloomfield, CN: Kumarian Press, 2007), p. 5.

46 Carpenter, *Born of War*, p. 5.

47 Betsy Pisik, "Congo: Men Told Not to Shun Raped Women," *The Washington Times*, September 9, 2009, available at www. washingtontimes.com/news/2009/sep/09/congo-men-told-not-to-shun-raped-women/#

48 Vanessa Farr and Kiflemariam Gebre-Wold (eds), *Gender Perspectives on Small Arms and Light Weapons: Regional and International Concerns* (Bonn International Center for Conversion, 2002), p. 19, available at www.iansa-women.org/ node/71, accessed on September 30, 2010.

49 Human Rights Watch, "We'll Kill You If You Cry."

50 Joanna de Berry, "The Sexual Vulnerability of Adolescent Girls during Civil War in Teso, Uganda," in Jo Boyden and Joanna de Berry (eds), *Children and Youth on the Front Lines: Ethnography, Armed Conflict, and Displacement* (New York: Berghahn Books, 2004), p. 47.

51 Iris Chang, *The Rape of Nanking* (New York: BasicBooks, 1997), p. 49.

52 Betsy Pisik, "Congo: Men Told Not to Shun Raped Women," *The Washington Times*.

53 Barbara Myerhoff, *Number Our Days: Culture and Community Among Elderly Jews in an American Ghetto* (New York: Simon and Schuster, 1978); Richard B. Lee, *The Dobe Ju/'hoansi (Case Studies in Cultural Anthropology)*, 2nd edn (New York: Harcourt, 1993); and Lawrence Cohen, *No Aging in India: Alzheimer's, The Bad Family, and Other Modern Things* (Berkeley: University of California Press, 1998).

54 Jean Ward, *Broken Bodies – Broken Dreams: Violence against Women Exposed* (United Nations Office for the Coordination of Humanitarian Affairs (OCHA) and the Integrated Regional Information Networks (IRIN), 2005), p. 165.

55 Chang, *The Rape of Nanking*, p. 119.

56 Bjørnlund, "A Fate Worse than Dying," pp. 16–58.
57 Sjoberg and Gentry, *Mothers, Monsters, Whores*, p. 195.
58 Bjørnlund, "A Fate Worse than Dying," p. 23.
59 Robert Sommer, "Forced Sex Labour in Nazi Concentration Camps," in Dagmar Herzog (ed.), *Brutality and Desire: War and Sexuality in Europe's Twentieth Century* (Palgrave Macmillan, 2009), pp. 168–73.
60 Na'ama Shik, "Sexual Abuse of Jewish Women in Auschwitz-Birkenau," in Dagmar Herzog (ed.), *Brutality and Desire: War and Sexuality in Europe's Twentieth Century* (Palgrave Macmillan, 2009), pp. 221–46.
61 Kamala Sarupk with Lys Anzia, "Lost Daughters – An Ongoing Tragedy in Nepal," *Women News Network-WNN*, December 5, 2008, available at http://womennewsnetwork.net/2008/12/05/lostdaughternepal808/, accessed on January 21, 2010.
62 Huma Ghosh-Ahmed, "Afghan Women: Stranded at the Intersection of Local and Global Masculinities." Paper presented at the annual meeting of the International Studies Association, Town & Country Resort and Convention Center, San Diego, California (March 22, 2006), p. 9.
63 Ghosh-Ahmed, "Afghan Women: Stranded at the Intersection of Local and Global Patriarchies," p. 12.
64 Vera Achvarina and Simon Reich, "No Place to Hide: Refugees, Displaced Persons, and the Recruitment of Child Soldiers," *International Security* 31(1) (2006): 127–64; Barbara Harrell-Bond, "Can Humanitarian Work with Refugees Be Humane?" *Human Rights Quarterly* 24 (2002): 51–85.
65 The LRA was founded in 1986 by Alice Lakwena as an Acholi resistance movement against the Uganda government forces of President Yoweri Museveni, and later taken over by Joseph Kony. Alice Lakwena claimed to be inspired by the Holy Spirit of God to create a messianic movement to liberate the world from sin and bloodshed, and professed to be a spirit and medium. See Telegraph.co.uk, "Alice Lakwena," January 20, 2007, available at www.telegraph.co.uk/news/obituaries/1539967/Alice-Lakwena.html, accessed on January 21, 2010.
66 See Najibullah Quraishi, *The Dancing Boys of Afghanistan* (Frontline Documentary Film, Public Broadcasting Service, April 2010, available at www.pbs.org/wgbh/pages/frontline/dancingboys/view/).

67 Achvarina and Reich, "No Place to Hide": 128.
68 See Coalition to Stop the Use of Child Soldiers, *Child Soldiers: Global Report 2008*, February 10, 2008, available at www. childsoldiersglobalreport.org/
69 Coalition to Stop the Use of Child Soldiers, *Child Soldiers: Global Report 2008*, p. 9.
70 Coalition to Stop the Use of Child Soldiers, *Child Soldiers: Global Report 2008*, p. 3.
71 Abigail Leibig, "Girl Child Soldier in Northern Uganda: Do Current Legal Frameworks Offer Sufficient Protection?" *Northwestern University Journal of International Human Rights* 3 (2005), available at www.law.northwestern.edu/journals/jihr/v3/6.
72 For the full text, see "The 1998 Statute of Rome," available at www.icc-cpi.int/Menus/ICC/Legal+Texts+and+Tools/.
73 H. Patricia Hynes, "On the Battlefield of Women's Bodies: An Overview of the Harm of War to Women," *Women's Studies International Forum* 27 (2004): 436.
74 As told by a witness to René Lemarchand in his book, *The Dynamics of Violence in Central Africa* (Philadelphia: University of Pennsylvania Press, 2009), p. 86.
75 Lemarchand, *The Dynamics of Violence in Central Africa*, p. 90.
76 Peter J. Hoffman and Thomas G. Weiss, *Sword and Salve: Confronting New War and Humanitarian Crises* (*New Millennium Books in International Studies*) (New York: Rowman & Littlefield Publishers, 2006), p. 91.
77 Hoffman and Weiss, *Sword and Salve*, p. 91.
78 Gendercide.org, "Case Study: The Srebrenica Massacre, July 1995," available at www.gendercide.org/case_srebrenica.html, accessed on October 23, 2009.
79 Janie Leatherman and Nadia Negrustueva, "Militarized Masculinity and Runway Norms: 1325 and the Challenge of Overcoming Extreme Violence." Paper delivered at the International Studies Association Annual Convention Honolulu, Hawaii, March 1–5, 2005. These points are drawn from Nadia Negrustueva's fieldwork in Sierra Leone in the spring of 2005.
80 Katherine Haver, "Duty of Care? Local Staff and Aid Worker Security," *Forced Migration Review* (2007): 10.
81 Humanitarian Policy Group, "Providing Aid in Insecure Environments: 2009 Update," HPG *Policy Brief 34*, April 2009, available at www.policypointers.org/Page/View/9132.

82 Julian Ponthus, "Rwandan Convicted of Killing Belgium Peacekeepers," *Reuters*, July 4, 2007, available at www.reuters. com/article/latestCrisis/idUSL04699005; Samantha Powers, "Bystanders to Genocide," *The Atlantic Monthly*, September 2001, available at www.theatlantic.com/doc/200109/power-genocide.

83 See IRIN, "In Brief: Darfur Aid Worker and Peacekeeper Security – 16 Statistics," September 10, 2009, available at http://ocha-gwapps1.unog.ch/rw/rwb.nsf/db900SID/MUMA-7VS3ZA?OpenDocument&Click=, accessed on September 10, 2009.

CHAPTER 3 SEXUAL VIOLENCE AND THE ONSET OF ARMED CONFLICT

1 Even in highly developed countries, fewer women than men are home-owners, and as recently as the 1970s, laws discriminating against women were still in place that prevented access to mortgages, credit, and loans. In the United States, only 9 percent of the agricultural landowners are women. Across Western Europe, the percentage of women owning agricultural land ranges from 9 percent in Norway to as high as 26 percent in Italy; Joni Seager, *Penguin Atlas of Women in the World*, 4th edn (New York: Penguin, 2008), pp. 86–8.

2 See United Nations Security Council, *Report of the Secretary General on Women, Peace and Security*, S/2002/1154, October 16, 2002; LaShawn R. Jefferson, "In War as in Peace: Sexual Violence and Women's Status," *Human Rights Watch World Report* (2004), available at http://hrw.org/wr2k4/15.htmhttp://hrw.org/wr2k4/15.htm.

3 Johan Galtung, "Violence, Peace and Peace Research," *Journal of Peace Research* 6(3) (1969): 171.

4 Johan Galtung, "Cultural Violence," *Journal of Peace Research* 27(3) (1990): 291–305.

5 See a systematic feminist critique of Galtung's work in Catia Confortini, "Galtung, Violence and Gender: The Case for a Peace Studies/Feminism Alliance." Paper presented at the 45th International Studies Annual Convention, Montreal, Quebec, March 17–20, 2004.

6 V. Spike Peterson and Anne Sisson Runyan, *Global Gender Issues in the New Millennium*, 3rd edn (Boulder, CO: Westview Press, 2010), p. 4.
7 Laura Sjoberg and Caron E. Gentry, *Mothers, Monsters, Whores: Women's Violence in Global Politics* (New York: Zed Books, 2007).
8 Confortini, "Galtung, Violence and Gender."
9 See Amy Allen, "Foucault on Power: A Theory for Feminists," in Susan J. Hekman (ed.), *Feminist Interpretations of Michel Foucault* (University Park: Pennsylvania University Press, 1996), pp. 265–82.
10 See Peterson and Runyan, *Global Gender Issues in the New Millennium*, p. 63.
11 Peterson and Runyan, *Global Gender Issues in the New Millennium*, p. 63.
12 Ricardo Hausmann, Laura D. Tyson and Saadia Zahidi, *The 2008 Global Gender Gap Report* (Geneva: World Economic Forum, 2008), p. 3.
13 Hausmann, Tyson and Zahidi, *The 2008 Global Gender Gap Report*, 22.
14 Erik Melander, "Gender Equality and Intrastate Armed Conflict," *International Studies Quarterly* 49(4) (2005): 695.
15 Jennifer Green, "Uncovering Collective Rape: A Comparative Study of Political Sexual Violence," *International Journal of Sociology* 34(1) (2004): 97–116.
16 World Bank, "Overview: Understanding, Measuring and Overcoming Poverty," available at http://go.worldbank.org/RQBDCTUXW0, accessed on November 4, 2009.
17 Seager, *The Penguin Atlas of Women in the World*, pp. 88–9.
18 Seager, *The Penguin Atlas of Women in the World*, pp. 76, 87.
19 Social Institutions and Gender Index, "Gender Equality and Social Institutions in Mozambique," November 4, 2009, available at http://genderindex.org/country/mozambique.
20 Klaus von Grebmer et al., *2009 Global Hunger Index. The Challenge of Hunger: Focus on Financial Crisis and Gender Inequality* (International Food Policy Research Institute, October 2009), p. 3.
21 Human Rights Watch, "Regional Overview of Women's Rights in Asia" (2006): 2, available at www.hrw.org/women/overview-asia, accessed on September 9, 2009.
22 Von Grebmer et al., *2009 Global Hunger Index*, p. 23.

23 Marie Vlachová and Lea Biason, *Women in an Insecure World: Violence against Women Facts, Figures and Analysis* (Geneva: Geneva Centre for the Democratic Control of Armed Forces, 2005), pp. 1–2, available at www.fmreview.org/.

24 "HIV in South Africa 'Levels Off,'" *BBC News*, June 9, 2009, available at http://news.bbc.co.uk/2/hi/africa/8091489.stm, accessed on July 3, 2010.

25 "South African rape survey shock," *BBC News*, June 18, 2009, available at http://news.bbc.co.uk/2/hi/8107039.stm, accessed on July 3, 2010.

26 Vlachová and Biason, *Women in an Insecure World*, p. 8.

27 WHO, *World Report on Violence and Health*, pp. 152–8; see also Nicholas D. Kristof and Sheryl WuDunn, *Half the Sky: Turning Oppression into Opportunity for Women Worldwide* (New York: Random House, 2009).

28 WHO, *World Report on Violence and Health*, pp. 149–50.

29 Human Rights Watch, "We'll Kill You If You Cry: Sexual Violence in the Sierra Leone Conflict," *Sierra Leone* 15(1) (A) (January 2003).

30 Physicians for Human Rights (with the support of UNSAMSIL (United Nations Mission in Sierra Leone)), *War-Related Sexual Violence in Sierra Leone: a population-based assessment* (November 4, 2009), available at http://physiciansforhumanrights.org/library/documents/reports/sexual-violence-sierra-leone.pdf.

31 Jeanne Ward, *If Not Now, When? Addressing Gender-based Violence in Refugee, Internally Displaced, and Post-Conflict Settings. A Global Overview* (Reproductive Health for Refugees Consortium (April 2002).

32 Ward, *Broken Bodies – Broken Dreams*, p. 74.

33 Mary Okumu, "The Critical Issues: Gender Based Violence in Africa," *Sexuality in Africa Magazine* 1(3) (2004): 8.

34 Amnesty International, "Nepal: Government Fails to Protect Women Human Rights Activists from Violent Attacks," press release, April 10, 2009, available at www.amnestyusa.org/document.php?id=ENGPRE20090410114&lang=e, accessed on June 30, 2010.

35 Irene Pietropaoli, "Sexual Violence Against Women in Nepal: Report on Rape Cases in 2007," available at www.childtrafficking.com/Docs/insec_sexual_violence_0109.pdf, accessed on June 10, 2008.

36 Human Rights Watch, *Sexual Violence and its Consequences among Displaced Persons in Darfur and Chad*. A Briefing Paper, 12 April 2005, available at www.hrw.org/legacy/backgrounder/africa/darfur0505/.

37 Human Rights Watch, "Regional Overview of Women's Rights in Asia," p. 4.

38 Ward, *Broken Bodies – Broken Dreams*, p. 135.

39 Ward, *Broken Bodies – Broken Dreams*, p. 135.

40 Human Rights Watch, "Regional Overview of Women's Rights in Asia."

41 Mukhtar Mai, with Marie-Thérèse Cuny, *In the Name of Honor*, trans. Linda Coverdale (New York: Washington Square Press, 2006).

42 Ward, *Broken Bodies – Broken Dreams*, p. 136.

43 See Nicholas D. Kristof, "Kristof: The Courage of Mukhtar Mai," videoclip, *The New York Times*, available at http://video.nytimes.com/video/2006/03/31/opinion/1194817113867/kristof-the-courage-of-mukhtar-mai.html, accessed on January 30, 2010.

44 Human Rights Watch, "Regional Overview of Women's Rights in Asia," p. 5.

45 Ghosh-Ahmed, "Afghan Women: Stranded at the Intersection of Local and Global Masculinities." Paper presented at the annual meeting of the International Studies Association, Town & Country Resort and Convention Center, San Diego, California (March 22, 2006), pp. 2–4; Krista Hunt, "Disciplining Women, Disciplining Women's Rights," in Janie Leatherman (ed.), *Discipline and Punishment in Global Politics: Illusions of Control* (New York: Palgrave Macmillan, 2008), pp. 41–64.

46 For example, see Nikki Van der Gaag, principal writer, *Because I Am a Girl: The State of the World's Girls 2008*: Special Focus – In the Shadow of War. Report by Plan UK. Plan is a leading children's NGO – Plan UK prepared the report referenced in note 199. The report was printed by Amadeus in Italy. See Plan at http:/plan-international.org/about.plan). See also Amnesty International, *Lives Blown Apart: Crimes against Women in Times of Conflict: Stop Violence Against Women* (Oxford: Alden Press, 2004).

47 Inger Skjelsbaek, "The Changing Politics of Gender: A Social Constructionist Approach to Bosnia Herzegovina." Paper presented at the 48th Annual Convention of the International

Studies Association, Hilton Chicago (Chicago, February 28, 2007), pp. 19–20, available at www.allacademic.com/meta/p181230_index.html, accessed on June 8, 2010.

48 Ismael Beah, *A Long Way Gone: Memoirs of a Boy Soldier* (New York: Farrar, Straus and Giroux, 2007), p. 121.

49 Amnesty International, *Lives Blown Apart*, see ch. 2.

50 Skjelbaek, "The Changing Politics of Gender," p. 18, italics in original.

51 See Jones, *Gender Inclusive: Essays on Violence, Men, and Feminist International Relations* (New York: Routledge, 2008), especially ch. 15, "Genocide and Humanitarian Intervention: Incorporating the Gender Variable."

52 Jones, *Gender Inclusive*, pp. 172–3.

53 See de Brouwer, *Supranational Criminal Prosecution of Sexual Violence: The ICC and the Practice of the ICTY (International Criminal Tribunal for the former Yugoslavia) and ICTR (International Criminal Tribunal for Rwanda)* (Intersentia, 2005).

54 Slavenka Drakulic, *The Balkan Express: Fragments from the Other Side of the War* (New York: W. W. Norton, 1993), p. 15.

55 Jennifer Rawlings, "One Women's Experience of War," March 26, 2007, referring to women she interviewed in postwar Bosnia. Available at www.youtube.com/watch?v=j11UoomJwyg

56 Author's field notes. Interview with Slobodan Milosevic. South Balkans Working Group (New York Council on Foreign Relations), Presidential Palace, Belgrade, Yugoslavia, November 1995.

57 Genocide in Rwanda, "The 'Hutu Ten Commandments'" as published in *Kangura*, no. 6 (December 1990), available at www.trumanwebdesign.com/~catalina/commandments.htm

58 Llezlie L. Green, "Gender Hate Propaganda and Sexual Violence in the Rwandan Genocide: An Argument for Intersectionality in International Law," *Columbia Human Rights Law Review* 33(3) (Summer 2002): 733.

59 Julie Mertus, *War's Offensive on Women: the Humanitarian Challenge in Bosnia, Kosovo and Afghanistan* (Bloomfield, CN: Kumarian Press, 2000), p. 42.

60 Mertus, *War's Offensive on Women*, pp. 12–13.

61 Mirjana Morokvasic-Müller, "From Pillars of Yugoslavism to Targets of Violence: Interethnic Marriages in the Former Yugoslavia and Thereafter," in Winona Giles and Jennifer

Hyndman (eds), *Sites of Violence* (Berkeley: University of California Press, 2004), pp. 134–51.

62 Mertus, *War's Offensive on Women*, p. 22.

63 Dyan Mazurana, Angela Raven-Roberts and Jane Parpart, with Sue Lautze, "Introduction: Gender, Conflict, and Peacekeeping," in Dyan Mazurana, Angela Raven-Roberts, and Jane Parpart (eds), *Conflict and Peacekeeping* (Lanham, MD: Rowman and Littlefield, 2005), p. 6

64 Mertus, *War's Offensive on Women*, p. 23.

65 Mazurana, Raven-Roberts and Parpart, with Lautze, "Gender, Conflict and Peacekeeping," p. 7; Carolyn Nordstrom, *Shadows of War: Violence, Power and International Profiteering in the Twenty-First Century* (Berkeley: University of California Press, 2004).

66 Mazurana, Raven-Roberts and Parpart with Lautze, "Gender, Conflict and Peacekeeping," pp. 8–9.

CHAPTER 4 SEEKING SAFE SPACE

1 Krisjon Rae Olson, "Children in the Grey Spaces Between War and Peace," in Jo Boyden and Joanna de Berry, *Children and Youth on the Front Line* (New York: Berghahn Books, 2007, reprinted), p. 154.

2 Yasmin Tambiah, "Sexuality and Women's Rights in Armed Conflict in Sri Lanka," *Reproductive Health Matters* 12(23) (2004): 80.

3 Mary H. Cooper, "Women and Human Rights," *Congressional Quarterly Researcher* 9(16) (April 30, 1999): 358.

4 Watch List on Children and Armed Conflict, "Caught in the Middle: Mounting Violations Against Children in Nepal's Armed Conflict," (January 2005), pp. 5–6, available at watchlist.org/reports/pdf/nepal.report.20050120.pdf, accessed on February 21, 2010.

5 IRIN, "Between Two Stones: Nepal's Decade of Conflict: IRIN Web Special," December 2005, available at www.irinnews.org/IndepthMain.aspx?IndepthId=11&ReportId=33611, accessed on February 21, 2010.

6 Mats Utas, "Victimacy, Girlfriending, Soldiering: Tactic Agency in a Young Woman's Social Navigation of the Liberian War Zone," *Anthropological Quarterly* 78(2) (Spring 2005): p. 408.

7 Jeremy Ginifer, "Armed Violence and Poverty in Sierra Leone: A Case Study for the Armed Violence and Poverty Initiative," Centre for International Cooperation and Security, Bradford University, March 2005, p. 24, available at www. googlesyndicatedsearch.com/u/SmallArmsSurvey?q=Armed+co nflict+and+poverty+in+Sierra+Leone&sa=go%C2%Ao, accessed on June 15, 2010.

8 Ishmael Beah, A Long Way Gone: Memoirs of a Boy Soldier (New York: Farrar, Straus and Giroux, 2007), p. 106.

9 Beah, A Long Way Gone, pp. 107–8.

10 All in the Mind, "In the Mind of the Child Soldier." Transcript of American Broadcasting Company Radio National interviews conducted by program host Natasha Mitchell with Michael Wessells and others. August 12, 2006, available at www.abc.net. au/rn/allinthemind/stories/2007/1812727.htm.

11 Coalition to Stop the Use of Child Soldiers, Child Soldiers: Global Report 2008, 9; See also Michaela Ludwig, Former Child Soldiers as Refugees in Germany (Geneva: Quaker United Nations Office), p. 5.

12 Utas, "Victimacy, Girlfriending, Soldiering."

13 Utas, "Victimacy, Girlfriending, Soldiering."

14 Deutsche Gesellschaft für Technische Zusammenarbeit (GTZ), Masculinity and Civil Wars in Africa – New Approaches to Overcoming Sexual Violence in War, Programme Promoting Gender Equality and Women's Rights (January 2009): 3, available at www.gtz.de/search/search.

15 Human Rights Watch, Soldiers Who Rape, Commanders Who Condone (2009): 29.

16 Pole Institute, "An Open Wound: Gender-based Violence in North Kivu," Regards Croises 11 (August 2004): 59, available at www.pole-institute.org/.

17 Mats Utas and Magnus Jörgel, "The West Side Boys: Military Navigation in the Sierra Leone Civil War," Journal of Modern African Studies 46(3) (2008): 487–511.

18 Utas and Jörgel, "The West Side Boys: Military Navigation in the Sierra Leone Civil War": 497–8.

19 Utas and Jörgel, "The West Side Boys: Military Navigation in the Sierra Leone Civil War": 497–9 and 505.

20 Ginifer, "Armed Violence and Poverty in Sierra Leone," p. 24.

21 GTZ, Masculinity and Civil Wars in Africa: 4.

22 Utas, "Victimacy, Girlfriending, Soldiering," p. 405.

23 United Nations Office on Drugs and Crime, "United Nations
    Convention against Transnational Organized Crime and its
    Protocols," March 1, 2010, available at www.unodc.org/unodc/
    en/treaties/CTOC/index.html.
24 Human Rights Watch, "We'll Kill You If You Cry: Sexual
    Violence in the Sierra Leone Conflict," *Sierra Leone* 15(1) (A)
    (January 2003): 19.
25 Amnesty International and Human Rights Watch,
    "'No One to Help Them': Rape Extends from Darfur
    into Eastern Chad," Sudan/CHAD AI Index: AFR
    54/087/2006, available at www.amnestyusa.org/document.
    php?id=ENGAFR540872006&lang=e, accessed on September
    30, 2010.
26 Ginifer, "Armed Violence and Poverty in Sierra Leone," p. 24.
27 Human Rights Watch, "We'll Kill You If You Cry": 9.
28 Amnesty International, "Darfur Camps Flooded with Weapons,"
    January 22, 2008, available at www.amnesty.org/en/news-and-
    updates/report/darfur-camps-flooded-weapons-20080122.
29 Amnesty International, "Darfur Camps Flooded with Weapons."
30 Human Rights Watch, "We'll Kill You If You Cry": 6.
31 Vera Achvarina and Simon Reich, "No Place to Hide: Refugees,
    Displaced Persons, and the Recruitment of Child Soldiers,"
    International Security 31(1) (2006): 140.
32 IRIN, "Bangladesh: Mohammad Ismail, 'Nobody Wants Us,'"
    January 28, 2009, available at www.irinnews.org/HOVReport.
    aspx?ReportId=82606.
33 Carinna Csáky, *No One to Turn To: The Underreporting of Child
    Sexual Exploitation and Abuse by Aid Workers and Peacekeepers*
    (Save the Children, United Kingdom, 2008), p. 5. Available at
    www.savethechildren.org.uk/en/54_5706.htm.
34 Dr Dennis Bright, "Sierra Leone, the Conflict and the World."
    Speech given by Dr Dennis Bright at the Conflict, Development
    and Peace Network Conference, June 18–20, 2001, London.
    Available at www.c-r.org/resources/occasional-papers/sierra-
    leone-conflict-world.php.
35 Bright, "Sierra-Leone, the Conflict and the World."
36 GTZ, *Masculinity and Civil Wars in Africa*: 5.
37 Lori Handrahan, "Conflict, Gender, Ethnicity and Post-conflict
    Reconstruction," *Security Dialogue* 35(4) (2004): 434.
38 Csáky, *No One to Turn To*, p. 6.

39 Csáky, *No One to Turn To*, p. 6.
40 Handrahan, "Conflict, Gender, Ethnicity and Post-conflict Reconstruction": 436; and C. Corrin, "Post-conflict Reconstruction and Gender Analysis in Kosova," *International Feminist Journal of Politics*, 3(1) (2000): 78–98.
41 Scott A. Levin, "Sexual Exploitation of Refugee Children by UN Peacekeepers," *New York Law School Journal of Human Rights* 19 (Summer 2003).
42 Handrahan, "Conflict, Gender, Ethnicity and Post-conflict Reconstruction": 436; and Corrin, "Post-conflict Reconstruction and Gender Analysis in Kosova": 78–98.
43 Corrin, "Post-conflict Reconstruction and Gender Analysis in Kosova": 84.
44 Csáky, *No One to Turn To*, p. 16.
45 Immigration and Refugee Board of Canada, "Nigeria: Levirate Marriage Practices among the Yoruba, Igbo and Hausa-Fulani; Consequences for a Man or Woman who Refuses to Participate in the Marriage" (March 16, 2006), available at *Refworld* at www.unhcr.org/refworld/topic,463af2212,469f2db72,45f1478811,0.html
46 Dyan Mazurana and Kristopher Carlson, "From Combat to Community: Women and Girls of Sierra Leone," Women Waging Peace: Hunt Alternatives Fund (January 2004). Available at smallarmssurvey.org/.
47 Carolyn Nordstrom, *Shadows of War: Violence, Power and International Profiteering in the Twenty-First Century* (Berkeley: University of California Press, 2004), p. 192; and M. Ross, "Oil, Drugs, and Diamonds: The Varying Roles of Natural Resources in Civil War," in Karen Ballentine and Jake Sherman, *The Political Economy of Armed Conflict: Beyond Greed and Grievance* (Boulder: Lynne Rienner, 2003).
48 Tambiah, "Sexuality and Women's Rights in Armed Conflict in Sri Lanka": 78–87.
49 Watch List on Children and Armed Conflict, *Caught in the Middle: Mounting Violations Against Children in Nepal's Armed Conflict* (January 2005), p. 6. Available at www.watchlist.org/reports/pdf/nepal.report.20050120.pdf.
50 Louise Shelley, "Human Security and Human Trafficking," in Anna Jonsson (ed.), *Human Trafficking and Human Security*, (New York: Routledge, 2009), p. 16.

51 Watch List on Children and Armed Conflict, *Caught in the Middle*, p. 31.
52 See US Department of State, "Sierra Leone," Bureau of Democracy, Human Rights, and Labor, February 28, 2005, available at www.state.gov/g/drl/rls/hrrpt/2004/41625.htm.
53 US Department of State, "Sierra Leone."
54 US Department of State, "Sierra Leone."
55 Nicole Lindstrom, "Regional Sex Trafficking Networks and International Intervention in the Balkans." Paper presented at the annual meeting of the International Studies Association, Le Centre Sheraton Hotel, Montreal, Quebec, Canada, March 17, 2004, available at www.allacademic.com/meta/p73476_index. html. Daan Everts, "Human Trafficking: The Ruthless Trade in Human Misery," *Brown Journal of World Affairs* 10(1) (2003): 149–58.
56 Teresa Iacobelli, "The 'Sum of Such Actions': Investigating Mass Rape in Bosnia-Herzegovina through a Case Study of Foca," in Dagmar Herzog (ed.), *Brutality and Desire: War and Sexuality in Europe's Twentieth Century* (New York: Palgrave Macmillan, 2009), p. 266.
57 Iacobelli, "The 'Sum of Such Actions,'" p. 267.
58 Iacobelli, "The 'Sum of Such Actions,'" pp. 267–8.
59 Dejan Anastasijevic, "Organized Crime in the Western Balkans," Occasional Paper 24, European Training and Research Center for Human Rights and Democracy (October 2009), p. 2. Available at www.etc-graz.at/typo3/index.php?id=74.
60 Human Rights Watch, "Trafficking of Women and Girls to Bosnia and Herzegovina for Forced Prostitution," 2002, available at www.crin.org/docs/resources/treaties/crc.39/ Bosnia_HRW_ngo_report.pdf, accessed on September 30, 2009.
61 Human Rights Watch, "Trafficking of Women and Girls to Bosnia and Herzegovina for Forced Prostitution," p. 2.
62 Human Rights Watch, "Trafficking of Women and Girls to Bosnia and Herzegovina for Forced Prostitution," p. 3.
63 Although a law passed in 2000 gives the US government jurisdiction over these types of cases, no action was taken. In October 2002, US personnel involved in the United Nations International Police Task Force (IPTF) in Bosnia who also committed trafficking abuses enjoyed protection under then

applicable US law from prosecution for criminal offenses while part of a UN mission. See Human Rights Watch, "Trafficking of Women and Girls to Bosnia and Herzegovina for Forced Prostitution," p. 2.

64 Manuela Colombini, "Gender-based and Sexual Violence against Women during Armed Conflict," *Journal of Health Management* 4(2) (October 2002): 171.

65 GTZ, *Masculinity and Civil Wars in Africa*: 4.

CHAPTER 5 SEXUAL VIOLENCE AND THE GLOBAL POLITICAL ECONOMY OF WAR

1 See Human Rights Watch, *The Curse of Gold*, available at www.hrw.org/en/reports/2005/06/01/curse-gold, June 1, 2005.

2 Johann Hari, "Congo's Tragedy: The War the World Forgot," *The Independent*, May 5, 2006, available at www.independent.co.uk/news/world/africa/congos-tragedy-the-war-the-world-forgot-476929.html, accessed on January 23, 2010.

3 Human Rights Watch 2009, *You Will be Punished: Attacks on Civilians in Eastern Congo* (December 13, 2009), p. 6, available at www.hrw.org/node/87151, accessed on March 10, 2010.

4 Congolese Women's Campaign Against Sexual Violence in the DRC, available at www.drcsexualviolence.org/site/en/node/37, accessed on July 9, 2010.

5 Harvard Humanitarian Initiative, with support from Oxfam International, *"Now the World is Without Me": An Investigation of Sexual Violence in Eastern Democratic Republic of Congo* (April 2010), available at www.oxfam.org.uk/resources/policy/conflict_disasters/sexual-violence-drc.html.

6 See United Nations Human Rights Council, *Technical Assistance and Capacity Building, Second Joint Report of Seven United Nations Experts on the Situation in the Democratic Republic of the Congo*, A/HRC/13/63 (March 8, 2010), p. 10.

7 See Congolese Women's Campaign Against Sexual Violence in the DRC, available at www.drcsexualviolence.org/site/en/node/37.

8 *The Greatest Silence: Rape in the Congo*, Lisa F. Jackson, film producer and director (Jackson Films Inc., 2007).

9 "DRC: Rape Crisis Set to Worsen Amid Kivu Chaos," IRIN

(November 19, 2008), available at www.irinnews.org/Report. aspx?ReportId=81549, accessed on July 14, 2010.

10 See Congolese Women's Campaign Against Sexual Violence in the DRC, available at www.drcsexualviolence.org/site/en/ node/37.

11 Human Rights Watch, *You Will be Punished*, p. 10.

12 Johann Hari, "Congo's Tragedy: The War the World Forgot," *The Independent*, May 5, 2006, available at www.independent. co.uk/news/world/africa/congos-tragedy-the-war-the-world-forgot-476929.html, accessed on January 23, 2010.

13 See Mareike Schomerus, "The Lord's Resistance Army in Sudan: A History and Overview. Small Arms Survey" (Graduate Institute of International Studies, Geneva: September 2007), available at www.smallarmssurveysudan.org, accessed on July 14, 2010.

14 Gwalgen Geordie Dent, "Canada in the Congo War," *The Dominion*, May 14, 2007, available at www.dominionpaper.ca/ articles/1177, accessed on July 16, 2010.

15 "List of Armed Groups in the Kivus," Congo Siasa (Blog), June 9, 2010, personal correspondence to author by email from Nadia Griffin, June 16, 2010.

16 Thijs Bouwknegt, "Laurent Nkunda's Fate still Unclear," *Radio Netherlands Worldwide*, January 19, 2010 available at www.rnw.nl/ int-justice/article/laurent-nkundas-fate-still-unclear.

17 See "Nkunda, Laurent," The Hague Justice Portal, at www. haguejusticeportal.net/eCache/DEF/11719.

18 Bouwknegt, "Laurent Nkunda's Fate still Unclear."

19 Hari, "Congo's Tragedy: The War the World Forgot."

20 *Final Report of the Group of Experts on the Democratic Republic of the Congo*. United Nations Security Council, S/2009/603, p. 24.

21 "Uganda: Rebel Commander's Defection 'A Boon' to Peace," IRIN (January 30, 2009), available at www.irinnews.org/Report. aspx?ReportId=82659, accessed on July 9, 2010.

22 *Final Report of the Group of Experts on the Democratic Republic of the Congo*, p. 60.

23 IRIN, "DRC: ICC Trial Screening Turns Sour in Bunia," January 27, 2009, available at www.irinnews.org/Report. aspx?ReportId=82586, accessed on February 5, 2009.

24 Global Witness, *Faced with a Gun, What Can You Do? War and the Militarization of Mining in Eastern Congo* (December 5, 2009), p. 24, available at www.globalwitness.org/fwag/index.html.

25 Gwalgen Geordie Dent, "Mining the Congo: Canadian Mining Companies in the DRC," *The Dominion* (Canada), May 26, 2007, available at http://saltspringnews.com/index.php?name=News&file=article&sid=19624, accessed on July 16, 2010.
26 See *Final Report of the Group of Experts on the Democratic Republic of the Congo*, p. 3; and Global Witness, *Faced with a Gun*, p. 24.
27 *Final Report of the Group of Experts on the Democratic Republic of the Congo*, p. 32.
28 *Final Report of the Group of Experts on the Democratic Republic of the Congo*, especially pp. 32–42.
29 For a fascinating up-close look into the local-to-global networks for the exploitation and trade in coltan in the Kivus, see Stephen Jackson, "Fortunes of War: the Coltan Trade in the Kivus," in Sarah Collinson (ed.), *Power, Livelihoods and Conflict: Case Studies in Political Economy Analysis for Humanitarian Action* (Overseas Development Institute/Humanitarian Policy Group Report 13, February 2003).
30 Global Witness, *Faced with a Gun*, p. 24.
31 Keith Harmon Snow, "Gertler's Bling Bang", February 8, 2008, Zmag.org, available at www.zmag.org/znet/viewArticle/16455, accessed on July 9, 2010.
32 See OSS announcement on www.spintelligent-events.com/minetech2009/en/booths/overseas-security.php.
33 Dominque Soguel, "Sexual Violence in the Congo," *womensenews.org*, June 1, 2009, available at www.womensenews.org/story/090601/rape-crisis-in-east-congo-tied-mining-activity.
34 Soguel, "Sexual Violence in the Congo."
35 R. W. Connell, "Masculinities, Change, and Conflict in Global Society: Thinking about the Future of Men's Studies," *The Journal of Men's Studies* 11(3) (Spring 2003): 3.
36 See www.barrick.com/, accessed on January 15, 2010.
37 Geordie Dent, "Mining the Congo."
38 William Reno, "Order and Commerce in Turbulent Areas: 19th Century Lessons, 21st Century Practice," *Third World Quarterly* 25 (2004): 608.
39 See especially V. Spike Peterson, *A Critical Rewriting of Global Political Economy: Integrating Reproductive, Productive and Virtual Economies* (New York: Routledge, 2006); and Cynthia Enloe, *Maneuvers: The International Politics of Militarizing Women's Lives* (Berkeley: University of California Press, 2000).

40 Anna M. Agathangelou, *The Global Political Economy of Sex: Desire, Violence, and Insecurity in Mediterranean Nation States* (New York: Palgrave Macmillan, 2004), p. 8.

41 John Ghazvinian, *Untapped: The Scramble for Africa's Oil* (New York: Harcourt, 2007).

42 However, see the growing literature on illicit economies and their relation to war in such works as Karen Ballentine and Jake Sherman, *The Political Economy of Armed Conflict: Beyond Greed and Grievance* (Boulder: Lynne Rienner, 2003); and Michael Nest, with François Grignon and Emizet F. Kisangani, *The Democratic Republic of Congo: Economic Dimensions of War and Peace* (Boulder: Lynne Rienner, 2006).

43 Carolyn Nordstrom, *Shadows of War: Violence, Power and International Profiteering in the Twenty-First Century* (Berkeley: University of California Press, 2004), p. 106, emphasis in original.

44 Nordstrom, *Shadows of War*, p. 85, emphasis in original.

45 Jackson, "Fortunes of War: the Coltan Trade in the Kivus," p. 29.

46 "UN Covered up Claims Corrupt Peacekeepers Sold Arms to Rebels in DR Congo," *Mail Online*, April 28, 2008, citing an 18-month investigation by the BBC TV news journal *Panorama*, available at www.dailymail.co.uk/news/article-562497/UN-covered-claims-corrupt-peacekeepers-sold-arms-rebels-DR-Congo.html.

47 See Global Witness, *Faced with a Gun*, especially pp. 27–33.

48 Carolyn Nordstrom, *Shadows of War*, pp. 106–8.

49 Audrey Macklin, "Like Oil and Water, with a Match: Militarized Commerce, Armed Conflict, and Human Security in Sudan," pp. 75–107 in Wenona Giles and Jennifer Hyndman (eds), *Sites of Violence: Gender and Conflict Zones* (Berkeley: University of California Press, 2004).

50 See Amy Eckert, "Outsourcing War," in Amy Eckert and Laura Sjoberg (eds), *Rethinking the 21st Century* (New York: Zed Books, 2009).

51 Achille Mbembe, *On the Postcolony* (Berkeley: University of California Press, 2001), pp. 78–9 (italics in original).

52 Mbembe, *On the Postcolony*, p. 13.

53 Joan Acker, "Gender, Capitalism and Globalization," *Critical Sociology* 30(1) (2004): 17–42.

54 See Nancy Rose Hunt, "An Acoustic Register, Tenacious

Images, and Congolese Scenes of Rape and Repetition," *Cultural Anthropology* (May 2008).

55 Jackson, "Fortunes of War," p. 36.

56 Maria Eriksson Baaz and Maria Stern, "Making Sense of Violence: Voices of Soldiers in the Congo (DRC)," *Journal of Modern African Studies* 46(1) (2008): 64–6 and 77.

57 Hugo Slim, *Killing Civilians: Method, Madness and Morality in War* (New York: Columbia University Press, 2008), p. 233.

58 Slim, *Killing Civilians*, p. 235.

59 Lisa S. Price makes this point in "Finding the Man in the Soldier-Rapist: Some Reflections on Comprehension and Accountability," *Women's Studies International Forum* 24(2) (2001): 216.

60 Price, "Finding the Man in the Soldier-Rapist": 218.

61 Price, "Finding the Man in the Soldier-Rapist": 218.

62 Rebecca Whisnant, "A Woman's Body is like a Foreign Country: Thinking about National and Bodily Sovereignty," in Rebecca Whisnant and Peggy DesAutels (eds), *Global Feminist Ethics: Feminist Ethics and Social Theory* (Lanham, MD: 2008): p. 167, quoting Jane Caputi.

63 Edward Croft Dutton, "Ritual, Taboo and Political Protest," *The Mankind Quarterly* 57(1–2) (Fall/Winter 2006): 42–3.

64 Dutton, "Ritual, Taboo and Political Protest": 43.

65 Whisnant, "A Woman's Body is Like a Foreign Country," in *Global Feminist Ethics*, pp. 176–86. See also Dutton, who, citing Douglas's work on taboo, notes "that ritual is frequently invoked as an antidote to the presence or influence of the taboo. In response to taboo, Douglas submits, 'ritual reconciles disorder.'" For example, in many cultures, puberty is understood as a time of disorder and, consequently, some type of ritual is required to confront it. Similarly, the period of engagement between a couple is outside of established order, so rituals are used to signal its end, as in wedding ceremonies, and the groom carrying the bride over the threshold of the new home. Dutton, "Ritual, Taboo, and Political Protest": 44.

66 Jackson, *The Greatest Silence*.

67 Whisnant, "A Woman's Body is Like a Foreign Country," in *Global Feminist Ethics*, p. 168.

68 Human Rights Watch, *You Will Be Punished*, see Part III. "Human Rights Abuses by FDLR and Allies."

69 Jeffrey Gettleman, "Symbol of Unhealed Congo: Male Rape Victims," *New York Times*, August 5, 2009, available at www. nytimes.com/2009/08/05/world/africa/05congo.html, accessed on September 5, 2009.

70 Gettleman, "Symbol of Unhealed Congo."

71 Mbembe, *On the Postcolony*, p. 4.

72 Whisnant, "A Woman's Body is Like a Foreign Country," in *Global Feminist Ethics*, p. 162, citing Andrea Dworkin.

73 Whisnant, "A Woman's Body is Like a Foreign Country," p. 165.

74 Paul Higate, "Peacekeepers, Masculinities, and Sexual Exploitation," *Men and Masculinities* 10(1) (2007): 107.

75 Higate, "Peacekeepers, Masculinities, and Sexual Exploitation": 108.

CHAPTER 6 FROM PROTECTION AND ACCOUNTABILITY TO AN ETHIC OF CARING

1 See the official website for the Kimberley Process at www. kimberleyprocess.com/.

2 Joan Acker, "Gender, Capitalism and Globalization," *Critical Sociology* 30(1) (2004): 29.

3 See Human Security Report Project data on state-based conflicts at www.hsrgroup.org/our-work/security-stats/State-Based-Armed-Conflicts.aspx.

4 V. Spike Peterson, *A Critical Rewriting of Global Political Economy: Integrating Reproductive, Productive and Virtual Economies*, 2nd printing (New York: Routledge, 2006), especially ch. 3, "The Productive Economy."

5 Phil Williams, "Transnational Organized Crime and the State," in Rodney Bruce Hall and Thomas J. Biersteker (eds), *The Emergence of Private Authority in Global Governance* (New York: Cambridge University Press, 2002), p. 177.

6 See Graham Knight and Jackie Smith, "The Global Compact and its Critics: Activism, Power Relations and Corporate Social Responsibility," in Janie Leatherman (ed.), *Discipline and Punishment in Global Politics: Illusions of Control* (New York: Palgrave Macmillan, 2008), pp. 191–214.

7 International Alert, *The Role of the Exploitation of Natural Resources in Fuelling and Prolonging Crises in the Eastern DRC*

(2009), p. 6, available at www.international-alert.org/pdf/ Natural_Resources_Jan_10.pdf.

8 Benedikt Korf, "Make Law, Not War? On the Political Economy of Violence and Appropriation," in Volker Beckmann and Martina Padmanabhan (eds), *Institutions and Sustainability* (Springer Science+Business Media B.V., 2009), p. 52.

9 International Alert, *The Role of the Exploitation of Natural Resources in Fuelling and Prolonging Crises in the Eastern DRC*, p. 6.

10 Acker, "Gender, Capitalism and Globalization": 28.

11 Jane Parpart, "Masculinity/ies, Gender and Violence in the Struggle for Zimbabwe," in Jane Parpart and Marysia Zalewski (eds), *Rethinking the Man Question* (London: Zed Books, 2008), p. 196.

12 Human Rights Watch, *Diamonds in the Rough: Human Rights Abuses in the Marange Diamond Fields of Zimbabwe*, June 2009. Available at www.hrw.org/en/news/2009/06/26/zimbabwe-end-repression-marange-diamond-fields.

13 Cynthia Enloe, *Globalization and Militarism: Feminists Make the Link* (Lanham, MD: Rowman and Littlefield, 2007), p. 109.

14 Adam Jones, "Straight as a Rule: Heteronormativity, Gendercide, and the Non-Combatant Male," Centro de Investigación y Docencia Económicas, November 2003, available at www.cide.edu; see also Carol Cohn, "Sex and Death in the Rational World of Defense Intellectuals," *Signs: Journal of Women in Culture and Society* 12(4) (1987): 687–718.

15 Harvard Humanitarian Initiative, with support from Oxfam International, *"Now, the World is Without Me": An Investigation of Sexual Violence in Eastern Democratic Republic of Congo* (April 2010), available at www.oxfam.org.uk/resources/policy/conflict_ disasters/sexual-violence-drc.html, p. 36.

16 Korf, "Make Law, Not War?" p. 46.

17 Harvard Humanitarian Initiative/Oxfam International, *"Now, the World is Without Me."*

18 Jones, "Straight as a Rule."

19 Yasmin Tambiah, "Sexuality and Women's Rights in Armed Conflict in Sri Lanka," *Reproductive Health Matters* 12(23) (2004): 82

20 This story is told in the film *Pray the Devil Back to Hell*, whose producer Abigail Disney recalled in an interview that "a warlord told me that when the women at the peace conference threatened

to strip naked in order to get the attention of the delegates, every man in the room saw them as their mothers. He said that to see them driven to this incredible desperation, it caused every single one of them to ask themselves: What did I do to get us here?" See Maria Garcia, "Devil in the Details," *Film Journal International*, September 22, 2008. www.filmjournal.com/filmjournal/content_display/esearch/e3id613851958f990729dfad19c6166d315?pn=1, accessed on July 20, 2010.

21 Cynthia Cockburn, *From Where We Stand: War, Women's Activism and Feminist Analysis* (New York: Zed Books, 2007), pp. 177–8.

22 Shelley Anderson, "'My Only Clan is Womanhood': Building Women's Peace Identities," Women's Peacemaker's Program, International Fellowship of Reconciliation, pdf available at www.ifor.org/WPP.

23 Wendy Cukier with Alison Kooistra and Mark Anto, "Gendered Perspectives on Small Arms Proliferation and Misuse: Effects and Policies," in Vanessa Farr and Kiflemariam Gebre-Wold (eds), *Gender Perspectives on Small Arms and Light Weapons: Regional and International Concerns* (Bonn International Center for Conversion, 2002), pp. 26–7, available at www.iansa-women.org/node/71.

24 Laura Heaton, "Rights Defender, Congo's 'Voice for the Voiceless', Silenced," *Human Rights Change*, June 4, 2010, available at http://humanrights.change.org/blog/view/rights_defender_head_of_congos_voice_for_the_voiceless_silenced, accessed on June 4, 2010.

25 Amnesty International, "Nepal's Government Fails to Protect Women Human Rights Activists," April 2009, available at www.amnesty.org/en/news-and-updates/news/nepal-government-fails-protect-women-human-rights-activists-20090410, accessed on July 15, 2010.

26 See an insightful critique in Helen M. Kinsella, "Gendering Grotius: Sex and Sex Difference in the Laws of War," *Political Theory* 34(2) (April 2006): 161–91.

27 Johann Hari, "Congo's Tragedy: The War the World Forgot," *The Independent*, May 5, 2006, available at www.independent.co.uk/news/world/africa/congos-tragedy-the-war-the-world-forgot-476929.html, accessed on January 23, 2010.

28 See Global Witness, "What is the Kimberley Process," available at www.globalwitness.org/pages/en/the_kimberley_process.html.

29 See International Alert, *The Role of the Exploitation of Natural Resources in Fuelling and Prolonging Crises in the Eastern DRC*; Nicholas Garret, Harrison Mitchel, Marie Lintzer, *Great Lakes Region – A Policy Guide on Professionalisation, Formalisation and Increased Transparency* (Resource Consulting Services, May 2010).

30 "Jobs Says Apple Products Not Tainted by 'Conflict' Minerals" (ipodnn, June 28, 2010), available at www.ipodnn.com/articles/10/06/28/confesses.no.way.for.suppliers.to.be.sure/.

31 Nicholas Kristoff, "Death by Gadget," *The New York Times*, June 26, 2010, available at www.nytimes.com/2010/06/27/opinion/27kristof.html?_r=1, accessed on June 26, 2010.

32 Vanessa Farr, "Women, Men and the Struggle to Disarm," *Conflict Trends* (2003): 26.

33 Vanessa A. Farr, "A Gendered Analysis of International Agreements on Small Arms and Light Weapons," in Vanessa Farr and Kiflemariam Gebre-Wold (eds), *Gender Perspectives on Small Arms and Light Weapons: Regional and International Concerns* (Bonn International Center for Conversion, 2002), p. 22, available at www.iansa-women.org/node/71.

34 United Nations Security Council, "Security Council Demands Immediate and Complete Halt to Acts of Sexual Violence Against Civilians in Conflict Zones, Unanimously Adopting Resolution 1820 (2008): Caps Day-Long Ministerial-Level Debate on 'Women, Peace and Security.'" Security Council's 5916th Meeting. *Department of Public Information, News and Media Division*, New York, June 19, 2008, available at http://un.org/News/Press/docs/2008/sc9364.doc.htm

35 See Halley's comments in Janet Halley, Prabha Kotiswaran, Hila Shamir, and Chantal Thomas, "From the International to the Local in Feminist Legal Responses to Rape, Prostitution/Sex Work, and Sex Trafficking: Four Studies in Contemporary Governance Feminism," *Harvard Journal of Law and Gender* 29 (Summer 2006): 22.

36 Halley, Kotiswaran, Shamir, and Thomas, "From the International to the Local in Feminist Legal Responses to Rape, Prostitution/Sex Work, and Sex Trafficking": 23.

37 Halley, Kotiswaran, Shamir, and Thomas, "From the International to the Local in Feminist Legal Responses to Rape, Prostitution/Sex Work, and Sex Trafficking": especially 20–4.

38 See Natalie Florea Hudson, *Gender, Security and the UN: Security*

Language as a Political Framework for Women (London: Routledge, 2010). See an annotated discussion for exploring the meaning of 1325 at www.womenwarpeace.org/1325_toolbox/1325_annotated.

39 See Laura Shepherd, *Gender, Violence and Security: Discourse as Practice* (New York: Zed Books, 2008), especially ch. 5.

40 "Disarmament, Demobilization and Reintegration (DDR)," Women, War, Peace, available at http://www.womenwarpeace. org/node/4.

41 Megan Mackenzie, "Securitization and De-securitization: Female Soldiers and the Reconstruction of Women in Post-Conflict Sierra Leone," in Laura Sjoberg (ed.), *Gender and International Security: Feminist Perspectives* (New York: Routledge, 2010), especially pp. 153–60.

42 See interview with Margot Wallström, "Tackling Sexual Violence Must Include Prevention, Ending Impunity," *UN News Centre*, April 27, 2010, available at www.un.org/apps/news/story. asp?NewsID=34502, accessed on April 29, 2010.

43 UN Security Council, "Security Council Resolution 1820 (2008): On Acts of Sexual Violence against Civilians in Armed Conflicts," June 19, 2008, S/RES/1820 (2008), available at www.un.org/ Docs/sc/unsc_resolutions08.htm, accessed on July 15, 2010.

44 UN General Assembly, "2005 World Summit Document," September 14, 2005, A/Res/60/1, available at http://daccessdds. un.org/doc/UNDOC/GEN/N05/510/94/PDF/N0551094. pdf?OpenElement, accessed on July 15, 2010.

45 UN Security Council, Security Council Resolution 1820 (2008); all italics are in the original.

46 See www.ocha.unog.ch/humanitarianreform/Default. aspx?tabid=70.

47 Jaya Murthy, "Responsibility to Protect: Lessons from South Kivu," *Forced Migration Review* 28 (2007): 12, available at www. fmreview.org.

48 Murthy, "Responsibility to Protect: Lessons from South Kivu" (2007): 2.

49 Andrea Binder, Véronique de Geoffroy, and Bonaventure Sokpoh, *Democratic Republic of Congo, IASC Cluster Approach Evaluation, 2nd Phase Country Study* (Global Public Policy Institute: April 2010).

50 IRIN, "Global: Defining the Rights of the Internally Displaced" (October 16, 2008), available at www.irinnews.org/Report. aspx?ReportId=80942.

51 On this point, see Jyl Josephson, "Sexual Citizenship, Sexual Regulation, and Identity Politics," draft chapter in *The Politics of Sexual Citizenship* (unpublished manuscript), presented at the Feminist Theory Workshop, Western Political Science Association, Vancouver, BC, Canada, March 31, 2009.

52 Virginia Held, *The Ethics of Care: Personal, Political, Global* (Oxford: Oxford University Press, 2006), p. 119.

53 Held, *The Ethics of Care*, p. 165.

54 Julius Ocen, "Can Traditional Rituals Bring Justice to Northern Uganda?" Institute for War and Peace Reporting, 2007), available at www.iwpr.net/?p=acr&s=f&o=337405&apc_state=henpacr.

55 Tim Allen, "Ritual (Ab)use? Problems with Traditional Justice," in Nicholas Waddell and Phil Clark (eds), *Courting Conflict? Justice, Peace and the ICC in Africa* (Royal African Society, 2007), p. 47, available at www.royalafricansociety.org/index.php?option=com_content&task=view&id=415.

56 See Judith Butler, *Undoing Gender* (New York: Routledge, 2004), pp. 180–2.

57 Butler, *Undoing Gender*, p. 180. I am indebted to Jyl Josephson for working out the argument in this paragraph.

58 Mark Drumbl, "Child Soldiers, Individual Agency, and International Criminal Law," International Studies Association Annual Conference, New York City, February 2009, p. 3.

59 See http://nairobi.iom.int/news3.htm.

60 For detailed descriptions of other traditional ceremonies, see Cecily Rose, "Looking beyond Traditional Justice and Reconciliation Mechanisms in Northern Uganda: A Proposal for Truth-telling and Reparations," *Boston College Third World Law Journal* 28 (2008): 345–400.

61 Ocen, "Can Traditional Rituals Bring Justice to Northern Uganda?"

62 Ocen, "Can Traditional Rituals Bring Justice to Northern Uganda?"

63 Michael Wessells, "In the Mind of the Child Soldier," *All in the Mind*, January 13, 2007, available at www.abc.net.au/rn/allinthemind/stories/2007/1812727.htm, accessed on November 2, 2010.

64 Lina Abirafeh, "Building Capacity in Sierra Leone," *Forced Migration Review* 28 (2007): 20–1.

65 Lucia Castelli, Elena Locatelli and Mark Canavera, *Psycho-Social Support for War Affected Children in Northern Uganda: Lessons Learned* (London: Coalition to Stop the Use of Child Soldiers, 2005), p. 5.

66 Harvard Humanitarian Initiative/Oxfam International, *"Now, the World is Without Me,"* p. 10.

67 Annalise Moser, "Women Building Peace and Preventing Sexual Violence in Conflict Affected Contexts: A Review of Community Based Approaches," UNIFEM (2007).

68 Kimberly Theidon, "Intimate Enemies: Reconciling the Present in Post-War Communities in Ayacucho, Peru," in Beatrice Pouligny, Simon Chesterman, and Albrecht Schnabel (eds), *After Mass Crime: Rebuilding States and Communities* (Tokyo, Japan: United Nations University Press, 2007), p. 108.

69 Theidon, "Intimate Enemies: Reconciling the Present in the Post-War Communities in Ayacucho, Peru," in *After Mass Crime*, p. 115.

Selected Readings

I have provided readers with many source materials in the endnotes, but here I will guide you more specifically to sources that allow you to explore in depth concepts developed in the book. I have selected for you the most interesting and oftentimes gripping reading.

Chapter 1 opens the book with an overview of many conflicts that have involved sexual violence. Some key works that give context include Iris Chang, *The Rape of Nanking* (New York: Basic Books, 1997); Danke Li, *Echoes of Chongqing: Women in Wartime China* (Chicago, IL: University of Illinois Press, 2010); Ritu Menon and Kamla Bhasin, *Borders and Boundaries: Women in India's Partition* (New Brunswick, NJ: Rutgers University Press, 1998); Clare Hatfield, "Drawing Boundaries on Bodies: The Use of Sexual Violence as a Tactic of War During the Partition of India," paper presented at the American Political Science Association Annual Convention, Chicago, IL, August 2007. Cynthia Enloe's book *Maneuvers: The International Politics of Militarizing Women's Lives* (Berkeley: University of California Press, 2000) will also give context for understanding gender under militarized globalization.

There have been a number of works that bring sexual violence in conflict into perspective over time, but the landmark study on which this whole body of literature rests is Susan Brownmiller's *Against Our Will: Men, Women, Rape* (New York: Simon and Schuster, 1975). Excellent sources to gain a historical overview for the twentieth century are Inger Skjelsbaek, *The Elephant in the Room: An Overview of How Sexual Violence Came to be Seen as a Weapon of War*, report to the Norwegian Ministry of Foreign Affairs (Peace Research Institute, Oslo, May 2010); and also Dagmar Herzog (ed.), *Brutality and Desire: War and Sexuality in Europe's Twentieth Century* (New York: Palgrave Macmillan, 2009). Jeanne Ward, *If Not Now, When? Addressing Gender-based Violence in Refugee, Internally Displaced, and Post-Conflict Settings. A Global Overview* (Reproductive Health for Refugees Consortium, April 2002) gives perspectives on GBV from many different cultural contexts and settings. "Stop Rape Now – UN Action Against Sexual Violence" provides testimonies that capture a wide range of experiences, suffering, and courage of survivors and witnesses at www.stoprapenow.org. Another useful tool is UNIFEM's portal, womenwarpeace.org. Finally, for an excellent history of the development of the scholarly literature in genocide studies and armed conflict on gender roles in violence, see Adam Jones, *Gender Inclusive: Essays on Violence, Men, and Feminist International Relations* (New York: Routledge, 2008).

Chapter 2 introduces the idea of a runaway norm to develop a typology of sexual violence in armed conflict. Students interested in classic studies on the role of norms in international relations may wish to consult Friedrich V. Kratochwil, *Rules, Norms, and Decision: On the Conditions of Practical Reasoning in International Relations and Domestic Affairs* (New York: Cambridge University Press, 1989). Two sources that provide more insight into the origins of the concept of civilians (or noncombatants) under international law, the gendering of this concept and its ambiguities are: Laura Sjoberg, "Gendered Realities of the Immunity Principle: Why Gender Analysis Needs Feminism," *International Studies Quarterly* 50 (2006); and Hugo Slim, *Killing Civilians: Method, Madness, and*

Morality in War (New York: Columbia University Press, 2008). An excellent resource for understanding the new wars is Tarak Barkawi, *Globalization and War* (Lanham, MD: Rowman and Littlefield, 2006), while Cynthia Enloe's works bring a gendered perspective to understanding. One of her classic works is *Bananas, Beaches and Bases: Making Feminist Sense of International Politics* (Berkeley, CA: University of California Press, 1990), while a more recent study that is an excellent read is *Globalization and Militarism: Feminists Make the Link* (Lanham, MD: Rowman and Littlefield, 2007). For background on the new wars, see works by Mary Kaldor who first stimulated this debate with her book, *New War and Old Wars: Organized Violence in a Global Era* (Stanford, CN: Stanford University, 1999). Another useful source is Michael Duffield, *Global Governance and the New Wars* (New York: Zed Books, 2001) and his book, *Development, Security and Unending War: Governing the World of Peoples* (Cambridge, UK: Polity, 2007).

Chapter 3 introduces concepts related to structural violence and gendered injustice. For a feminist grounding to these issues as they relate to global politics, see V. Spike Peterson and Anne Sisson Runyan, *Global Gender Issues in the New Millennium*, 3rd edn (Boulder, CO: Westview Press, 2010). An excellent resource for gaining a global perspective on these issues is Joni Seager, *Penguin Atlas of Women in the World*, 4th edn (New York: Penguin, 2008). Other valuable resources include Ricardo Hausmann, Laura D. Tyson, and Saadia Zahidi, *The 2008 Global Gender Gap Report* (Geneva: World Economic Forum, 2008), and Klaus von Grebmer et al., *2009 Global Hunger Index. The Challenge of Hunger: Focus on Financial Crisis and Gender Inequality* (International Food Policy Research Institute, October 2009), which are annual publications. A best-seller on the topic is also Nicholas D. Kristof and Sheryl WuDunn, *Half the Sky: Turning Oppression into Opportunity for Women Worldwide* (New York: Random

House, 2009). The book by Muktar Mai, with Marie-Thérèse Cuny, *In the Name of Honor*, trans. Linda Coverdale (New York: Washington Square Press, 2006) offers an inspiring account of how one young woman took on an entire cultural and legal system in Pakistan to seek justice for herself and her family, and inspired many other women along the way. Two autobiographical accounts that convey the sense of how war encroaches on a community, and what it means to have to flee, are Ishmael Beah, *A Long Way Gone: Memoirs of a Boy Soldier* (New York: Farrar, Straus and Giroux, 2007), and a set of short essays by Slavenka Drakulic, *The Balkan Express: Fragments from the Other Side of the War* (New York: W. W. Norton, 1993).

Chapter 4 turns its focus on how sexual violence in armed conflicts erodes all manner of safe space. One of the key concepts covered in this chapter is how both men and women subvert sexual hierarchies in war. Laura Sjoberg and Carone E. Gentry challenge traditional stereotypes of women's roles with their provocative book, *Mothers, Monsters, Whores: Women's Violence in Global Politics* (New York: Zed Books, 2007). Mats Utas provides another perspective on this with his account of Bintu in "Victimacy, Girlfriending, Soldiering: Tactic Agency in a Young Woman's Social Navigation of the Liberian War Zone," *Anthropological Quarterly* 78(2) (Spring 2005): 403–30. The role of humanitarian actors exploiting refugees is another tragic turn in the lives of people fleeing conflict. Paul Higate's field research that includes interviews with United Nations peacekeepers provides extraordinary insight into the way power differentials are expressed through sexual exploitation. See his article "Peacekeepers, Masculinities, and Sexual Exploitation," *Men and Masculinities* 10(1) (2007).

In chapter 5, the focus turns to understanding how the social construction of masculinity is related to a global political economy that profits from sexual violence in mineral-rich war zones and other shadow enterprises. A very interesting volume that explores this theoretically in a related economic context is Anna M. Agathangelou, *The Global Political Economy of Sex: Desire, Violence, and Insecurity in Mediterranean Nation States* (New York: Palgrave Macmillan, 2004). A short article by Joan Acker also provides a succinct overview of the ways that globalization is gendered, especially in the context of the productive and reproductive economies. See Joan Acker, "Gender, Capitalism and Globalization," *Critical Sociology* 30(1) (2004): 17–42. For an encompassing gender analysis of the global political economy, see also V. Spike Peterson, *A Critical Rewriting of Global Political Economy: Integrating Reproductive, Productive and Virtual Economies* (New York: Routledge, 2006, 2nd printing). The analysis in chapter 5 begins with a short case study of the civil wars in Eastern Congo. A few good resources for further background reading include Gérard Prunier, *Africa's World War: Congo, the Rwandan Genocide and the Making of a Continental Catastrophe* (New York: Oxford University Press, 2009); Thomas Turner, *The Congo Wars: Conflict, Myth and Reality* (New York: Zed Books, 2007); René Lemarchand in his book, *The Dynamics of Violence in Central Africa* (Philadelphia: University of Pennsylvania Press, 2009); and Michael Nest, with François Grignon and Emizet F. Kisangani, *The Democratic Republic of Congo: Economic Dimensions of War and Peace* (Boulder, CO: Lynne Rienner, 2006).

There are also a number of excellent reports that background the connections between the global political economy, the exploitation of natural resources in Eastern Congo, and the pervasive human rights violations. These include Global Witness, *Faced with a Gun, What Can You Do? War and the Militarization of Mining in Eastern Congo* (July 23, 2009); the Harvard Humanitarian Initiative, with support from Oxfam International, *"Now, the World is Without Me": An*

Investigation of Sexual Violence in Eastern Democratic Republic of Congo (April 2010); Human Rights Watch 2009, You Will be Punished: Attacks on Civilians in Eastern Congo (December 13, 2009) and the Final Report of the Group of Experts on the Democratic Republic of the Congo, United Nations Security Council, S/2009/603. Chapter 5 also explores the reasons why combatants rape. There are some excellent studies of this, including interviews with combatants and theoretical discussions. One of the most thought-provoking works on the topic is by Lisa S. Price, "Finding the Man in the Soldier-Rapist: Some Reflections on Comprehension and Accountability," Women's Studies International Forum 24(2) (2001).

Chapter 6 begins the task of synthesizing the arguments in the book and focusing on the way various solutions to the problem of sexual violence in armed conflict have been framed or approached by the international community. International law provides one piece of the puzzle, and an important discussion of its strengths and weaknesses is found in Janet Halley, Prabha Kotiswaran, Hila Shamir, and Chantal Thomas, "From the International to the Local in Feminist Legal Responses to Rape, Prostitution/Sex Work, and Sex Trafficking: Four Studies in Contemporary Governance Feminism," Harvard Journal of Law and Gender 29 (Summer 2006). Catharine Mackinnon has been one of the leading radical feminist voices as evidenced by such works of hers as Are Women Human? And Other International Dialogues (Cambridge: Harvard University Press, 2006). For works examining the United Nations Security Council Resolution 1325 and its impact, see Natalie Florea Hudson, Gender, Security and the UN: Security Language as a Political Framework for Women (London: Routledge, 2010); and also Laura Shepherd, Violence and Security: Discourse as Practice (New York: Zed Books, 2008). For a variety of perspectives on concepts and theories relating to women and security, an important volume is Laura Sjoberg (ed.), *Gender and International Security: Feminist Perspectives* (New York: Routledge, 2010). Regarding the ethics of care as a theoretical approach to undergird international responses to sexual violence in armed conflict, see especially Virginia Held, *The Ethics of Care: Personal, Political, Global* (Oxford: Oxford University Press, 2006). For a different perspective, see Daniel Engster, *The Heart of Justice: Care Ethics and Political Theory* (Oxford: Oxford University Press, 2007). And finally, excellent volumes on women's activism in response to the types of violence this book has covered include Cynthia Cockburn, *From Where We Stand: War, Women's Activism and Feminist Analysis* (New York: Zed Books, 2007); and Sanam Naraghi Anderlini, *Women Building Peace: What They Do, Why it Matters* (Boulder, CO: Lynne Rienner, 2007).

Index

Lightning Source UK Ltd.
Milton Keynes UK
UKOW030607210312

189320UK00004B/3/P